10/19
DF

Submarines of the Imperial Japanese Navy

Submarines of the Imperial Japanese Navy

By Dorr Carpenter
and Norman Polmar

CONWAY
MARITIME PRESS

First published in Great Britain 1986 by
Conway Maritime Press Ltd
24 Bride Lane, Fleet Street
London EC4Y 8DR

ISBN 0 85177 396 6

Printed and bound in Great Britain by The Bath Press,
Bath

In the Pacific, the Indian Ocean, and the Atlantic we remember the multitude of resentful sleeping warriors; in our ears we hear the whisper of the "voice from the bottom of the sea."

—Commander Mochitsura Hashimoto,
Imperial Japanese Navy,
16 August 1945

Contents

Foreword

When you read this history, you will feel curious about the wide variety of Japanese submarine classes and types.

During World War II, the U.S. Navy mass-produced basically one kind of submarine in order to faithfully execute the submarine's main objective, which is to destroy enemy supply lines. This brought great success to their submarine warfare.

On the other hand, the traditional application of submarines in the Japanese Navy was to operate in fleet warfare; therefore, the cruiser-type submarines were developed to participate in lengthy cruising operations, the fleet type to accompany the battle fleet, and the medium size for use in coastal defense. These submarines brought some tangible and intangible successes in the beginning of the war.

During the middle and latter parts of the war, however, the conditions of warfare in the Pacific were drastically changed due to the unexpected efficiency of antisubmarine tactics in the U.S. Navy. Although belatedly, changes in submarine application and improvements in ship design and equipment were launched. Consequently, there was a reduction in the aircraft-carrying type, the emergence of the transport type, the building of the underwater high-speed type, and cancellation of the mass production of the medium-size submarine. But due to the unfavorable war situation and the lack of raw materials, the shipbuilding plans were changed again and again, causing chaos.

Toward the end of the war, as a trump card for defense of the Japanese homeland, the small-size, special-attack midget submarine and the *kaiten* human torpedo were mass-produced, but the war ended before they could be effectively employed. So devastating was the antisubmarine warfare that when the conflict ended, there were only nine large attack-type submarines in service.

This history may be a reminder of glory to some. To others it may appear as deep shadows of past tragedy. To me, this stirs emotion in my heart because these pages appear as grave-markers for the Japanese submarines and for the men who crewed them.

Zenzi Orita,
former Commander,
Imperial Japanese Navy

Preface

This review seeks to describe the submarine force of the Imperial Japanese Navy from the acquisition of its first undersea craft in 1904–1905 to the end of World War II.

At the outbreak of the Pacific War, the Japanese Navy had the largest and most-capable undersea force in the Pacific. Japanese submarines were relatively modern, their crews were well trained, and their torpedoes were the best in the world. Further, reconnaissance floatplanes were an integral part of the submarine force.

During the course of the war, the Japanese developed several remarkable submarine designs—the I-201 high-speed attack craft, the I-400 underwater aircraft carriers, several submarine cargo/transport classes, plus an array of midget submarines and human-torpedo craft.

Some Japanese naval leaders, including Admiral Isoroku Yamamoto, Commander in Chief of the Combined Fleet from September 1939 until his death in combat in April 1943, looked to this submarine force for great accomplishments. There were predictions by some flag officers that submarines could accomplish more in the Pacific War than could aircraft carriers.

The performance of the Japanese submarines, however, was quite poor in comparison with those of the United States, Great Britain, or Nazi Germany. Not even the much-touted *kaiten* human torpedoes could inflict significant damage on the U.S. naval forces attacking Japan. Indeed, it could be said that Japanese submarines had no significant impact on the Pacific War except for a few successes against U.S. aircraft carriers in 1942. During a period when U.S. naval forces were required in the Atlantic, Mediterranean, and Pacific theaters, and few aircraft carriers were available to the Allies, Japanese submarines were able to sink the USS WASP and USS YORKTOWN (the latter already damaged by Japanese aircraft), and twice damage the USS SARATOGA, forcing her to withdraw from combat for significant periods.

These successes—and several of lesser significance—were small compensation for the one hundred and twenty-nine Japanese submarines and several thousand crewmen lost in the Pacific War.

FORMAT

This volume uses the same format developed for the reference books *The Ships and Aircraft of the U.S. Fleet* and *Guide to the Soviet Navy*, edited by Mr. Norman Polmar. Hull numbers for U.S. ships that appear in the text are provided in the Ship Name Index.

Japanese names in this book are given in the Western style with the given name first followed by the surname, the reverse of the Japanese style.

Hyphens are inserted in Japanese and German submarine designations for the convenience of readers (e.g., I-161, RO-62, U-215).

Abbreviations and jargon have been avoided where possible. Standard terminology is used: *Standard displacement* was established by the London Naval Treaty as the displacement of the ship, complete, fully manned, equipped and ready for sea, with all armament and ammunition, but without fuel on board; *surfaced* and *submerged* displacements are *normal*, similarly fully equipped and ready for sea but with one-quarter fuel, one-half to two-thirds stores and provisions, and a one-half to three-quarters supply of ammunition.

Specific abbreviations used in the book are:

oa	overall
hp	horsepower
MG	machine gun
shp	shaft horsepower
S/m	submarine

ACKNOWLEDGMENTS

Many individuals have assisted in the research and preparation of this book: Paul H. Silverstone and Lieutenant Commander Toshio Tamura assisted in developing contacts in Japan. Captain George R. Wendt, USNR, Robert Carlisle, and Charles Haberlein assisted in obtaining photography from U.S. sources. Dr. Dean Allard made the files of the Naval Historical Center available to the authors. Colonel Gregory Boyington, USMC (Ret), made available his experience in being captured by a Japanese submarine. Kohji Ishiwata made available much of the material in the files of the magazine *Ships of the World*, as did Masanobu Harigae of *Maru Magazine*, while Patty Maddocks and Mary Sprawls made available the photographic files of the U.S. Naval Institute. Again, we are in debt to Beverly Baum and Carol Swartz for putting this all together. The Imperial War Museum also kindly assisted in providing photographs, as did Martin E. Holbrook, Albert Macko, Kenneth MacPherson, Robert C. Mikesh, Zenji Orita, Earl Reinert, Dick L. Seely, Robert C. Stern, and Anthony J. Watts.

Also, our thanks to Arnold S. Lott, who helped get this project started.

Dorr Carpenter
Norman Polmar

1 Strategy and Operations Through 1941

Japanese interest in submarines began with the Russo-Japanese conflict of 1904–1905. Both Russia and Japan purchased submarines from the United States, but these small craft were not used in combat (see chapter 7). Japan continued to purchase foreign-built submarines and designs, and the Imperial Japanese Navy subsequently initiated a most impressive program to develop submarines.

Submarines had considerable importance in the Atlantic and Mediterranean theaters in World War I. After the war, at the Washington Naval Conference of 1921–1922, the major governments sought agreements on naval strength ratios as an alternative to the massive warship construction programs underway at the time. The conference resulted in a ratio of 5:5:3 for capital ships—battleships and battle cruisers—and in aircraft carriers of the navies of the United States, Britain, and Japan, respectively.[1] The Japanese Navy and government had initially sought parity with the United States, but considered 10:10:7 an acceptable ratio because the United States and Britain had naval commitments beyond the Pacific. The United States, however, with the ability to read the Japanese diplomatic communications by having access to the Japanese diplomatic code, was in a position to force the 5:5:3 ratio.

The Washington conference also sought accords on lesser warships, including submarines. At one point the British asked that all submarines be abolished. There were subsequent and more realistic discussions of just how much submarine tonnage each navy could have. But all hopes for an agreement on the size of submarine fleets ended when the French refused to consider a force of less than a total of 90,000 tons (surface displacement) as part of the price for accepting the comparatively small French quota for capital ships.

DEVELOPMENT OF SUBMARINE CONCEPTS

In this period both the U.S. and Japanese navies accepted the strategic thesis of their fleets crossing an ocean for a major duel of capital ships. This concept had been articulated earlier in the widely read writings of American naval strategist Alfred Thayer Mahan. Both navies soon realized, however, that the movement of the U.S. Fleet westward would be a long and tenuous effort. To accomplish this the U.S. Navy sought

to establish forward bases for replenishment and repairs at Pearl Harbor in the Hawaiian Islands, Cavite in the Philippines, and possibly Apra Harbor at Guam. The Japanese believed that large, long-range submarines could attack the U.S. Fleet as it moved westward, reducing its strength through attrition while at the same time reporting its movements in preparation for the fateful duel at sea. Thus was born the strategic concept for the Japanese submarine force.

After the Washington conference and until the end of 1924, the Japanese Navy had to adjust its capital-ship programs to bring them in line with the conference accords. At that point Japanese submarine strength consisted of the following:

First-class submarines	1	1,400 tons
Second-class submarines	39	30,842 tons total
Third-class submarines	10	3,259 tons total

Early Japanese submarine programs drew heavily on foreign designs, as the Vickers-built submarine No. 12 shown here in Saeki Bay on 26 November 1915. The submarine is down by the stern, with a line forward to the submarine tender KARASAKI. (Shizuo Fukui)

---

1. The French and Italian fleets were each accorded a ratio of 1.75 in the conference. Germany, disarmed after World War I, and Russia, in the midst of a civil war, were not parties to the conference.

At the end of the First World War the Allies awarded Japan seven former German U-boats for Japan's participation in the conflict, which included an antisubmarine squadron operating in the Mediterranean. Here are the Japanese O-7 (left) and O-2, formerly the German UB-143 and U-46, with the Japanese ensign flying over the Imperial standard. These and the other U-boats provided the Japanese with considerable input for later designs. (Imperial War Museum)

By late 1930 a large submarine construction program would provide Japan with the following:

First-class submarines	22	34,788 tons total
Second-class submarines	45	36,185 tons total

But the Japanese strategy of employing long-range, first-class submarines to serve as scouts and as the first line of attack against the American or British fleets was threatened by the London Naval Conference of 1930. The conference sought to provide limitations on cruisers, destroyers, and submarines to complement the earlier limitations on the larger warships. Japan tenaciously struggled for a submarine allocation of 78,000 tons (surface displacement). The debates at the London conference, like those earlier in Washington, were heated, with Britain and the United States generally siding against Japan. Finally the participants agreed that each of the three major navies could have a submarine tonnage of 52,700. According to one Japanese commentary on the outcome of the conference:

> The Naval General Staff in Tokyo was enraged at this. Equality of submarine tonnage was totally unsatisfactory. Japan's war games had shown that she needed an absolute minimum of 78,000 tons. A strength of 52,700 tons would leave her short by two squadrons of submarines—sixteen boats—of what her planners considered necessary to the strategy of attrition. The results of the London Conference were thus looked upon as having placed Japan's national defense in jeopardy.[2]

The debate on this issue in Japan was considerable. The first-class (I-class) submarines were subsequently produced at a significant rate.

2. Masanori Ito and Roger Pineau, *The End of the Imperial Japanese Navy* (New York: W. W. Norton, 1956), p. 23.

The Japanese Navy was one of the first to have specialized ships to support submarines. Here the tender or depot ship KARASAKI at Malta on 6 April 1919 has alongside four former U-boats; from left they are the Japanese O-2 (U-46), O-3 (U-55), O-4 (UC-90), and O-6 (UB-125). The KARASAKI was also a war prize, from the 1904–1905 Japanese war with Russia. (Shizuo Fukui)

They could cruise from the Japanese home islands to the United States, without refueling, to scout out and begin the attrition of the westward-moving U.S. Fleet.

SUBMARINE PROGRAMS

Based on the limitations of the London conference, in October 1930 the Japanese Navy minister presented to the government a new naval program that would completely readjust and replenish naval strength. The 1931 plan—the First Naval Armament Replenishment Plan—called for the construction of nine submarines, to be delivered in 1937:

Long-range cruising	(J2)	1	1,900 tons[3]
Large size	(KD6A)	6	1,400 tons each
Medium size	(K5)	2	700 tons each

This aggregate of 11,700 tons for submarines can be compared with the 1931 plan's 34,000 tons for cruisers (four ships) and 16,416 tons for destroyers (twelve ships) and lesser ships. Even before this plan was completed, however, world events in the early 1930s led the Jap-

anese to implement the Second Naval Replenishment Plan to bring the fleet up to treaty limits as soon as possible. The second plan was to be completed in just four years, from 1934 to 1937. It was significantly reduced, however, during negotiations between the Navy and Finance Ministry because of cost considerations. Most of the 1934 plan was devoted to carrier, cruiser, and destroyer construction. Only four additional submarines were provided:

Long-range cruising	(J3)	2	2,231 tons each
Large size	(KD6B)	2	1,420 tons each

In December 1934 the Japanese government submitted notification of the abrogation of the Washington treaty. The Japanese leadership believed that the naval ratios accepted in both the Washington and London accords were unreasonable and would not guarantee the security of Japan. Another five-power naval conference convened in London in December 1935, seeking to reinstate constraints on warship construction. Because Britain and the United States ignored Japan's contention that the previous treaties were unreasonable, the Japanese withdrew from that conference in January 1936.

The Third Naval Replenishment Plan was then drawn up, to be carried out in five years, from 1937 to 1941. It provided for the superdreadnoughts YAMATO and MUSASHI, the largest battleships ever built, as well as many lesser warships. Thirteen submarines were included:

---

3. Tonnages are standard surface displacement, listed as in the specific replenishment plans; see chapter 8 of this volume for actual displacements.

One of the early Japanese long-range submarines, I-3 (formerly submarine No. 76) is shown about 1930. These submarines were developed to intercept U.S. warships steaming westward to attack Japanese interests in the Pacific during wartime. (*Ships of the World*)

The Japanese Navy rapidly integrated long-range submarines into fleet operations. These are the KD6A-type submarines I-68 (foreground) and I-69 at Ariake Bay in March 1936; at left is the large aircraft carrier KAGA and at right the light cruiser KINU, serving as a submarine flotilla flagship. (K.R. MacPherson)

Three KD3A-type submarines of Submarine Squadron 18 at anchor in 1928. These were streamlined submarines, here with their periscopes and radio masts raised. From left, the I-55, I-53, and I-54. These and other submarines had their numbers increased by one hundred in May 1942 in an effort to reduce the confusion of Japanese submarine numbering. (Shizuo Fukui)

Long-range cruising	(A1)	2	2,434 tons each
Large size	(B1)	6	2,198 tons each
Large size	(C1)	5	2,184 tons each

These submarines would have a complementary role in long-range operations against an enemy fleet. The A1 type would be command or headquarters submarines for coordinating operations, the B1 type scouting submarines specifically for locating the enemy, and the C1 type the attack unit. The A1 would have additional communications facilities and space for staff, and the A1 and B1 would have hangars for floatplanes. The B1 and C1 would be similar except for the deletion of hangar and aircraft facilities in the latter. All three types, of course, would be armed with torpedo tubes and deck guns. These submarines would be completed by October 1941.

Beginning with the Third Replenishment Program, Japanese ships were assigned order numbers; the thirteen submarines were listed as Nos. 35 to 48.

In the following year the Navy Ministry started to develop what might best be described as the wartime shipbuilding programs, commencing with the Fourth Replenishment Program and concluding with the 1944–1945 war program, none of which were completed. Chapter 6 provides a detailed list of Japanese submarines of the war programs.

AIRCRAFT ABOARD SUBMARINES

A key component of Japanese submarine tactics was the use of reconnaissance aircraft launched from submarines, from specially configured "underwater aircraft carriers" as the A1 and B1 types. As early as 1923, using a German Caspar-Heinkel U-1 biplane fitted with floats, the Japanese experimented with operating the plane from a submarine. While the British, French, and U.S. navies similarly experimented with floatplanes aboard submarines, only the Japanese pursued this operational concept.

By 1925 a prototype floatplane, based on the Heinkel U-1, had been developed specifically for submarine operation, the Yokosuka Type 1 biplane. It was test-flown from the minelaying submarine I-121. The aircraft's wings folded back for storage in a hangar, and with a maximum speed of eighty miles per hour it could remain aloft for two hours.

The Watanabe E9W1—later given the code name Slim by the U.S. military—was developed specifically for fleet use. It was test-flown in 1935 and entered production after successful evaluation. From 1938 these twin-float biplanes operated from large submarines. While the more-capable Yokosuka E14Y1 (Glen) entered service as a replacement in the late summer of 1941, several of the E9W1 aircraft would see operational use early in the war and then serve as trainers. But it would be the E14Y1, with a maximum speed of 153 mph at sea level and an endurance of five and a half hours, that would have a significant impact on Japanese submarine operations in World War II.

A related aircraft operation would be the use of submarines to refuel and rearm flying boats at forward bases. The Germans would be the only others to use this scheme during the war, but Japanese operations with submarines at forward bases were much more ambitious and complex than those of the Germans.

SUBMARINE PERSONNEL

Submarine personnel were among the elite of the Imperial Japanese Navy. Almost all submarine officers were graduates of the naval academy at Etajima. Life for Japanese midshipmen and junior officers was strict, harsh, and spartan. Even junior officers had to request permission of the Navy Ministry to get married.

Officers tended to serve for at least two years in surface ships, reaching the rank of lieutenant (junior grade), before being accepted to the submarine school at Otake near Kure. Courses for officers and enlisted men were taught there by a staff of forty former submarine commanding officers, one hundred officer specialists, and twenty warrant officers. There were basic and specialized officer courses in submarine warfare, a course for prospective commanding officers, and specialist enlisted courses. The courses varied in length, with the commanding officer

The Caspar-Heinkel U-1 floatplane was acquired by the Japanese and U.S. navies for experiments with submarines. This shows one of the American planes, flown from the U.S. submarine S-1. Under optimum conditions, four men could prepare the stored aircraft for takeoff in just over one minute. The S-1 was the only U.S. submarine fitted to carry an aircraft.

The Yokosuka E6Y1 was used mainly by Japanese surface ships, but was evaluated for submarine use. The Japanese letter "SU" on the fuselage stood for *Suzuka Kotutai,* the unit to which the plane was attached, and the code number 5 for a carrier-borne aircraft, although in this instance it was also used for submarine aircraft.

The Yokosuka Type 1 floatplane was a direct copy of the German U-1, equipped with a more powerful Le Rhone rotary engine. Two other Yokosuka-built aircraft were also designated Type 1 in this period; the submarine aircraft could be distinguished by the absence of bracing wires between the upper and lower wings.

The Wantabe E9W1 was the first widely used submarine floatplane. The biplane's primary drawback was that it required the submarine to remain on the surface for 20 minutes while the aircraft was assembled. Although the E9W1 was used mainly for training during World War II, several flew combat reconnaissance early in the conflict.

course running three or four months in peacetime as well as during the war.

Facilities at Otake included two submarine hulls fixed in concrete, and attack and damage control training devices in buildings, plus operational submarines and hulks that were assigned to the school.

Officers and enlisted men were strictly segregated in the Japanese Navy. Of course, in the narrow confines of a submarine the division between officers and enlisted men tends to break down, and it appears in retrospect that they seemed to have had a close association. Still, in all parts of the armed forces discipline came second only to loyalty to

The E14Y1 was the most widely used submarine aircraft in history. The aircraft could be assembled and readied for flight by seven men in about ten minutes, about twice as fast as the best time with a submarine biplane. The "E" in the designation indicated a reconnaissance aircraft, the first number the fourteenth E-series aircraft, the second letter the manufacturer (First Naval Air Technical Arsenal at Yokosuka), and the second number the model.

An E14Y1 Glenn floatplane is poised for takeoff from an I-boat. The fold-down crane used to assemble and recover the aircraft is clearly visible. The photo was taken in 1942 as only the deck and hangar top have been painted black and the *Hinomaru* flag is still laced to the conning tower.

the emperor as a way of life; officers could discipline enlisted men without appeal, and physical punishment, in many cases abusive, was normal. Human-torpedo pilot Yutaka Yokota, in his autobiography, wrote of his treatment as a junior petty officer while in training for suicide attacks:

> Several of us had not folded the blankets on our beds properly. When Ensign Miyoshi demanded that the guilty ones step forward, about six men did so. I remembered that I had not folded mine properly, either, but was still thinking about it as the others moved ahead of ranks. There was a five-second interval between the time they stepped forward and the time that I did. Ensign Miyoshi, who always gave orders outside the barracks in a very loud voice to cover up his true gentleness, came down the line and struck all of us once each. The others then stepped back into ranks, but Ensign Miyoshi called out to me.
>
> "Yokota! Wait!"
>
> He stood in front of me. "You were the last to step forward," he said. "Did you think I would favor you before the others, just because we are going out on a mission together? You should have been the first man out! I don't think I want to take you along with me now!"
>
> He began to hit me, and continued until he knocked me down. When I got to my feet my cheeks were beginning to puff out. When he dismissed me, I was deeply ashamed. I knew why he had struck me. I had shamed him, Ensign Kato and the two other men on our [forthcoming] mission. He asked whether I expected favors, but he had already favored me by selecting me for a mission. I forgave him, mentally, at once.[4]

4. Yutaka Yokota and Joseph D. Harrington, *The Kaiten Weapon* (New York: Ballantine Books, 1962), p. 90.

Submarine crewmen scurry as the E14Y1 is given a last-minute check before being catapulted from the B1-type submarine I-29 and (bottom) climbs slowly away from the submarine. The catapult cradle is visible at the submarine's bow. (*Ships of the World*)

In addition to operating floatplanes, several Japanese submarines were modified (and later specially built) to refuel and rearm flying boats. Here the I-22 (later I-122) is refueling a Kawanishi H6K Mavis flying boat. In this peacetime view, the minelaying submarine has awnings spread and many of her crew are present on deck. (Anthony J. Watts)

Submarine crews, as well as the rest of the seagoing navy, tended to have preferential treatment with respect to food and cigarettes. At sea the submariners had a diet of boiled white rice, pickled vegetables, dried seaweed, eggs, beef, pork, various fish, and usually for breakfast, *miso-shiro,* a vegetable soup. Refrigeration space was severely limited, and fresh meat, fish, and vegetables would be exhausted in about a week, after which canned food was the staple. There was little coffee but plenty of tea. Officers and men generally ate the same food, their daily submarine ration amounting to some 3,300 calories, quite high for wartime Japan. *Sake* and beer were available to submarine crews ashore, while at sea a commanding officer could issue alcohol under special conditions. Drunkenness ashore or afloat was not tolerated.

Life in the cramped, unairconditioned submarines was difficult. On long deployments bags of rice and canned food filled every available space, and just moving through the submarine was a difficult task. The newer boats had cooling systems; the older craft were always very humid. Rats were common on board.

The *fundoshi* or loin cloth was the standard clothing for submarine sailors during the hot, humid deployments to the South Pacific area.

Crews showered and clothes were washed only every few days, and clothes were rarely fully dried. At the forward bases of Truk and Rabaul, officers and sailors took coveted baths on submarine tenders. At the forward bases there were movies, swimming, and fishing for all hands, and tennis for the officers. At Singapore and Penang (Malaya) and other bases in built-up areas, there were additional amenities, including major recreation areas where female companionship was provided. At the bases in Malaya and Java there was ample fresh fruit for the sailors.

SUBMARINES AT WAR

The Japanese Navy first used I-class submarines as an integral part of their fleet in the war with China, which began in the 1930s. While submarine operations against China were limited in scope and size, they did help prepare the Navy for combat. But in the U.S. Navy the Japanese would face a capable and innovative opponent who, despite losses at Pearl Harbor, was quick to go on a limited offensive. Further, the large numbers of warships being built under the Two-Ocean Navy Act voted by Congress in 1940 would provide a U.S. fleet far larger than Japan could produce by 1943 or even 1945. This situation would force the

Submariners were among the elite of the Japanese Navy. This is the interior of the conning tower of the RO-50, with the officer at the periscope probably Lieutenant Commander Masao Kimura. He claimed to have sunk a U.S. escort carrier and a destroyer on 25 November 1944, but no such ships were lost on that date.

Japanese enlisted submariners having a meal in their living quarters on board the large, cruiser-type submarine I-69. Officers and enlisted men ate the same rations. Although life in the submarines was arduous, morale was high into 1943 when the submarine force began to suffer heavy losses and largely engaged in supply missions. (*Ships of the World*)

The control room of the I-69. Despite Japanese submarines being highly capable and innovative, and armed with the world's most effective torpedoes, their lack of radar and effective radar warning devices coupled with leadership problems severely reduced their effectiveness in the test of combat. (*Ships of the World*)

The Japanese Navy trained at a hard pace, accepting significant losses in men, aircraft, and, at times, ships. The I-61 was lost after a collision with a gunboat during maneuvers northwest of Kyushu on 2 October 1941. Some of her crew survived. The submarine was later raised and scrapped. (Associated Press)

Japanese submarine force to change its tactical concepts six times in the four years of conflict with the United States. And it was the Japanese Navy's repeated use of submarines for purposes for which they were not designed that was a major reason for the failure of the submarine force to achieve a creditable combat record.

The tactical concepts employed by Japanese submarines in World War II can be considered in the following phases:

• Phase I—1931 to April 1942: Submarines operated with the surface fleet; their major role was reconnaissance and attacks against warships.
• Phase II—April 1942 to November 1944: Submarines concentrated their efforts on attacking merchant shipping.
• Phase III—mid-November 1942 to mid-August 1945: Submarines were employed primarily to supply bypassed island outposts.
• Phase IV—November 1944 to April 1945: Submarines were converted to carry *kaiten* one-man torpedoes, and operated in groups against warships at anchor.
• Phase V—April 1945 to August 1945: Submarines carrying *kaiten* operated in groups in the open sea, primarily against tankers and troop ships.
• Phase VI—July to August 1945: In a concept initiated but not completed, STo-class and AM-class submarines were to carry aircraft to strike U.S. bases.
• Phase VII—considered, but not initiated: the use of the new high-speed ST-class submarines.

STRENGTH AND ORGANIZATION

At the start of the Pacific War in December 1941, the Japanese Navy had sixty-three operational submarines—forty-eight of the larger I-class

and fifteen smaller RO-class submarines.[5] In addition, at the outbreak of hostilities Japan had another twenty-nine submarines under construction, to complete in 1942–1943, and thirty-eight more were approved for construction but not yet started. Thus, without losses, by early 1944 the Japanese Navy could have up to 130 undersea craft in service.

The submarines were organized into squadrons and divisions. Squadrons were normally commanded by rear admirals and divisions by captains, with lieutenant commanders generally in command of submarines. Squadron and division commanders normally went to sea in their squadron flagships, submarines especially fitted with extensive communications gear.

When the war began, the overall responsibility for submarine operations rested with the commander of the Sixth Fleet, Vice Admiral Mitsumi Shimizu. Under the direct control of the Sixth Fleet were the 1st, 2nd, and 3rd Submarine Squadrons, which had the Navy's most-capable submarines (see table 1). The primary mission of these three squadrons of long-range submarines was to destroy the U.S. Pacific Fleet based at Pearl Harbor and on the West Coast of the United States. At the start of the war Admiral Shimizu was on board his light cruiser-flagship KATORI at Kwajalein in the Marshall Islands.

5. By comparison, in December 1941 the U.S. Navy had 111 submarines in commission and another seventy-three under construction. Fifty-one U.S. undersea craft were in the Pacific—29 assigned to the Asiatic Fleet and based at Manila in the Philippines (23 modern fleet boats and six older S-boats), and 22 with the Pacific Fleet based at Pearl Harbor (16 modern fleet boats and six older S-boats). Also in the Pacific on 7 December 1941 were twelve Dutch submarines; there were no British undersea craft in the Pacific.

The 4th and 5th Submarine Squadrons were next in first-line strength, but included some older craft of limited capability. These squadrons, assigned directly to Combined Fleet Headquarters, were charged with the destruction of Allied surface ships in southern waters, and were also to support the planned invasions of the Philippines and British Malaya.

The 6th Submarine Squadron, with minelaying submarines, was attached to the Third Fleet (Blockade and Transport Force) and was initially to support the Japanese landings in the Philippines, Dutch East Indies, and British Malaya.

The 7th Submarine Squadron, with both first-line and second-line boats, was attached to the Fourth Fleet for the defense of the Mandate Islands and Japanese home waters.

Several second-line submarines that were unsuitable for operations in the open sea were attached to the Kure Naval District for homeland defense and training submarine crews.

In general, the Japanese submarines were well built and their crews well trained, with Japanese peacetime exercises being far more realistic (and dangerous) than those of any western navy. Several Japanese submarines were fitted to carry floatplanes for reconnaissance, while some were fitted with special communications for serving as group flagships. When the war began, Japanese torpedoes were the most reliable of those available to the major navies, with the oxygen-propelled Type 95 that was entering service having a longer range, higher speed, and larger warhead than any western torpedo of the war period (see chapter 16).

THE PEARL HARBOR ATTACK PLAN

The Japanese naval high command realized that to go to war in the Far East the American Pacific Fleet would have to be immobilized, if not destroyed, at the outset to prevent its interference with the drive to the southern resource areas. Accordingly, a highly secret plan was devised to attack the fleet at its home base of Pearl Harbor in the Hawaiian Islands.

The plan to attack Pearl Harbor (Hawaii Operation), which included the use of submarines in the Phase I tactical concept, was contained in the Special Combined Fleet Secret Operations Order No. 1, issued by an Imperial Conference on 5 November 1941. The tentative date of attack was 7 December (Sunday, U.S. time; one day later Tokyo time). On 1 December it was determined that the attack would actually be made on that date.

TABLE 1. SUBMARINE FORCE, DECEMBER 1941*

COMBINED FLEET

4th Submarine Squadron
flagship: KINU (CL)
tender: NAGOYA MARU (AS)

18th Submarine Division	I-53, I-54, I-55
19th Submarine Division	I-56, I-57, I-58
21st Submarine Division	RO-33, RO-34

5th Submarine Squadron
Rear Adm. Etuzo Yoshitomi
flagship: YURA (CL)
tender: RIO DE JANEIRO MARU (AS)

28th Submarine Division	I-59, I-60
29th Submarine Division	I-62, I-64
30th Submarine Division	I-65, I-66

THIRD FLEET/BLOCKADE AND TRANSPORT FORCE

6th Submarine Squadron
Rear Adm. Chimaki Kono
tender: CHOGEI (AS)

9th Submarine Division	I-123, I-124
13th Submarine Division	I-121, I-122

FOURTH FLEET (Japanese Mandate islands)

7th Submarine Squadron
Rear Adm. Shinzo Onishi
tender: JINGEI (AS)

26th Submarine Division	RO-60, RO-61, RO-62
27th Submarine Division	RO-65, RO-66, RO-67
33rd Submarine Division	RO-63, RO-64, RO-68

SIXTH FLEET/SUBMARINE FLEET

Vice Adm. Mitsumi Shimizu
flagship: KATORI (TS)

1st Submarine Squadron
Rear Adm. Sato Tsutomu
flagship: I-9
tender: YASUKUNI MARU (AS)

1st Submarine Division	I-15, I-16, I-17
2nd Submarine Division	I-18, I-19, I-20
3rd Submarine Division	I-21, I-22, I-23
4th Submarine Division	I-24, I-25, I-26

2nd Submarine Squadron
Rear Adm. Yamazaki Shigeteru
flagships: I-7, I-10
tender: SANTOS MARU (AS)

7th Submarine Division	I-1, I-2, I-3
8th Submarine Division	I-4, I-5, I-6

3rd Submarine Squadron
Rear Adm. Miwa Shigeyoshi
flagship: I-8
tender: TAIGEI (AS)

11th Submarine Division	I-74, I-75
12th Submarine Division	I-68, I-69, I-70
20th Submarine Division	I-71, I-72, I-73

KURE NAVAL DISTRICT FORCE

Assigned to headquarters	I-52, RO-31 (training)
6th Submarine Division	RO-57, RO-58, RO-59

*AS = Submarine tender.
CL = Light cruiser.
TS = Training Ship (the KATORI was one of three light cruiser-type ships built by the Japanese Navy in the late 1930s specifically for use as training ships).

While air strikes from six aircraft carriers were considered the primary means of attacking U.S. warships anchored in Pearl Harbor, the submarines were considered vital for (1) pre-attack reconnaissance, (2) tracking down and sinking any U.S. warships that escaped the air strikes, and (3) interception of any U.S. counterattack against the Japanese carriers. Rear Admiral Shigeru Fukudome, Chief of Staff of the Combined Fleet, wrote after the war: "As the General Staff estimated the chance of a successful aerial attack by the Task Force to be fifty percent, they considered it necessary to have the Submarine Force participate in the Hawaii Operation and launch underwater attacks coordinated with the aerial attacks."[6]

Fukudome continued,

It was my belief that, even if the Task Force's aerial attack ended in failure, the Submarine Force's operation would not fail. My belief was based on the expectation that no hitch would arise in the submarines' operations. They had a cruising radius of 10,000 miles, with no need of refueling at sea. Besides, submarines were best suited for stealthy movements, and a blockading operation of Hawaii would be very easy for the highly trained Japanese submarines. Furthermore, I expected that more damage would be inflicted by submarine attacks, which would be continued over a longer period, then by the air attacks, which would be of comparatively short duration.[7]

Thirty large, first-line submarines of the Sixth Fleet participated in the Pearl Harbor attack, five of which carried Type A two-man submarines. These "midget" submarines were to penetrate the harbor in advance of the air attack, adding to the general confusion and destruction. Admiral Isoroku Yamamoto, Commander in Chief of the Combined Fleet, had initially opposed the use of the two-man midgets. He was against their use as suicide craft and insisted that they be recovered by the submarines carrying them after the attack; also, Yamamoto feared that the midgets would be detected attempting to penetrate the harbor and would give warning of the impending attack—as indeed happened just prior to the air attack on the morning of 7 December.

The Japanese carrier striking force, under Vice Admiral Chuichi Nagumo, sailed from an isolated anchorage in the Kurile Islands on 26 November. It consisted of six aircraft carriers, supported by two battleships, one light and two heavy cruisers, eight destroyers, and eight tankers and supply ships. The Patrol Unit of three submarines, the I-19, I-21, and I-23 of the 1st Submarine Squadron, was assigned to the carrier striking force. These submarines were to patrol some fifty miles ahead of the main body, rescue the crews of downed aircraft, and help defend the carriers against counterattacks.

The remaining submarines of the Sixth Fleet were to deploy around the Hawaiian Islands in accord with the following plan.

The 1st Submarine Group under Rear Admiral Sato Tsutomu, composed of the I-9, I-15, I-17, and I-25, was to patrol in a line north of Oahu to track down any U.S. ships escaping to the north, and to intercept any counterattacks against the carrier striking force.

6. Vice Admiral Shigeru Fukudome, "Hawaii Operation," U.S. Naval Institute *Proceedings* (December 1955), p. 1326.
7. *Ibid.*

The 2nd Submarine Group under Rear Admiral Yamazaki Shigeteru, consisting of the I-1, I-2, I-3, I-4, I-5, I-6, and I-7, was to patrol between the islands of Molokai and Oahu (where Pearl Harbor is located). The 3rd Submarine Group, directed by Rear Admiral Shigeyoshi Miwa with the I-8, I-68, I-69, I-70, I-71, I-72, I-73, I-74, and I-75, was to patrol the area south of Oahu. The two latter groups also were to intercept U.S. ships and prevent a counterattack on the carriers. In addition, the I-71, I-72, and I-73 were to make a reconnaissance of the Lahaina anchorage in Maui prior to the attack to determine if any U.S. warships were anchored there.

The submarines of the 1st and 2nd Groups departed from the Kure and Yokosuka naval bases beginning on 10 November. They sailed southward to Kwajalein to top off their fuel and then headed eastward toward the Hawaiian Islands. Eleven of these submarines carried small floatplanes for reconnaissance.

The Special Attack Unit or "Sasaki Group"—named for Captain Hanku Sasaki, commander of the 3rd Submarine Division—contained the I-16, I-18, I-20, I-22, and I-24. These submarines departed the naval base of Kure on 18 November, each with a two-man submarine clamped to her deck. The Special Attack Unit was to deliver the midget submarines to the approaches of Pearl Harbor on the morning of the attack. The I-boats would remain in the area to recover the craft that night.

In conjunction with the Pearl Harbor attack, the final two submarines of the Sixth Fleet, the I-10 and I-26, were to perform reconnaissance of the Aleutian Islands and U.S. possessions in the South Pacific areas, respectively, on 5 December. If no U.S. warships were detected, they were to move to a position between Hawaii and the United States by the outbreak of war. The I-10 left Yokosuka on 16 November, and the I-26 departed three days later. The I-10 did sight the U.S. cruiser ASTORIA in the Fiji Islands, but saw no other U.S. naval forces. Since the sighting was made before the Pearl Harbor attack, the I-10 avoided the cruiser and sailed eastward.

The overall submarine participation in the Pearl Harbor attack was directed by the Commander Sixth Fleet. Immediately after the air strikes, the commander of the carrier striking force was to assume operational control of the submarine force for a three-day period, as it was anticipated that the two forces would be operating in the same area. The three I-boats of the Patrol Unit would remain with the carriers as long as necessary for their protection on the return transit to Japan.

Following the Pearl Harbor attack, submarines of the 1st and 2nd Squadrons would remain in the Hawaiian area as long as practical for reconnaissance and to attack U.S. ships. The boats of the 3rd Squadron were to sail eastward to attack shipping between Hawaii and the United States.

As the Japanese carrier striking force steamed eastward toward Pearl Harbor, the coded signal "Climb Mount Niikata" was transmitted to the force on 2 December (Japanese time). It was the order to carry out the attack on the U.S. Fleet at Pearl Harbor on 7 December at 8 A.M. Hawaiian time.

The aircraft from Admiral Nagumo's carriers made two highly effective strikes against the seven U.S. battleships moored alongside Ford Island in the center of Pearl Harbor (one other was in a dry dock in Pearl

The submarines I-68 and I-70 at high speed; both were among the large Japanese submarine participation in the Pearl Harbor attack with the I-70 being the only Japanese ship lost in the attack. The submarine contribution to the attack was virtually nil. (*Ships of the World*)

Harbor). While a number of U.S. ships sortied from Pearl Harbor after the air strikes, and two U.S. carrier groups—centered on the ENTERPRISE and LEXINGTON—were at sea, none was intercepted by the ring of Japanese submarines.

Immediately after the second air strike, Admiral Nagumo's carriers turned westward and, with jubilant crews, steamed toward Japan (with two carriers making a detour to strike Wake Island). They successfully recovered almost all of the attacking planes. After darkness fell on 7 December, the five I-boats off Pearl Harbor surfaced to recover their midgets. None appeared. The Japanese submarines submerged at dawn on 8 December and resurfaced that night. Again the seas off Oahu were empty of the ill-fated midgets.

SAGA OF THE MIDGETS

The Japanese Navy had developed midget submarines from 1934 onward, and by the late 1930s the Type A midgets were being mass-produced, and their two-man crews trained, under exacting secrecy (see chapter 11). At the end of October 1941—barely a month before the attack—Admiral Yamamoto approved their use in the Pearl Harbor attack *if* their crews could be recovered. The midgets' two-man crews had undergone several months of intensive training and were fully confident in their ability to carry out any mission assigned.

The commanding officers of the five submarines chosen to carry the midgets were not told of their mission until, a few days before departure, their I-boats were ordered into shipyards for the modifications necessary to carry and launch the midgets. Captain Sasaki, commander of the Special Attack unit, was a strong supporter of the midget operations and had helped to convince Yamamoto of the viability of the concept.

Each midget, manned by a crew of two, was fitted with two 18-inch torpedo tubes. They were not, as with later midget submarines, suicide craft; they were to penetrate Pearl Harbor in conjunction with the air attack, add their ten "fish" to the devastation of the U.S. battle fleet, and then escape back to sea to be recovered, or at least their crews rescued, by their mother submarines.

The five I-boats, each with a Type A midget carried abaft the conning tower, slipped out of the Kure naval base on the night of 25 November. They set course directly for Pearl Harbor, not going via Kwajalein, as were the other I-boats, because of their reduced speed while carrying the midgets.

The five mother submarines comprised the C1 class, all recently completed and with relatively untrained crews. The newest boat, the I-24, was almost lost during the transit to Pearl Harbor when a valve to a trim tank froze in the open position. Only quick action by one of the I-24 officers saved the boat from plunging below her collapse depth. Because of the time factor, these boats travelled on the surface in daylight as well as at night until they came within range of American air patrols. Afterwards they travelled on the surface only at night. The five mother submarines reached a point some one hundred miles from the entrance to Pearl Harbor on the evening of 5 December. They surfaced that night to charge their own batteries and those of the midgets, and make other preparations for the operation.

As the mother submarines approached the southern coast of Oahu on the night of 6 December, their crews could see the landing lights at the U.S. Army's Hickam Field as well as those along Waikiki Beach. Crewmen of the I-24 claimed they could hear jazz being played on a radio ashore. Shortly after midnight, while the I-boats were on the surface, the crewmen climbed into the midgets, the clamps that secured the midgets were released, and the mother submarines submerged some ten miles off the entrance to the harbor.

The midget submarine crewmen believed that they would not return from the mission. An officer in one of the mother submarines wrote,

> The officers commanding the [midget] craft seemed to have set out with the idea that they would not return. After launching, their private possessions, left in the parent submarine, had been set in order. They had duly left messages of farewell to their parents and directions for forwarding certain private effects. Their money was all left with their servants [stewards].[8]

8. Mochitsura Hashimoto, *Sunk!* (New York: Henry Holt and Company, 1954), p. 31.

All five midgets floated free as the mother submarines submerged. One midget, that of Ensign Kazuo Sakamaki (from the I-24), had a faulty gyrocompass, and he remained at periscope depth to navigate.

In the early morning of Sunday, 7 December, two U.S. Navy minesweepers were conducting a routine sweep off the entrance to Pearl Harbor. At 3:42 A.M. one of them, the USS CONDOR, sighted a submarine periscope; the commanding officer, a reserve ensign, immediately signaled by flashing light to the destroyer WARD, which was patrolling nearby. The destroyer took up the search. At 6:33 a U.S. Navy PBY Catalina flying boat sighted the same or another submarine periscope in the area and dropped smoke pots to mark the spot. This submarine appeared to be trailing the repair ship ANTARES, which was towing a barge into Pearl Harbor. The antisubmarine nets at the entrance would be open to permit the ship to enter. The ANTARES also sighted the submarine and along with the PBY contacted the WARD.

The WARD closed on the contact and attacked with gunfire. Her second salvo of 4-inch shells struck the submarine. The midget rolled over and disappeared. The WARD continued to close and released depth charges. She sank the midget at 6:45. A few minutes later the destroyer radioed the Commandant of the 14th Naval District (Pearl Harbor headquarters): "We have attacked, fired upon, and dropped depth charges upon submarine operating in defensive sea area." Thus, the midgets did in fact announce the start of the attack, and the first shots fired by the U.S. Navy in the Pacific War were against a Japanese submarine.

Because of a delay in decoding at Pearl Harbor, the WARD's message did not reach the headquarters duty officer until 7:12 A.M. The district commandant was immediately informed, and another destroyer, the MONAGHAN, was ordered to move out of the harbor to assist the WARD in searching for further contacts. The report was also passed to Admiral

The midget submarine HA-19 after the Pearl Harbor attack as beached for the last time on the eastern shore of Oahu. Her pilot, Ensign Kazuo Sakamaki, became America's first prisoner of war; his enlisted crewman drowned. (U.S. Navy)

The midget submarine that entered Pearl Harbor after being raised, showing the "washboard" effect of depth charging as well as the damage from being rammed. The Japanese Navy expected that major damage would be inflicted on the anchored U.S. fleet by the five midget submarines used in the attack. (U.S. Navy)

Husband E. Kimmel, the Pacific Fleet commander. He was on his way to headquarters when, at 7:55 A.M., the first bombs fell on Pearl Harbor.

Meanwhile, for unexplained reasons the antisubmarine nets to the harbor had been opened for the two minesweepers at 4:58 A.M. and not closed again until 8:40. A second midget submarine entered the harbor through the open nets a few minutes before the air attack began.

While the air attack was underway, the destroyer MONAGHAN, inside the harbor and steaming toward the entrance, saw a signal flying from the moored seaplane tender CURTISS that an enemy submarine was in the area. The CURTISS and the repair ship MEDUSA, moored nearby, opened fire at this second midget. The MONAGHAN sighted the midget just as she fired a torpedo at the CURTISS. The torpedo sped past the seaplane tender to explode against a dock at Pearl City, at the northern end of Pearl Harbor.

The midget sighted the approaching destroyer and fired the second torpedo. This one also missed its target and exploded against Ford Island in the center of the harbor. The MONAGHAN rammed the submarine at 8:43 A.M., following up with a barrage of depth charges, destroying the two-man craft.[9] The destroyer fired off another shot at what was thought to be a midget, but a harbor buoy was the cause of that false alarm. The MONAGHAN continued toward the entrance.

9. This midget was raised and used as fill material for a pier being built at Pearl Harbor. The two crewmen were given a military funeral as their battered craft was entombed.

Outside of the harbor the WARD now detected a third midget submarine, the one piloted by Sakamaki, which had no gyrocompass. Based on sonar contact, the WARD released five depth charges over this submerged midget. Their detonations knocked Sakamaki unconscious for a few moments, and the submarine filled with smoke, but continued running submerged. Sakamaki soon regained control of the midget, but almost immediately ran aground on a reef east of the harbor entrance. The destroyer HELM apparently fired on this midget at 8:17 A.M. The midget was able to slip off the reef, but soon ran aground again. A torpedo had been damaged in the earlier grounding, and now the torpedo firing mechanism was found to be broken and the boat was filling with gas from its electric storage batteries.

After transferring weights inside the submarine, Sakamaki and his crewman got the midget afloat sometime in the afternoon. He now planned to ram his boat—with two torpedoes in the bow—against a U.S. warship. But the midget could not be controlled and, with the two crewmen sick from the battery-gas fumes and stifling heat, as well as from the battering of depth charges, the boat drifted eastward, running onto a reef on the eastward side of Oahu, near Bellows Airfield. Sakamaki set the self-destruct charge in the boat, and he and his crewman began to swim the mile to shore. The crewman drowned; exhausted, Ensign Sakamaki reached shore. The next day, 8 December, he was captured by U.S. soldiers, becoming the first Japanese prisoner of war.

The self-destruct charge failed to destroy the abandoned midget, and it was attacked by a Navy PBY. The plane's depth charges dislodged the submarine from the reef. The boat then drifted ashore and was recovered by U.S. Navy.[10]

A fourth midget sank off the entrance to Pearl Harbor after a depth-charge attack. The destroyers BREESE, HELM, MONAGHAN, and WARD all carried out depth-charge attacks against it. The midget's crewmen had escaped from the craft after it sank; the two torpedoes were still in their tubes.[11] There is no record of what happened to the fifth midget. Most likely that craft also fell victim to a U.S. destroyer's depth charges or to an operational accident. It is possible that either the fourth or fifth midget also managed to gain entrance to the harbor, but this seems unlikely.

The midget submarines—for all the bravery and perseverance of their two-man crews—made no contribution to the Japanese assault on Pearl Harbor. They scored no successes with their topedoes, and their detection outside of the harbor almost gave warning of the impending Japanese attack. The midgets were the only Japanese submarines to see action of 7 December.

FOLLOW–UP OPERATIONS

In the four days following the Pearl Harbor raid, the submarines I-9, I-10, and I-26 each sank a merchant ship. At about 4 A.M. of 10 December the I-6, stationed in the Kauai Channel, reported sighting an aircraft carrier of the LEXINGTON class, escorted by two heavy cruisers. Admiral Shimizu, in his flagship KATORI at Kwajalein, ordered several submarines of the 1st Submarine Group to pursue and sink the carrier. The submarines pursued her for two days on the surface at speeds of up to twenty knots. In two separate, submerged attacks the submarines did fire torpedoes at the carrier, actually the ENTERPRISE, but no hits were made. On the morning of 10 December, however, the I-70 was sighted on the surface some two hundred miles northeast of Oahu by an SBD Dauntless dive bomber from the ENTERPRISE. The submarine was bombed and suffered sufficient damage to prevent her from submerging: that afternoon another SBD from the ENTERPRISE sank her, the first Japanese submarine loss of the war.

Admiral Shimizu directed the 1st Submarine Group and the I-10 and I-26 to continue eastward and attack shipping along the U.S. West Coast. These submarines had some successes against merchant ships. Various towns, cities, and navigation lights were still illuminated at night, to the surprise of the submariners. In late December, as these submarines were about to depart American waters, they were ordered to shell mainland targets; however, the order was rescinded just before the nine submarines involved were about to withdraw.

The 3rd Submarine Group concluded operations off the Hawaiian Islands in mid-December and headed back for Kwajalein. On 22 December three of these submarines shelled the Johnston and Palmyra islands with their deck guns.

10. This craft was brought to the United States for use in the war-bond campaign; after the war it went on display at Key West, Florida.

11. This craft was salvaged in 1960; because the corroded torpedoes could not be removed, the bow section was unbolted and the remaining portion of the midget was subsequently returned to Japan, where it was fitted with a new bow and placed on display.

The 2nd Submarine Group continued to patrol off the approaches to Pearl Harbor. On 17 December a floatplane from the I-5 carried out a dawn reconnaissance over Pearl Harbor, obtaining valuable information on the results of the air attack. The I-5 was one of the eleven I-boats in the Hawaiian Operation that carried one floatplane each. (The I-9 later made another floatplane reconnaissance of Pearl Harbor while returning to Kwajalein from patrolling the U.S. West Coast.) In late December these submarines also departed, shelling the islands of Hawaii, Maui, and Kauai. No damage was inflicted by any of these submarine bombardments.

Japanese submarines had thus made virtually no contribution to the attack on Pearl Harbor. The Japanese did claim that the midget submarine that had penetrated Pearl Harbor had, in fact, sunk a battleship; the claim was false. The submarine accomplishments, however, might have been quite different had the two U.S. carrier groups in the area attempted to counterattack the Japanese striking force. U.S. Navy anti-submarine tactics and capabilities were quite limited, while the subsequent Japanese submarine successes against U.S. carriers during 1942 demonstrated the effectiveness of the I-boats in that role. (Also, the highly experienced and unscathed air groups on board Admiral Nagumo's six carriers would probably have defeated the untested American carrier squadrons.)

Pearl Harbor began three years and eight months of conflict between the United States and Japan. Of the twenty surface warships, thirty submarines, and eight oilers that had participated in the Japanese attack, only one oiler would survive the war to surrender to U.S. naval forces.

THE ASSAULT ON WAKE ISLAND

Wake Island was an American outpost two thousand miles northwest of Oahu; the atoll had a seaplane anchorage and small air strip. Wake was defended by a battalion of Marines and a dozen fighter planes that had just been flown in from the aircraft carrier ENTERPRISE. The atoll was within bomber range of Japanese bases on Kwajalein, six hundred mile away. Five hours after the attack on Pearl Harbor, Japanese bombers from Kwajalein struck, destroying seven and damaging one of the twelve Marine fighter planes. Bomber attacks continued on a daily basis, followed by air strikes from two of the carriers that attacked Pearl Harbor and, finally, a landing that captured the atoll on 23 December.

The Fourth Fleet's 27th Submarine Division, consisting of the RO-65, RO-66, and RO-67, departed Kwajalein on 6 December for duty with the Wake Island invasion force. They reached the atoll on the 10th and conducted reconnaissance operations. Two days later, after the American defenders had defeated the first Japanese landing attempt, the submarines were ordered back to Kwajalein. The RO-66, however, failed to receive the recall order.

The 26th Submarine Division, consisting of the RO-60, RO-61, and RO-62, departed Kwajalein for Wake on 12 December to support the second invasion effort. On the night of 17 December the RO-62 collided with the RO-66; the hapless RO-66 sank immediately. All of her crew were saved. The RO-62, with only minor damage, continued on patrol.

After the successful Japanese landing on Wake, which surrendered on 23 December, the 26th Division was ordered back to Kwajalein. En route the RO-60 lost her bearings in rough weather, ran aground off Kwajalein, and sank on 29 December.

The remaining seven RO-type submarines of the 7th Squadron supported the Japanese assault on Rabaul in the Gilbert Islands, and then were assigned to defend the Marshall and Gilbert Islands against possible incursions by U.S. carrier forces. Also, submarines from this squadron shelled the U.S. Howland and Baker islands on 10–11 December, but inflicted no damage.

TO THE SOUTH SEAS

The eighteen boats of Submarine Squadrons 4, 5, and 6 were assigned to support operations in the South Seas. At the outbreak of hostilities, the minelaying I-123 and I-124 of the 6th Submarine Squadron sailed into Philippine waters to sow mines at the approaches to Manila Bay and to report on weather conditions, with the I-124 also rescuing aircraft crews after the initial air strikes against the Philippines. The remaining submarines supported the invasion of Malaya, performing patrol, reconnaissance, and the protection of shipping; the 6th Squadron's two other submarines, the I-121 and I-122, laid mines in the southern approaches to the British naval base at Singapore.

The I-121 subsequently laid mines at the northern entrance to the Surabaja Strait. The I-121 made another trip to Manila Bay to sow additional mines, but was deterred by U.S. naval patrols. The I-6, however, was able to lay mines through her torpedo tubes.

Japanese troop landings along the Malay coast began on 8 December (local time). The Japanese aircraft reconnoitering Singapore reported sighting two British capital ships in port, the just-arrived battleship PRINCE OF WALES and battle cruiser REPULSE. Late that night the two big-gun ships, in company with four escorting destroyers, slipped out of Singapore and steamed down the Strait of Johore, heading toward the Japanese landings.

The following day rain squalls and low clouds prevented Japanese planes from sighting them. At 3:15 P.M. the following afternoon, 9 December, the submarine I-65 sighted the two capital ships, screened by destroyers, proceeding north at approximately 5° North latitude and 105°30′ East longitude.

The I-65's report was broadcast to all submarines in the area, and at about 9 P.M. that evening several I-boats formed a barrier line to intercept the British ships. At 3:40 A.M., some twenty-three miles west of the earlier I-65 sighting, the two British capital ships were detected by the I-58. The Japanese submarine, on the surface, was almost run down by the British warships. She fired five torpedoes, but without effect. The I-58, unable to keep contact with the PRINCE OF WALES and REPULSE, sent off a sighting signal that the British ships were heading *south*. The British commander had decided that because his ships had been sighted and it was too late to attack the Japanese transports before they unloaded their troops, he would return to Singapore. Late that morning, guided by the Japanese submarine sightings, Japanese naval bombers from airfields in Indochina searched out and attacked the two British ships. For the loss of just three aircraft, both of the large British warships were sunk with heavy loss of life.

Even before the Malayan campaign was concluded, Japanese naval forces, supported by submarines from the 4th Squadron, began the invasion of British Borneo. The outnumbered Allied warships in the Far East consisted of cruisers and destroyers from the American, British, and Dutch navies. They fought gallantly, but were heavily outnumbered in the air and on the sea. The Allied forces were supported by several U.S. and Dutch submarines, and it was the Dutch submarine K-XVI off the northwest coast of Borneo that torpedoed and sank the first Japanese warship to fall victim to a submarine's torpedoes, the destroyer SAGIRI, on 24 December. The K-XVI was sunk soon after by Japanese surface ships. Several of the Dutch submarines were sunk in this period, with the K-XVII probably being sunk by the submarine I-66 in mid-December. As normally occurred in such sinkings, there were no survivors among the Dutch submariners.

The year 1941 ended with Japanese triumph on all fronts. At small cost the Imperial Japanese Navy had inflicted grievous injury on the U.S. and British battle fleets, and landed assaults in the Philippines, Malaya, and Borneo as well as on several Pacific islands. The Japanese submarine force, for the loss of three boats, had performed admirably in the reconnaissance role. But they had sunk only merchant ships and one Dutch submarine, when the policy of the Japanese Navy at this time was to concentrate on attacking warships. The list of ships attacked and sunk by submarines up until 15 January 1942 was not very impressive. The Japanese claimed a total of seventeen merchant ships sunk and three damaged, but even those claims must be balanced against the postwar Allied records that reveal only six ships lost in the Pacific area during that period. This poor exchange occurred even though Japanese submarines had the most reliable, most powerful, and longest-range torpedoes of any navy. The submarines themselves were well built and reliable, and their crews included some of the best-trained and most dedicated men of the Japanese armed forces. The new year would bring the greatest triumphs of the Japanese submarine force.

2 Strategy and Operations, 1942

With the New Year, the Imperial Japanese Army and Navy were on the offensive throughout Southeast Asia. In an effort to improve the operational control of submarines that would participate in the campaigns planned for early 1942, in late December the head of the Navy's Southern Force had organized Submarine Group A from the 6th Submarine Squadron and Group B from the 5th Submarine Squadron. This would place the activities of these undersea craft under his direct command.

Group A would operate in the Dutch East Indies and in Australian waters east of 117° longitude, with Davao in the Philippines as its base. This group was to intercept Allied warships in the area and lay mines off Australian ports.

Group B's operational area would be the Indian Ocean west of 106° longitude with the mission of destroying Allied shipping passing through the Malacca Strait and in the Indian Ocean. Its base was established at Penang, an island off the west coast of Malaya. Japanese troops had occupied the island in December. It would become a major Japanese *and German* submarine base.

In addition, several submarines assigned to the Malayan invasion force would operate in the Java Sea, covering the area between 117° and 106° East longitude. These boats were to provide direct support to the invasion forces.

The first major operation of the new year by the submarines of Group A was the laying of mines in Australian waters off Port Darwin and in Torres Strait by the large I-121 and I-122. As they were en route back to Davao they and all other I-boats in the region were notified by radio that the U.S. Asiatic Fleet was believed to be in the Flores Sea, east of Java. On 14 January the I-124 sighted the heavy cruiser HOUSTON, the largest U.S. warship in the Western Pacific, and two accompanying destroyers. The I-123 and I-124 attempted to trail the U.S. ships, but were unable to close for an attack. Additional U.S. ships were sighted in the area by these and other submarines, but the Japanese were able to torpedo only one transport. The I-121 and I-124 next laid mines at the western entrance of the Clarence Strait in northern Australia, and the I-123 at the northern entrance of Torres Strait between Australia and New Guinea.

During these operations the I-124 was lost off the Australian port of Darwin on 20 January. The U.S. destroyer EDSALL and a trio of Australian minesweepers sank the large minelaying submarine. The I-124, with the division commander, Captain Keiyu Endo, embarked, sank with all those on board in water only forty feet deep. U.S. Navy divers were sent down, entered the submarine, and removed naval code books, a godsend for the Navy codebreakers at Pearl Harbor.

Submarines of Group B began the new year by sailing from Davao and Camranh Bay for operations in the Indian Ocean. On January 17 the I-60 was attacked and sunk by the British destroyer JUPITER in the southern entrance to Sunda Strait.[1] Other submarines passed through the strait and had several successes in the Bay of Bengal and along the eastern coast of India. The British, hard-pressed in the Atlantic and Mediterranean theaters, could provide few antisubmarine ships and aircraft for this region.

Two more Japanese submarines were sunk in January, both in the Hawaiian area. Following the attack on Pearl Harbor the Sixth Fleet had maintained relays of submarines in Hawaiian waters. The fleet's strength had been reduced, as the 2nd Submarine Squadron's six I-boats returned to Japan during January for overhaul; they were then dispatched to the south to help with operations in the Indian Ocean (to become Submarine Group C), and several submarines from the other squadrons were sent to shipyards in Japan for overhaul and maintenance. En route to and from their operational area from their base at Kwajalein, these submarines generally shelled U.S. outposts, principally Johnston and Midway islands.

Those boats that operated in Hawaiian waters achieved few sinkings. However, on 10 January the I-6 located and torpedoed the large U.S. carrier SARATOGA about 500 miles southeast of Oahu. Six men in the carrier were killed in the explosions, and three of the ship's sixteen firerooms were flooded. The carrier and her sister ship LEXINGTON were the U.S. Navy's largest warships.[2] At the time, the Japanese believed the carrier to have been sunk. Only damaged, however, the "Sara" limped into Pearl Harbor under her own power for emergency repairs and then proceeded to Bremerton, Washington, for further repairs and modernization. The I-6's two torpedo hits had put the carrier out of action

---

1. Both the USS EDSALL and HMS JUPITER were sunk by Japanese forces during March 1942.
2. The submarine I-6 reported damaging the LEXINGTON. The two U.S. carriers were virtually identical in appearance; in 1930 the U.S.Navy had painted a vertical stripe on the SARATOGA's funnel and a horizontal stripe around the top of the LEXINGTON's funnel to help U.S. Navy units distinguish the sister ships during peacetime operations.

for five months in a critical period for the U.S. Navy in the Pacific. Two weeks later, on 23 January, another Japanese submarine torpedoed and sank the Navy oiler NECHES. Her loss 135 miles west of Oahu forced the cancellation of a planned raid by the carrier LEXINGTON against the Japanese forces on Wake Island.

Retribution for these U.S. losses came a few days later when the U.S. submarine GUDGEON sank the I-73. The GUDGEON had made the first U.S. submarine patrol into Japanese home waters, having departed Pearl Harbor on 11 December. She was now coming home, with no Japanese ships sunk because of faulty torpedo exploders (which plagued U.S. submarines for the first two years of the war). The GUDGEON's luck changed late on 26 January when she was advised by the submarine force commander at Pearl Harbor that one of the Japanese submarines that had just shelled Midway would pass across her track.[3] Early the next morning the GUDGEON, operating submerged, detected a Japanese submarine on sonar. A periscope check revealed the Japanese submarine travelling on the surface at about 15 knots. Ten minutes later the GUDGEON reached an attack position and fired three torpedoes. The I-73 blew up and sank with her entire crew. She was the first Japanese warship to be sunk by an American submarine. (The first Japanese warship to be sunk by any submarine had been the destroyer SAGIRI, torpedoed by the Dutch K-XVI.)

The day after the GUDGEON's success, U.S. destroyers caught and sank the I-23 north of Hawaii. This brought to seven the number of Japanese submarines lost since the war began. There would be no further submarine losses for the next three months.

February and March 1942 were marked by the defeat of U.S., British, and Dutch naval forces in the Far East, with the U.S. cruiser HOUSTON and several other Allied warships being sunk in the Java Sea battle of 27 February–1 March. The long range of the Type 95 torpedoes fired by Japanese cruisers and destroyers in the battle so surprised Allied naval officers that they believed they were under attack by nearby submarines.

The Allied naval forces were devastated in the one-sided Battle of the Java Sea. Then, except for the few U.S aircraft carriers with their limited screen of destroyers and cruisers, the Allies had no significant naval surface forces between the U.S. West Coast and the Suez Canal. Japanese losses in obtaining this had been minimal—no battleships, carriers, or modern cruisers had been lost in the first month of the war. Even the six large carriers of Admiral Nagumo's striking force had suffered few casualties among their 350-odd aircraft; just twenty-nine planes had been lost in the Pearl Harbor strike. After a respite in Japan, several of those carriers would steam south, for operations in support of Japanese aggression in the East Indies and to strike at British interests in the Indian Ocean.

No Japanese submarines participated directly in the Java Sea battle. However, the I-boats and smaller RO-type undersea craft were active from the Indian Ocean to the West Coast of the United States.

ATTACKS ON AMERICA

On 24 February the submarine I-17, under Commander Kozo Nishino, shelled the Elwood oil fields near Santa Barbara, California. It was the first direct attack on the continental United States since 1814. This was the I-17's second war patrol off the American coast. About 5:30 in the evening the submarine surfaced and fired seventeen rounds of 5.5-inch ammunition at the oil storage tanks. In addition, the I-17 sank two merchant ships.[4]

Even before Nishino's bombardment an even more daring raid was being prepared—a submarine-supported air strike against the Pearl Harbor naval base. Planning began in January 1942 for this second air raid on Pearl Harbor, the code name Operation K being assigned.

In early February the submarines I-15, I-19, and I-26 were fitted to refuel large flying boats, in this case two four-engine Kawanishi H8K1, which were given the Allied code name Emily. This would be the first combat mission for these aircraft. The planes would depart Japanese-held Jaluit Island before dawn on the day of the attack and reach the French Frigate Shoal—roughly half the distance between Midway and Oahu—at about sunset. The I-9 would serve as a radio beacon halfway between the two points. At the shoal the planes would be refueled by

The 5.5-inch (140-mm) gun was the largest mounted on Japanese submarines and was used in the attacks against the U.S. West Coast in early 1942. The U.S., French, and British navies all carried larger deck guns on their submarines, with the British M-class submarine monitors having 12-inch guns that could be fired while the submarines ran submerged with only the muzzles exposed. (U.S. Navy)

3. This information on the I-73's movements was obtained by radio intercept of Japanese communications—a key factor in U.S. Navy success in the Pacific; see W.J. Holmes, *Double-Edged Secrets* (Annapolis, Md.: Naval Institute Press, 1979), p. 57.

4. Excerpts from the diary of a crewman aboard the I-17 describe the shelling in detail in Zenji Orita and Joseph D. Harrington, *I-Boat Captain* (Canoga Park, Calif.: Major Books, 1976), pp. 52–54.

Kawanishi H8K flying boats, refueled and supported by submarines, flew the second Japanese air attack against Pearl Harbor. But this strike inflicted no damage, with later Operation K flights being cancelled. (U.S. National Archives)

the submarines and take off for the 500-mile flight to Pearl Harbor, each with one ton of bombs. Seven hours after sunset they were to make a surprise attack on Pearl Harbor and return directly to Jaluit. The I-15 would stand by off Pearl Harbor to rescue the crews if the planes had to come down after the attack. The ill-fated I-23 was to have provided weather reports to the bombers. The first Operation K occurred on 4 March with the planes arriving over Oahu at 1 A.M. A low overcast prevented the bombers from finding their target in the center of the naval base and they released their bombs "blindly." One plane's bombs fell into the sea and the other's near the city of Honolulu; U.S. military aircraft were blamed for the latter.

Both Japanese flying boats returned safely to Jaluit after a flight of over 4,000 miles that took twenty-four hours. Additional Operation K missions were planned but did not occur. The following August a different type of submarine air strike occurred when the I-25 arrived in waters off Cape Blanco, Oregon. With Commander Meiji Tagami in command, the large submarine made a perfect landfall. Before dawn the submarine surfaced and crewmen scrambled onto the deck, opened the hangar, and rapidly fitted wings, stabilizers, rudder, and floats to the Yokosuka E14Y Glen reconnaissance aircraft. A pair of special incendiary bombs were attached to wing racks, and Warrant Flying Officer Nobuo Fujita and Petty Officer Shoji Okuda climbed into the cockpit and were catapulted into the air.

The floatplane flew inland some fifty miles, and the fliers released the two fire bombs over the Oregon forests. The plane returned to come down safely on the water alongside the I-25, and was taken back on board the submarine. A second fire-bombing mission was flown. These were the first air attacks ever made against the continental United States.

The I-25 continued to operate off the West Coast, with Commander Tagami sinking two American freighters and damaging another. With one torpedo remaining, Tagami was preparing to conclude his patrol when, on 11 October, he detected two submarines travelling on the surface some 500 miles west of Seattle, Washington.

Tagami fired his last torpedo and one of the submarines exploded. He thought that he had sunk an American submarine. His victim, however, was the Soviet submarine L-16. At that time the United States was at war with Japan and Germany while the Soviet Union was at war with Germany but not with Japan. The Soviets decided to send the submarines L-15 and L-16 from Vladivostok on the Siberian coast to the Baltic Sea where they could be used against the Germans. The craft were to make the voyage via the Aleutians, San Francisco, and the Panama Canal.

The men on the bridge of the L-15, following the L-16, heard three sharp explosions from the L-16. The stricken submarine reportedly broadcast a message, "We're sinking from. . . . " The smoke dispersed and the L-16 was gone from sight.

A lookout on the bridge of the L-15 sighted a submarine periscope. The L-15, according to Soviet reports, opened fire with the craft's 4-inch deck gun, but without effect. There were no survivors from the sunken L-16.

(The Soviets—ever paranoid—stated at the time that the "cruel and foul blow" against the L-16 could have been struck by *either* a U.S. submarine or a submarine belonging to Japan—"which was neutral as far as we were concerned.")

Warrant Flying Officer Nobuo Fujita, who with his enlisted air crewman, flew the only bombing missions against the continental United States. He was conscripted into the Japanese Navy in 1932 and soon took flight instruction. He served in the submarines I-23 and I-25 before becoming an instructor during the remainder of the war.

A CHANGE IN TACTICAL CONCEPT

By the spring of 1942 senior Japanese naval officers were largely in agreement that submarines had not been used to their best advantage. With U.S. forces now on the alert, the prewar strategy of approaching U.S. ports to attack existing warships was now extremely hazardous. The use of submarines with the fleet in action against combatant ships was also questioned, but there was no change in tactics until April.

Phase I tactical concepts ended on 16 March 1941, when Admiral Shimizu was relieved as commander of the Sixth Fleet. Shimizu had been wounded when U.S. carrier planes attacked Kwajalein on 1 February. (None of the Japanese submarines at Kwajalein at the time were damaged.) In April, Phase II of Japanese submarine tactics went into effect. The new Sixth Fleet commander, Vice Admiral Teruhisa Komatsu, directed that merchant shipping was to be his submarines' primary target.

Subsequent submarine blockades of Allied harbors met with some success. Five submarines of the newly formed 8th Squadron under Rear Admiral Noboru Ishizaki sailed from Penang for the Indian Ocean at the end of April 1942. This group (I-10, I-16, I-18, I-20, I-30) sailed across the Indian Ocean, being refueled at sea by the accompanying armed merchant cruisers AIKOKU MARU and HOKOKU MARU. Three of the I-boats carried Type A midget submarines; the I-10 and I-30 carried floatplanes. Once off the coast of Africa the I-10's Glen floatplane reconnoitered Aden, Durban, Djibouti, Zanzibar, Dar-es-Salaam, and Diego-Suarez seeking out British naval and merchant ships.

Based on the floatplane's information, Admiral Ishizaki ordered an attack against the British naval base at Diego-Suarez on the morning of 31 May. The I-16 and I-20 each launched a midget submarine to attack ships in the harbor. The I-18 failed to launch the third midget because she suffered engine problems. The two midgets entered the harbor and damaged the British battleship RAMILLIES and sank a large tanker. Neither of the two-man craft returned to rendezvous with the I-boats.

After the Diego-Suarez raid, the submarines operated off the coast of Africa, sinking several Allied merchant ships. On 30 June all of the submarines took on fuel and supplies from the AIKOKU MARU and HOKOKU MARU some 600 miles southeast of Madagascar. All but the I-30 remained off the coast of Africa until early July, when the four submarines returned to Penang, conducting reconnaissance missions en route. Their three months' patrol in the Indian Ocean was followed by an upkeep period in Japan beginning in late August.

The I-30, which had been patrolling off Madagascar, proceeded on her own to the Cape of Good Hope in early July, thence around into the Atlantic, entering the Bay of Biscay on 2 August. Three days later, under an escort of German minesweepers, the I-30 arrived at the submarine pens at Lorient, France. There Commander Shinobu Endo was decorated by the Germans for his voyage. Then, loaded with technical equipment for the Japanese armed forces, the I-30 set out on the return trip. She arrived safely at Singapore in October 1942, but her journey ended on 13 October as she left that port en route to Japan and struck a British mine. All but thirteen of her crew of one hundred men were

rescued. This was the first of several efforts of the two Axis nations to employ submarines for the exchange of technical personnel and critical materials.

TABLE 2. SUBMARINE FORCE, 10 APRIL 1942

COMBINED FLEET	
5th Submarine Squadron	
flagship: YURA	
tender: RIO DE JANEIRO MARU	
19th Submarine Division	I-56, I-57, I-58
28th Submarine Division	I-59, I-62
30th Submarine Division	I-64, I-65, I-66
FOURTH FLEET (Japanese Mandate islands)	
7th Submarine Squadron	
tender: JINGEI	
21st Submarine Division	RO-33, RO-34
26th Submarine Division	RO-61, RO-62, RO-65, RO-67
33rd Submarine Division	RO-63, RO-64, RO-68
SIXTH FLEET/SUBMARINE FLEET	
flagship: KATORI	
13th Submarine Division*	I-121, I-122, I-123
1st Submarine Squadron	
flagship: I-9	
tender: HEIAN MARU	
2nd Submarine Division	I-15, I-17, I-19
4th Submarine Division†	I-25, I-26
2nd Submarine Squadron	
flagship: I-7	
tender: SANTOS MARU	
7th Submarine Division	I-1, I-2, I-3
6th Submarine Division	I-4, I-5, I-6
3rd Submarine Squadron	
flagship: I-8	
tender: YASUKUNI MARU	
11th Submarine Division	I-74, I-75
12th Submarine Division	I-68, I-69
20th Submarine Division	I-71, I-72
8th Submarine Squadron	
flagship: I-10	
tender: HIE MARU	
1st Submarine Division	I-16, I-18, I-20
3rd Submarine Division	I-21, I-22, I-24
14th Submarine Division	I-27, I-28, I-29, I-30
KURE NAVAL DISTRICT FORCE	
	I-52, RO-31
6th Submarine Division	RO-57, RO-58, RO-59
18th Submarine Division	I-53, I-54, I-55

*The 6th Submarine Squadron was deactivated on 10 April 1942; its 13th Submarine Division was placed directly under command of the 6th Fleet, and its 21st Division was transferred to the 7th Squadron.
†I-23, assigned to the 4th Submarine Division, was sunk on 10 April 1942.
Note: Twenty-seven submarines numbered between I-52 through I-85 were renumbered from I-152 through I-185 on 20 May 1942.

At the time of the Diego-Suarez raid, five other submarines from the 8th Squadron (I-21, I-22, I-24, I-27, I-29), under Captain Sasaki, were operating off the eastern coast of Australia. These five I-boats each carried a Type A midget submarine. The I-22, I-24, and I-27 launched their midgets into Sydney Harbor on the afternoon of 31 May, but they accomplished no significant results despite the presence of U.S. and Australian cruisers and lesser warships there. None of the midgets survived the attack. There were other midget attacks against Allied forces in the region, but without result. The Japanese I-boats shelled Sydney and Newcastle in early June, sank a few merchant ships, and then withdrew, going on to Japanese yards for maintenance and repairs.

Also during the spring of 1942, the change of command in the Sixth Fleet, the loss of seven submarines since the war began, and the completion of additional undersea craft led to a reorganization of Japanese submarine forces (see table 2). The Sixth Fleet retained the 1st, 2nd, and 3rd Submarine Squadrons, and the 8th Squadron was established under the Sixth (Submarine) Fleet. The 4th Squadron was deactivated on 10 March; only the 5th Squadron remained under the Combined Fleet headquarters; the 6th Squadron, which had the large I-121-class minelayers, was deactivated on 10 April, its submarines being assigned to the operational control of the Sixth Fleet commander (as the 13th Submarine Division); the 7th Squadron remained under the Fourth Fleet in the Mandate Islands, based at Truk; and the Kure Naval District retained several older submarines for training and area defense.

CORAL SEA INTERLUDE

From the beginning of April 1942, most of the 7th Submarine Squadron's boats were in Japan undergoing overhaul and repairs. Only the RO-33 and RO-34 were at Truk. In mid-April these submarines sailed to Rabaul, on New Ireland at the northern end of the Solomon Sea, and were placed under the direct command of the South Seas Force to search for suitable convoy routes and anchorages for the planned assault on Port Moresby, New Guinea—designated Operation MO (for Moresby) by the Japanese. Subsequently, the RO-33 and RO-34 were assigned to blockade the port and guide Japanese ships to the region. Meanwhile, the 8th Squadron's I-22, I-24, I-28, and I-29 were directed to deploy some 250 miles southwest of Guadalcanal Island to guard against possible interference by Allied warships. Afterwards, they were to load midgets at a Solomons anchorage for further operations off eastern Australia. Two other submarines, the I-21 and I-27, would initially accompany these I-boats, but their mission was to conduct reconnaissance of Australia and the South Sea islands. The latter boats were of the B1 aircraft-carrying type. The sortie of these six I-boats south from Japan was interrupted on 18 April when they were about four hundred miles south of Honshu. In response to the Doolittle-Halsey raid on Japan, they were directed to form a scouting line east of the Bonin Islands, but they saw nothing of the U.S. carriers.[5] The submarines resumed their course to the naval base at Truk to refuel and then headed on to the Coral Sea area (below the Bismarck Sea).

In early May, Japanese forces landed on the island of Tulagi, adjacent to Guadalcanal, to establish a seaplane base to support the planned invasion of Port Moresby, an important Allied base on New Guinea. A U.S. carrier force centered on the LEXINGTON and YORKTOWN sought to engage these forces, thus precipitating the Battle of Coral Sea. On the afternoon of 2 May, the I-21 was sighted by a carrier aircraft some thirty-two miles from the YORKTOWN. The SBD Dauntless attacked the submarine, but the submarine escaped, apparently without having sighted the U.S. carrier group. The I-21 was not operating her floatplane, which would have certainly found the carriers.

Instead, the Japanese forces in the area, including the light carrier SHOHO, and their distant supporting force of two large fleet carriers were surprised by the presence of the U.S. naval ships. There followed history's first carrier-versus-carrier battle.[6] The Coral Sea battle was a tactical victory for the Japanese, as their carrier aircraft sank the large carrier LEXINGTON and damaged the YORKTOWN, in return for the loss of a light carrier. However, the large Japanese carrier SHOKAKU was damaged, and her sister ship ZUIKAKU suffered severe losses in aircraft and air crews. After the battle they withdrew to Japan for rehabilitation, thus causing the two carriers to be absent at the subsequent Battle of Midway. And because of their absence at Midway and the resulting lack of Japanese planes for the Port Moresby invasion, the Coral Sea engagement was a strategic victory for the United States.

Despite their readiness to intercept the U.S. carrier force, the Japanese submarines were not in a position to participate in the battle. The brand-new I-28, returning to Truk, reported engine trouble on 16 May while 250 miles north of Rabaul. She was sunk the following day by the U.S. submarine TAUTOG. (There were eleven old U.S. S-class submarines assigned to support the defense of Port Moresby; only four were able to go to sea, and those boats sank a Japanese minelayer and cargo ship after the carrier battle.)

The Coral Sea battle was history's first naval engagement in which only the attacking aircraft saw the opposing fleet. The opposing ships never saw their enemies. The lack of contribution of the available Japanese submarines in this first carrier battle was a harbinger of the coming Midway battle.

THE BATTLE OF MIDWAY

Although the Japanese Navy's tactical concept for the use of submarines had shifted in the spring of 1942—instead of U.S. warships being the primary target, they launched a campaign against merchant shipping—it was still the strategic concept of the Japanese Navy to force the U.S. Fleet into a major sea battle where, under advantageous conditions, the Japanese could inflict a decisive defeat. Following the Doolittle-Halsey raid against Japan in April 1942, the Japanese military leadership

5. Led by Colonel James (Jimmy) Doolittle, sixteen U.S. Army B-25B bombers flew from the carrier HORNET on 12 April 1942 in a token bombing raid against Japan; Vice Admiral William F. (Bull) Halsey, embarked in the accompanying carrier ENTERPRISE, commanded the operation.

6. In April 1942 the five Japanese carriers in the Indian Ocean had encountered the British HERMES, the first ship built by any nation from the keel up as an aircraft carrier. She had no aircraft embarked when the Japanese found her on 9 April, and she was quickly destroyed—the first carrier to be sunk by carrier aircraft.

decided to push forward with the invasion of Midway Island. This assault, they felt, would force the United States to commit its remaining battleships and carriers to the defense of the main Hawaiian Islands. With a predeployed screen of submarines and the advantages of superior numbers of battleships and carriers—and with aircraft based ashore at Midway after it was captured—the Combined Fleet would defeat the Americans. Just before the Midway operation there would be a diversionary assault on the western Aleutian Islands in the hope of drawing what U.S. warships were available away from the Hawaiian Islands.

The Midway operation—code-named Operation MI for Midway—would include massive submarine participation. Under Vice Admiral Komatsu, the Sixth Fleet's 3rd and 5th Submarine Squadrons and the 13th Submarine Division would participate in the Midway campaign, while the 1st Submarine Squadron would take part in the Aleutians operation. Thus, the plan was for nineteen I-boats to participate in the Midway-Aleutians operation (as listed in table 2, plus the new I-11, assigned to the 3rd Squadron; also, the I-8 was shifted to the 8th Squadron). In addition, the submarine carriers CHIYODA and NISSHIN would accompany the invasion force, the former with eight Type A midget submarines and the latter with five motor torpedo boats for the defense of Midway after the island was captured.[7] Six other I-boats would support the Aleutians campaign.

Several of the 3rd Squadron's I-boats, however, that had left Japanese ports to refuel and stand by at Kwajalein suffered mechanical problems and had to return to base. And the I-64, departing Sasebo for Kwajalein on 16 May, was sunk by the U.S. submarine TRITON on 17 May while travelling on the surface off the Japanese coast. The TRITON had fired a single torpedo at a range of 6,200 yards to hit the I-64. (Four days later the TRITON fired four torpedoes at another submarine, but all missed their target.)

In preparation for the Midway campaign, a second Operation K was scheduled. Two Kawanishi H8K Emily flying boats were to reconnoiter Pearl Harbor to determine the status of the U.S. naval forces there. The planes would be refueled by submarines at the French Frigate Shoal. The I-121, I-122, and I-123 would refuel the seaplanes upon their arrival; the I-171 would serve as a radio beacon to guide the flying boats to the tankers; the I-174 would cruise southwest of Oahu to rescue the flying boat crews if they were forced to ditch near the target; and the I-175 was to report weather from southwest of Oahu. The seaplane reconnaissance operation was cancelled, however, on the evening of 31 May when U.S. ships were reported in the French Frigate Shoal area. Thus, the Combined Fleet was denied information on the number of U.S. ships at Pearl Harbor.

By 4 June the I-boats were taking their prearranged stations to form barrier lines ahead of the Japanese main force in order to intercept U.S. warships that would sortie from Pearl Harbor to intercept the Combined Fleet *after* the Midway invasion began. On the eve of the great carrier battle, the submarine patrol lines were manned by:

3rd Submarine Squadron	5th Submarine Squadron
I-169	I-156
I-171	I-157
I-174	I-158
I-175	I-159
	I-162
	I-165
	I-166

In addition, the I-121, I-122, and I-123 of the 13th Divison were to patrol near Laysan Island and the French Frigate Shoal. And the I-168 was to scout out Midway Island, bringing to fifteen the number of I-boats participating in the Midway operation.

But because of repairs to submarines of the 5th Squadron and the participation of the 3rd Squadron in the cancelled Operation K, the submarine deployments were behind schedule. The unsatisfactory condition of the boats in the 5th Submarine Squadron was fully understood by the staff of the submarine force before the battle. A submarine specialist on the Naval General Staff, Commander Shojiro Iura, has been quoted as protesting the use of the boats of Submarine Squadron 5; he is said to have "predicted that they would not be able to do the jobs given them."[8] The submarines did not reach their assigned stations on time, and it was toward this hole in the Japanese reconnaissance screen that the U.S. carrier task forces approached.[9]

Since U.S. Navy intelligence had determined in advance through radio intercept the Japanese plans for the Midway invasion, the available U.S. warships had already departed Pearl Harbor. Indeed, three U.S. carriers were advancing against the Japanese force—the ENTERPRISE, HORNET, and the hastily repaired YORKTOWN. These carriers, with a small screen of cruisers and destroyers, would face four first-line Japanese carriers that were supported by a host of battleships, cruisers, and destroyers, and screened by the Sixth Fleet's submarines.

Through superior U.S. intelligence of Japanese activities, support from Midway-based planes, good tactical leadership, and luck, U.S. dive bombers at Midway sank all four large Japanese carriers on the afternoon of 4 June. In return, a small strike group that flew from the carrier HIRYU before she was sunk managed to score bomb hits on the USS YORKTOWN. The U.S. carrier was left dead in the water, prematurely abandoned by her crew. Subsequently, while six destroyers screened her, a minesweeper took her in tow and repair crews went to work on the damaged carrier.

With the loss of the four fleet carriers in his main striking force, Admiral Isoroku Yamamoto, CinC of the Combined Fleet, directed the I-168 (Lieutenant Commander Yahachi Tanabe), which had scouted Midway on 1 June, to conduct a surface bombardment of the island after sundown on 4 June with her single 3.9-inch deck gun. Tanabe was to be joined that night by four heavy cruisers carrying a total of forty 8-inch

---

7. These ships were former seaplane tenders, modified in 1941–1942 to carry midget submarines. Most histories, however, incorrectly listed them as seaplane tenders at the time of the Midway operation. See chapter 15.

8. Orita and Harrington, *I-Boat Captain,* p. 71.

9. Similarly, the subsequent Japanese aerial reconnaissance on the eve of the battle failed to locate the American carriers because the cruiser floatplane assigned to the specific sector where the U.S. ships were located developed engine trouble, and there was a delay until a substitute could be launched.

guns, whose broadside could send about five tons of high explosives crashing into the island with each salvo.

The I-168 arrived off Midway and opened fire. The submarine's shelling, however, was quickly halted when defensive gun batteries, aided by searchlights, took the submarine under fire. Tanabe was forced to submerge after firing only six rounds, all of which hit the lagoon. The bombardment by the four cruisers, which might have been able to smash Midway installations in a night attack, was cancelled and the cruisers withdrew. After her brief firing run, the I-168 was pursued briefly by an American ship.

Early on 5 June the Japanese fleet commander determined that the damaged carrier YORKTOWN was about 150 miles northeast of Midway, and the I-168, following her abortive attack on the island, was directed to attack the carrier. The I-168 set off in the direction of the U.S. ship at the best underwater speed that would permit her to run submerged during daylight hours. With darkness on 5 June the I-168 surfaced and searched for the YORKTOWN. The search was conducted visually, as the submarine had no radar. "So it was that, at 0530 on 6 June, the 12-mm binoculars of my best-trained lookout picked up YORKTOWN. She was a black shape on the horizon, about 11 miles distant."[10] The I-168 stalked her prey for several hours after the carrier was detected. One U.S. destroyer, the HAMMANN, was alongside the carrier, and five others were cruising about one mile out to provide defense against air and submarine attack. Some of the destroyers were "pinging" with their active sonar, but did not detect the I-168. Tanabe continued:

By 1100, I had decided that the enemy [sonar] equipment was not very sensitive. This gave me confidence as the range shortened; I kept moving in. Suddenly my sound operator reported that the Americans had stopped emitting detection signals. I couldn't understand this but, since it was now nearly noon, I tried to make my voice light and told my crew, "It appears the Americans have interrupted their war for lunch. Now is our chance to strike them good and hard, while they are eating!" There were small jokes made about what to give them for dessert.[11]

Tanabe maneuvered the I-168 to less than six hundred yards from the carrier on his first approach, and fearing the distance was insufficient for his torpedoes to arm, he made a complete circle and gained another attack position of 1,200 yards. At 1:30 P.M. the I-168 fired four torpedoes at the YORKTOWN. These were the older Type 89 torpedoes, with only 660-pound warheads.[12] To maximize their effect, Tanabe decided to fire his torpedoes close together instead of in a normal spread of perhaps six degrees. Two torpedoes were fired with a two-degree spread, and then two more were fired in their wakes.

One torpedo missed the carrier, two went under the HAMMANN and exploded against the carrier, and the fourth hit the destroyer, the explosion breaking her in two. The HAMMANN sank in four minutes, taking with her eighty-one of her crew of 241. Several more of her crew would later die of wounds. The YORKTOWN initially remained afloat as the salvage crew on board fought to stem the inrush of water. At 6 A.M. on 7 June the carrier sank.

After this torpedo attack, the U.S. destroyers began an intensive

10. Yahachi Tanabe and Joseph D. Harrington, *I Sank the Yorktown at Midway*, U.S. Naval Institute *Proceedings* (May 1963), p. 61.

11. *Ibid.*, p. 62.
12. Most Japanese submarines at this time had Type 95 torpedoes with 891-pound warheads.

The U.S. carrier YORKTOWN sinking after being torn apart by two torpedoes from the submarine I-168. The submarine's captain, Yahachi Tanabe, was hailed as a national hero upon returning to Japan. His torpedoes and bombs from aircraft flying from the carrier HIRYU scored the only Japanese success in the Battle of Midway. (U.S. Navy)

assault on the I-168. Some sixty depth charges were dropped on the submarine, inflicting serious damage. The I-168's batteries and air supply were low, at one point electrical power was lost, water was coming in through a damaged torpedo tube, and the boat was sinking below her safe operating depth. Finally forced to surface, Tanabe was able to evade the destroyers long enough to charge his batteries, using smoke to help hide his craft until he could again submerge—while under fire from the U.S. destroyers. In time, the destroyers gave up the hunt, and Tanabe was able to escape. Upon his arrival at Kure, Tanabe was hailed as a national hero and given command of the new I-176. His achievement was the only bright moment for the Japanese in the otherwise disastrous Battle of Midway.[13]

The 1st Submarine Squadron I-boats sent to the Aleutians saw little action. Some subsequently approached the American coast. The I-26 shelled Estewan Point in Canadian Vancouver, while the I-25 shelled Fort Stevens, Oregon. Only two merchant ships were sunk by these submarines.

After Midway, Japanese forces withdrew from the Central Pacific. The 1st Submarine Squadron in the Aleutians was replaced in late June by the seven I-boats of the 2nd Squadron. These boats reconnoitered the U.S. bases and sought to intercept U.S. naval ships in the region, but only one transport was sunk. On 20 July all but the I-6 were ordered back to Japan, ending all vestiges of the Midway-Aleutians operation.

The Battle of Midway is considered to have been the turning point in the naval war against Japan, as it ended the period of Japanese offensive action. Japanese naval air strength was severely damaged by the loss of four large aircraft carriers with all of their aircraft and many highly trained pilots. Nineteen Japanese submarines were involved in the Midway-Aleutians action, but their contribution was to sink only the already damaged Yorktown and, inadvertently, a destroyer lying alongside the carrier.

The American carriers had been able to reach their holding position, awaiting the arrival of the Japanese carriers, without being detected by Japanese submarine or search aircraft. The I-boats of the 5th Squadron arrived too late on their patrol station. But neither did U.S. submarines make a contribution to the battle. The U.S. Navy had deployed nineteen fleet-type submarines off Midway—four in a barrier line north of the main Hawaiian Islands, in the event U.S. intelligence misread the Japanese intentions and a strike against Pearl Harbor was intended; three between the Hawaiian Islands and Midway; eleven off Midway; and a picket submarine farther west. (Six older U.S. S-boats were in the Aleutians, but had no part in the action.) The U.S. submarine deployments off Midway were poor, and only one, the Nautilus, made contact with the main Japanese force. She was taken under attack several times; she fired several torpedoes at Japanese ships, including one burning carrier, but without any effect. One report contended that the torpedo from the Nautilus, after hitting the Soryu, broke apart, the warhead sinking and the after body remaining afloat. Several Japanese are said to have been seen clinging to the after body of the dud torpedo.

At the time U.S. sources incorrectly credited the Nautilus with having given the *coup de grâce* to the bomb-devastated carrier Soryu. Another U.S. submarine, the Tambor, sighted the four cruisers that were to have bombarded Midway, but she did not attack them because she was unable to identify them as enemy ships.

THE WAR IS LOST

The Japanese leaders had begun the war to ensure the availability of resources from the East Indies and freedom of action in China. Those men in Tokyo believed that by inflicting major losses on the U.S. Fleet at Pearl Harbor and rapidly overrunning the American, British, and Dutch possessions in the Western Pacific, the Allied nations, locked in an intense struggle with Nazi Germany, would accept Japan's position in the Western Pacific as a *fait accompli*.[14]

The Coral Sea battle, the April 1942 Doolittle-Halsey bomber raid on Japan, and Midway demonstrated instead that the United States would continue to fight in the Pacific. Further, despite the victories of Japanese forces over the impotent Allied air, ground, and naval forces in the Far East when the war began, Midway demonstrated that the Imperial Japanese Navy could be decisively defeated in a battle that occurred at a time and place, and essentially under circumstances of Japanese choosing, and in which the Combined Fleet had superiority in all categories of warships. At Midway the Japanese were decidedly defeated, losing four fleet carriers with all of their air wings plus one heavy cruiser sunk and a second badly damaged, in return for the American loss of one carrier and one destroyer.

Never again would the Japanese have overwhelming superiority in numbers. There would be approximate parity in the naval engagements of the Solomons area in the second half of 1942, and certainly the Japanese would still enjoy a great superiority in the Far Eastern theater. But the American shipyards and aircraft factories would provide the steady flow of warships and aircraft that would, by mid-1943, give the U.S. Pacific Fleet overwhelming numerical and qualitative superiority over the Japanese Fleet. (Of course, those same yards were also producing the many hundreds of escort carriers, escort ships, amphibious ships, and landing craft as well as merchant ships needed for the Allied victories in the Atlantic, Mediterranean, and European theaters as well as in the Pacific.)

At the beginning of the war Japanese naval leaders had envisioned that their submarines would have a major role in the Pacific conflict—locating and attriting U.S. naval forces as they steamed westward against superior Japanese naval forces. The Japanese submarine force failed completely to perform these missions effectively during the first six months of the war. At Pearl Harbor and again at Midway the submarines could have changed the outcome to a Japanese victory.

Japanese victories in 1942 and 1943 could delay but never change the outcome of the conflict once the Americans resolved to fight the Pacific war to the defeat of Japan. As British military historian H.P. Willmott astutely observed, "Midway was fought between one navy at

---

13. The Japanese naval high command never revealed the extent of the disaster at Midway to the Japanese people or to the Army's leadership, who were running the country.

14. The Japanese had occupied air and naval bases in French Indochina after France fell to the Germans in 1940.

the peak of its strength and another if not at its nadir then close to it."[15]

Thus, Japanese grand strategy had failed to intimidate the Americans and force them to accept the Japanese "new order" in the Pacific; the Japanese Navy had failed to win total victory, despite its overwhelming superiority, at Pearl Harbor, Coral Sea, or Midway; and, in particular, the Japanese submarine force failed to accomplish its vital missions— *which could have changed each of these battles into a Japanese victory.*

FLEET REORGANIZATION

The Combined Fleet was reorganized on 10 July 1942 in the aftermath of Midway. At the same time, the submarine force was being reorganized. In August the standard size of a submarine division was increased from three to six boats, the maximum it was believed possible for a commander to control in raids against enemy communication routes. There was at the time considerable debate within the Navy as to whether the division structure should be retained at all.

The Navy had planned to send more submarines into the southern area, to operate against Australia. However, the need to train crews for new submarines being built required several boats to be sent to the Kure Naval District, curtailing the planned increase of activity off Australia. The 19th Division (I-156, I-157, I-158, I-159) was sent to Kure; the remainder of the 30th Division plus the squadron flagship, the trouble-plagued I-8, was assigned to the Southwest Area Fleet (and the 5th Submarine Squadron was disbanded on 10 July 1942).

The 2nd Squadron, with submarines I-1 through I-7, was reassigned to the Sixth Fleet (and would be disbanded on 20 August 1942). On 14 July the 26th Submarine Division (RO-61, RO-62, RO-65, RO-67) and the 33rd Submarine Division (RO-63, RO-64, RO-68), which had been operating in the South Seas area as part of the 7th Squadron, was reassigned to the Fifth Fleet. These boats would operate in Aleutian waters in place of the I-boats. They would use Kiska as a base to defend Japanese holdings in that frigid area. Most of the RO-boats arrived at Kiska in early August. One, the RO-65, was lost on 4 November when she submerged in Kiska Harbor during a U.S. air attack and struck rocks.

At the other end of the Japanese empire, the area of South Seas operations was considered too large for control by one fleet commander. The 4th Fleet became the Inner Seas Fleet, and the Eighth Fleet was established to direct operations in the area south of Rabaul, including the Solomons. On 14 July the 7th Squadron was assigned to the Eighth Fleet. The old RO-type boats were replaced, the squadron now comprising the 13th Submarine Division (I-121, I-122, I-123) and 21st Submarine Division (RO-33, RO-34). When the squadron was reorganized, the five submarines were in Japan undergoing overhaul and repairs. The two RO-boats reached Rabaul late in July and immediately departed for the Coral Sea. In early August the RO-33 sank a transport in the Gulf of Papua. The three I-boats followed and were at Rabaul on 7 August when the alarm was sounded that U.S. troops were landing on Tulagi. The three I-boats were ordered to proceed immediately to the Solomons.

15. H.P. Willmott, *The Barrier and the Javelin* (Annapolis, Md.: Naval Institute Press, 1983), p. 519.

SUBMARINES ON THE DEFENSIVE

Immediately after the Battle of Midway, the U.S. Navy's leadership realized that the United States had temporarily gained the initiative in the Pacific. The Navy was already planning an assault on the Solomon Islands, with the newly established Japanese air base at Rabaul on New Britain as its ultimate objective. In the southern Solomons the Japanese had

TABLE 3. SUBMARINE FORCE, 14 JULY 1942

FIFTH FLEET	
26th Submarine Division	RO-61, RO-62, RO-65, RO-67
33rd Submarine Division	RO-63, RO-64, RO-68
SIXTH FLEET/SUBMARINE FLEET flagship: KATORI	
1st Submarine Squadron flagship: I-9 tender: HEIAN MARU	
2nd Submarine Division	I-15, I-17, I-19
4th Submarine Division	I-25, I-26
15th Submarine Division	I-31, I-32, I-33
2nd Submarine Squadron flagship: I-7 tender: SANTOS MARU	
7th Submarine Division	I-1, I-2, I-3
8th Submarine Division	I-4, I-5, I-6
3rd Submarine Squadron flagship: I-11 tender: YASUKUNI MARU	
11th Submarine Division	I-174, I-175
12th Submarine Division	I-168, I-169, I-172
8th Submarine Squadron flagship: I-10 tender: HIE MARU	
1st Submarine Division	I-16, I-18, I-20
3rd Submarine Division	I-21, I-22, I-24
14th Submarine Division	I-27, I-29, I-30
EIGHTH FLEET	
7th Submarine Squadron tender: JINGEI	
13th Submarine Division	I-121, I-122, I-123
21st Submarine Division	RO-33, RO-34
SOUTHWEST AREA FLEET	
flagship: I-8 tender: RIO DE JANEIRO MARU	
30th Submarine Division	I-162, I-163, I-166
KURE NAVAL DISTRICT	
tender: CHOGEI	
6th Submarine Division	RO-57, RO-58, RO-59
18th Submarine Division	I-153, I-154, I-155
19th Submarine Division	I-156, I-157, I-158, I-159
YOKOSUKA NAVAL DISTRICT	
	RO-31

established a seaplane base on Tulagi, and in early July began construction of an airfield on nearby, jungle-covered Guadalcanal. These bases would support a renewed offensive to capture Port Moresby on New Guinea and a general thrust south, toward Australia.

On the night of 6 August 1942 a U.S. invasion force entered the Solomon Sea. The U.S. force, supported by three aircraft carriers and one fast battleship, carried a Marine division to assault Guadalcanal and capture the unfinished airfield from the Japanese. At 8 A.M. on 7 August, under the protection of carrier planes, U.S. Marines stormed ashore at Tulagi and one hour later at Guadalcanal against virtually no resistance from the Japanese troops and laborers. The Japanese area commander at Rabaul immediately responded with air strikes against the American beachhead. These were followed by surface warships and submarines as the Japanese sought to expel the invaders in what would become a lengthy and costly campaign.

The RO-33 and RO-34, already in the Solomon-Bismarck Sea area when the landings began, were rapidly reinforced by additional submarines, initially the large minelayers I-121, I-122, and I-123. The RO-33 sank a transport, but air strikes and then Japanese surface ships making hard-hitting night attacks were the real threat to the U.S. invasion forces. By 24 August 1942, when opposing forces were converging for the Battle of the Eastern Solomons, the Japanese submarines already in the Guadalcanal area were joined by the I-9, I-15, I-17, I-19, I-26, I-31, and I-33, all coming down from Japan via Truk. Subsequently, the I-11, I-174, and I-175 moved up from the coast of Australia. These brought to fifteen the number of Japanese submarines on the prowl in the area, mostly southeast of Guadalcanal. None of these submarines had any successes during this period; two submarines were attacked by U.S. forces and escaped. Japanese aircraft damaged the U.S. carrier ENTERPRISE that day, forcing her to withdraw; the U.S. Navy could still deploy three other carriers in the Solomons, and their planes were able to damage two I-boats.[16]

Japanese submarines were effective in reporting U.S. ship movements, and such information was useful in the later battles of Santa Cruz and Guadalcanal, in which the Japanese surface fleet did win impressive victories. However, the Japanese submarines scored no kills in this phase of the Solomons campaign, and the I-123 was sunk by the U.S. destroyer-minelayer GAMBLE on 29 August in the Guadalcanal area.

(Two other Japanese submarines were sunk in late August: the RO-33 was killed on 29 August by the Australian destroyer ARUNTA off Port Moresby, and the RO-61 was sunk on 31 August by the U.S. destroyer REID and land-based aircraft at Nazan Bay, Atka Island, in the Aleutians.)

On the Morning of 31 August, while on patrol northwest of Espiritu Santo, the I-26 torpedoed and damaged the carrier SARATOGA. The I-26 had been detected moments before she fired a salvo of six torpedoes at the carrier and had actually scraped a U.S. destroyer. After hitting the "Sara" with one torpedo, the I-26 evaded counterattacks by several

destroyers. The SARATOGA suffered only twelve men injured, but her propulsion plant was damaged and she had to withdraw, to spend the next three months in a shipyard. This left the HORNET and WASP as the only Allied aircraft carriers operational in the Pacific area.

On 6 September the I-11 attacked the HORNET, but inflicted no damage. An astute SBD pilot, who had just taken off from the carrier, released a depth charge in the path of one torpedo, causing it to detonate. But in that same area on 15 September, the I-19 (Commander Takaichi Kinashi) fired what was probably the most effective torpedo salvo in submarine history.

As Kinashi made a submerged approach on the WASP task group, he was unaware that another U.S. task group with the carrier HORNET and battleship NORTH CAROLINA was beyond his periscope view, but within the 13,000-yard range of his Type 95 torpedoes. In all, twenty-three U.S. warships were within range of Kinashi's torpedoes.

A full salvo of six torpedoes was fired by the I-19 at 2:42 P.M. from a range of only five hundred yards. Three of them slammed into the side of the carrier WASP. The three others missed the carrier and raced toward the other U.S. task group, more than five miles away. One of these torpedoes passed under the NORTH CAROLINA, another struck the battleship forward, and one struck the destroyer O'BRIEN. The WASP was wracked by explosions and sank five hours later. The damaged NORTH CAROLINA—the only modern Allied battleship in the Pacific—and O'BRIEN limped away for repairs. The NORTH CAROLINA suffered a 36-foot tear in her outer hull and lost five men in the torpedo's explosion. She listed to port five and one-half degrees, but this was quickly corrected by shifting fuel and the battleship was in no danger. She could still maintain twenty-four knots for short periods with eighteen knots considered a safe sustained speed. The dreadnought did, however, have to withdraw to Pearl Harbor for repairs.

One of the I-19's torpedoes passed close astern of the O'BRIEN, and moments later another hit the destroyer on the port bow. There was relatively little observable damage to the ship, but she suffered severe structural stress. Emergency repairs were made to the ship at Espiritu Santo. She then proceeded to Noumea, New Caledonia, for additional repairs, after which she proceeded to Fiji. She left that port on 16 October, en route to the United States, but progressive structural failures led to flooding, and the destroyer sank at sea three days later (without loss of life).

The I-15 made a torpedo attack against the HORNET at about the same time as the I-19 attack, but her torpedoes missed. That submarine was originally given credit for the hits on the NORTH CAROLINA and O'BRIEN.

The WASP lost 193 of her crew of 2,247 officers and enlisted men when she sank, and her demise left only one fully operational U.S. carrier in the Pacific, the HORNET. (Repairs were rushed to the bomb-damaged ENTERPRISE, and she was able to depart Pearl Harbor for the Solomons on 16 October.)

In view of these submarine successes and continued U.S. activity in the Solomons, a second group of I-boats was assigned to this area and was on station by 19 October. The following night the I-176 fired a spread of four torpedoes at a column consisting of the U.S. cruisers

---

16. These carriers were the HORNET, WASP, and SARATOGA, the last back in service after repairs to the torpedo damage inflicted by the I-6 in January 1942.

The most devastating torpedo salvo of the war was fired by Commander Takaichi Kinashi in the I-19. At left the carrier WASP erupts in flames, while another torpedo from the same salvo strikes the destroyer O'BRIEN in foreground. The third victim was the battleship NORTH CAROLINA. (U.S. Navy)

SAN FRANCISCO, HELENA, and CHESTER east of San Cristóbal. One torpedo hit the heavy cruiser CHESTER amidships inflicting severe damage, sending her into a shipyard in the United States for several months. The three other torpedoes just missed the other cruisers; the screening destroyers were unable to locate the attacker. (The submarine's skipper reported sinking a TEXAS-class battleship.) The I-7 shelled Espiritu Santo in nuisance raids on 14 October and again on the 23rd. The carrier battle of Santa Cruz on 25–26 October was over two hundred miles northeast of the Japanese submarine positions, and none saw action.

Following these battles the Japanese submarines in the Solomons-Bismarck area were ordered to destroy any damaged U.S. ships and then to stay in the American shipping lanes and interrupt the flow of supplies to Guadalcanal. The Japanese efforts were of limited success, and the flow of U.S. supplies and personnel was not stopped. In the only Japanese submarine action after the main battle, the I-21 torpedoed and sank the destroyer PORTER while she was rescuing a downed pilot off Santa Cruz on 26 October.

The last major Japanese submarine success of the year occurred on 13 November off Guadalcanal. During an intense night duel on 12–13 November between U.S. and Japanese surface ships, the antiaircraft cruiser JUNEAU suffered major damage from a ship-launched torpedo. Just before noon on the 13th the JUNEAU was limping away from the battle area at thirteen knots with one of her two screws dragging when the I-26 fired three torpedoes at the nearby cruiser SAN FRANCISCO. That cruiser escaped the torpedo spread, but one torpedo struck the JUNEAU. The JUNEAU blew up "with all the fury of an erupting volcano," according to one witness. Within twenty seconds the JUNEAU was gone—only ten

men surviving from a crew of more than six hundred. Among those lost were the five Sullivan brothers, who had enlisted in the Navy together and insisted on serving in the same ship.

SUBMARINES AS SUPPLY SHIPS

It was still the official Japanese naval policy to attack merchant shipping, but the situation for the Japanese troops on Guadalcanal had become so serious that the Japanese Army's leadership sought to employ submarines for their resupply. Although Phase II continued on into 1944, the majority of active submarines were diverted into Phase III, which officially began on 16 November 1942, when all available I-class submarines were ordered to Rabaul on New Britain and placed under the command of Rear Admiral Hisao Mito to take part in *mogura* or supply operations. The boats that proved most effective in that phase of the war effort were the aircraft-carrying submarines. With their floatplanes removed, each one could carry more than fifty tons of provisions and ammunition, a two-day supply for the troops on Guadalcanal. It should be noted that by that time their floatplane reconnaissance flights had become vulnerable because of the increased use of radar by the U.S. Navy.

Supply duty was very distasteful to submarine crews, who, having been trained to fight, were relegated to acting as storekeepers on runs to island bases, and caring for sick and wounded men on the return trips to forward bases or Japan. The result was a significant drop in the morale of the submarine crews.

Sixteen submarines were initially assigned to the Guadalcanal supply operation. The first supply run, from Bougainville to Guadalcanal, was

Looking down from the conning tower of the I-171 while underway. This boat participated in the K operations and then served as a supply ship. The supply runs, first to Guadalcanal, sapped the strength and morale of the Japanese submarine force.

made by the I-176 under Lieutenant Commander Yahachi Tanabe. By the end of February 1943 the submarines carried 1,500 tons of supplies to Guadalcanal in twenty-eight runs. These *mogura* or "mule" operations were eventually expanded to include runs to New Guinea and the Aleutians as American troops assaulted the Japanese holdings in those areas, and a number of the smaller RO-class boats were used in the operation. Through September 1943, a total of ninety-five supply runs delivered 3,500 tons to New Guinea. During the remainder of the Pacific war, submarines were pressed into supply service to support bypassed garrisons in other areas. They carried in food and medical supplies and,

to a lesser extent, munitions. Coming away from the beaches, they brought off wounded and sick troops, technicians, and most importantly, pilots who were needed for upcoming battles. At times staffs and, as at Truk, some munitions and critical parts were taken back to Japan by submarine as the Americans threatened. The largest evacuation would be at Kiska in May of 1943 when the entire garrison of some seven hundred soldiers was safely removed in fifteen submarine trips (see chapter 3).

A U.S. Navy assessment of the supply operations stated:

> This use of submarines was an extremely controversial issue in Japan, causing many stormy sessions in the joint discussions of the Army and Navy General Staffs. However, when the Navy was forced to divert a large number of submarines to this use, it seems to have plunged into the problem of perfecting the techniques involved. They developed special cargo tubes, watertight boxes, special gun cases, and rubber cargo bags to be carried on deck, in addition to carrying oil drums on deck.[17]

In response to the supply requirement, the Navy modified several submarines and developed special supply devices as short-term solutions. For the long-term resupply problem the Navy and the Army built specialized transport submarines (see chapters 12 and 13). Attack submarines pressed into this role had their deck guns, ammunition, and reload torpedoes removed to provide space and weight for supplies. Even provisions for the crew were cut to the minimum for the mission as another means of providing more space for supplies. Beyond what could be carried internally, buoyant rubber sacks of rice and oil drums were carried on deck, to be carried ashore in small boats or floated off.

The *unpoto* or cannon carrier was developed to carry artillery on the submarines. Consisting of a platform some 71 by 13 feet lashed to two hollow cylinders, a cannon and shells could be secured to the platform. Two torpedo propulsion units were fitted under the platforms to propel them ashore. The craft, weighing twenty tons, could carry almost that much cargo and had enough fuel (oxygen) to sail it some two miles. This device was followed by the *unkato* or stores carrier, a cylindrical structure 136 feet long with a diameter of 16 feet. There was watertight space within the *unkato* for 337 tons of cargo plus a series of ballast tanks. This device was towed behind submarines at depths to four hundred feet. When the submarine surfaced near the beach, the *unkato* would be unhooked and towed to shore by small craft. A number of other devices and schemes were proposed and some tried, among them were firing rubber containers of rice from out of torpedo tubes.

The employment of attack submarines as supply ships was a necessary expedient, but a classic example of the misuse of submarines. Several submarines were lost and others damaged in these supply operations; some calculations list at least twenty-five submarines lost in all areas during the war while making supply runs.

Japanese submarine losses in the Solomons campaign during the latter part of 1942 were severe. Although there are some disagreements on the cause of I-boat losses, it appears that a U.S. destroyer sank the

17. U.S. Naval Technical Mission Japan, Ship and Related Targets, Japanese Submarine Operations (S-17), February 1946, p. 13.

The *unkato*-L supply canister was intended to be towed by submarines and then floated ashore to help supply isolated or surrounded garrisons. After reaching their objective they were to be sunk. It was difficult to maintain trim while being towed, and only a few ever reached their destinations.

I-15 off Guadalcanal on 10 November; a destroyer-minesweeper sank the I-172 in the same area the following day; and the I-22 was lost to U.S. PT-boats a day later off New Guinea as was the I-3 off Cape Esperance on 9 December. The I-4 was probably sunk by the U.S. submarine SEADRAGON on 21 December. (The SEADRAGON fired three torpedoes, two of which struck the I-boat with the explosion from one hit damaging the SEADRAGON, causing her to lose depth control and starting up a torpedo in one of the submarine's tubes; the "fish" was hastily launched and control was regained.)

The PT-boats appear to have been a particular concern of the Japanese submariners. Carrying four antiship torpedoes plus an assortment of light guns and a few depth charges, these high-speed craft lacked sonar. Their radar, however, gave them a great advantage over Japanese submarines. One submarine captain wrote:

> American PT boats turned out to be the unconquerable enemy of Japanese submarines. They were very small, which made them hard to see, either at sea or against a shoreline. It did no good to fire torpedoes at them, as the Model 95's passed well beneath them. And they had radar. While they could hide under the smallest cover cast by an overshadowing cloud or in a cove, they could still see us at a great distance with their electronic eyes. They could dart in and attack with machine guns, torpedoes or depth charges, then race away at high speed before a submarine could do anything.[18]

18. Orita and Harrington, *I-Boat Captain*, pp. 148–49.

In addition to the submarine losses described above, the I-33 was sunk at the Truk naval base in a U.S. Army Air Forces strike on 26 September 1942, three months after the submarine was completed. The I-33 was refloated in 1943 and towed to Kure for rebuilding. (She would be sunk a second time in 1944.)

Thus, seventeen submarines were lost to all causes in 1942; two others, the outdated RO-30 and RO-32, were retired on 1 April 1942. With the loss of these submarines, the war had so far cost the Japanese Navy twenty-one submarines. Twenty submarines were delivered to the Japanese Navy during 1942, approximately double the number of submarines completed in 1941. Therefore, Japanese submarine strength at the end of the first full year of war with the United States was sixty-one, two less than at the start of the war. Further, the quality of the submarines and their crews had improved, although neither radar nor radar warning receivers were yet being fitted to Japanese submarines, a critical shortcoming. In 1941–1942 the Navy Ministry had listed submarines as the second highest Navy priority, following "air strength" (aircraft carriers, aircraft, and pilots), but in terms of submarines this was translated into numbers of boats and crews and not necessarily qualitative improvements.

The record of Japanese submarines in 1942 had not been impressive, especially their failure to provide effective reconnaissance of U.S. carrier forces at Coral Sea and Midway, or to inflict more damage on American forces. Their major triumphs—which were significant in the course of

U.S. motor torpedo boats were particularly effective against Japanese submarines. The PT-boats were small, fast, heavily armed with guns and torpedoes, with a few depth charges in some boats, and were fitted with radar. The radome "pot" is clearly visible in this view of a PT-boat on the prowl off the coast of New Guinea. (U.S. Navy)

1942—were the sinking of the carriers YORKTOWN and WASP, and the twice torpedoing of the SARATOGA as well as the torpedo damage to the British battleship RAMILLIES. In 1942 Japanese submarines also sank a damaged U.S. antiaircraft cruiser, two U.S. destroyers, one U.S. naval oiler, and approximately 125 Allied merchant ships (most in the Indian Ocean), plus the Soviet submarine L-16. Perhaps a final observation of submarine operations in the Pacific during 1942 is that Japanese submarines, despite their less-than-expected achievements, were considerably more effective than U.S. submarines.

One of the more innovative—and unsuccessful—ideas tried by the Japanese submarine force was the carrying of tanks armed with torpedoes for attacking surface ships. The amphibious tanks were to be carried into the battle area by submarines, floated free, and then travel overland to attack amphibious ships off the beach. At top, during tests, an I-class submarine loads two of the craft, then submerges, and surfaces with her stern ballasted down so that the crews can climb aboard and the tanks can be floated off. In the final view the submarine submerges with the torpedo-armed tanks ready to get underway. (Shizuo Fukui)

3 Strategy and Operations, 1943

The primary missions of the Japanese submarine force in 1943 were to attack Allied merchant ships and to supply Japanese troops ashore in combat areas where surface transports could not safely operate. In reality, because of losses suffered in the first year of the war and because many of the newly delivered submarines were not yet fully operational, the supply runs left few I-boats available for offensive operations.

Meanwhile, the air and surface strength of the Combined Fleet were being built up in the continued hope of bringing about a major engagement with the U.S. Pacific Fleet. Unlike the battles at Coral Sea and Midway, this one would be fought within range of Japanese land-based aircraft and, it was hoped, with submarines fulfilling the roles for which they were intended in a fleet action—first reconnaissance and then sinking or damaging enemy warships before they reached the battle. But neither the Japanese nor U.S. fleets were ready for a major battle in 1943. From November 1942 until February 1943 both navies concentrated on the struggle for Guadalcanal. Reinforcements were poured in, and there were several savage gun duels, usually at night, between opposing surface ships. Finally, in February 1943 the Japanese gave up the island, withdrawing almost 13,000 troops, all exhausted and most of them starving and suffering from malaria (several hundred died before they could receive proper medical attention). Almost 24,000 more Japanese troops died on Guadalcanal or in the waters around the island, and about a thousand more were captured.

In addition to the loss of the I-3 while on a supply run to Guadalcanal late in 1942, the I-1 was sunk in the same area by New Zealand anti-submarine trawlers on 29 January 1943. The I-1, badly battered, was run aground, and fifty survivors led by the executive officer managed to get ashore on Guadalcanal. In all, the Japanese had lost six submarines in the Guadalcanal campaign. After the fall of Guadalcanal, U.S. forces moved up the Solomon archipelago, landing successively at New Georgia, Vella Lavella, and Bougainville.

To the west of the Solomons, at the head of the Coral Sea, were the 1,300-mile-long island of New Guinea and, to the east of that island, New Britain. Near the southern "tail" of New Guinea, on its western coast, is Port Moresby, held by the Allies and the goal of the Japanese forces that fought in the Coral Sea in May 1942. The Japanese high command had considered their setback at Coral Sea only temporary and drew up plans for attacking Port Moresby overland (over the Owen Stanley Mountains) from Buna and Milne Bay on New Guinea's southeastern coast. The new Japanese assault against Port Moresby would begin in July 1943 with unopposed troop landings at Buna. But the attempts to land at Milne Bay marked the first Japanese assault of the war that was repulsed (other than the initial landing attempt at Wake). The ground and naval battles at Milne Bay in August and September marked the start of the Allied offensive up the coast of New Guinea.

Allied air power in the area forced the Japanese to employ submarines to supply their troops in New Guinea from September 1943 through January 1944. Several surface ships were sunk while attempting to run supplies and fresh troops into the battle, and the submarines were regularly called upon to rescue survivors of these sinkings. At times the boats took on board some two hundred survivors in addition to their own crews of half that number—a total of more than three hundred men per submarine on some rescue missions.

As Japanese submarines sought to stem the flow of American troops and supplies into this region as well as to support the troops ashore, they suffered heavy losses: the I-18 was sunk on 11 February 1943 in the Coral Sea by a U.S. destroyer and a cruiser's scouting aircraft; the RO-34 was sunk in the Solomons by a U.S. destroyer on 5 April 1943; the RO-102 was lost in the same general area on 14 May 1943 to U.S. PT-boats; the I-178 was sunk by a submarine chaser on 29 May; and the RO-107 by a destroyer in July. The I-168, which had sunk the YORKTOWN, was torpedoed by the U.S. submarine SCAMP on 27 July in the Solomons, both submarines having fired at the other. The RO-103 was probably sunk by a mine in July, the RO-35 by U.S. destroyers on 25 August, the I-182 by a U.S. destroyer on 1 September, the I-25 by a U.S. destroyer on 3 September, and the RO-101 by a destroyer and aircraft on 15 September. The I-20 was lost in this area, but details are lacking—in September or October 1943 she was apparently lost to a U.S. destroyer attack or was an operational casualty. Several other boats were damaged by U.S. antisubmarine forces. These Japanese submarines accomplished little and certainly were unable to stem the tide of battle in the Solomons–Bismarck Sea area.

Meanwhile, U.S. troops landed on Attu on 11 May 1943 to begin the recapture of the two Aleutian Islands that the Japanese had taken the year before. The submarines I-9, I-21, I-24, I-155, I-157, I-169, RO-104, and RO-105, under Rear Admiral Takeo Konda, were sent to the Aleutians to reinforce the seven RO boats already in that area. Operating

TABLE 4. SUBMARINE FORCE, 1 JANUARY 1943

FIFTH FLEET	I-34, I-35
SIXTH FLEET/SUBMARINE FLEET flagship: KATORI	I-8
7th Submarine Division	I-1, I-2, I-5, I-6, I-7
1st Submarine Squadron flagship: I-9 tender: HEIAN MARU	
2nd Submarine Division	I-17, I-19, I-25, I-26
15th Submarine Division	I-31, I-32, I-36
3rd Submarine Squadron flagship: I-11 tender: YASUKUNI MARU	
11th Submarine Division	I-174, I-175, I-176
12th Submarine Division	I-168, I-169, I-171
8th Submarine Squadron flagship: I-10 tender: HIE MARU	
1st Submarine Division	I-16, I-18, I-20, I-21, I-24
14th Submarine Division	I-27, I-29
EIGHTH FLEET	
7th Submarine Squadron tender: JINGEI	RO-34, RO-100, RO-101, RO-102, RO-103
13th Submarine Division	I-121, I-122
SOUTHWEST AREA FLEET	
tender: RIO DE JANEIRO MARU	
30th Submarine Division	I-162, I-165, I-166
KURE NAVAL DISTRICT tenders: CHOGEI SANTOS MARU	
Kure Submarine Squadron	I-177, I-178, RO-106, RO-107
6th Submarine Division	RO-57, RO-58, RO-59
18th Submarine Division	I-153, I-154, I-155
19th Submarine Division	I-156, I-157, I-158, I-159
26th Submarine Division	RO-61, RO-62, RO-67
33rd Submarine Division	RO-63, RO-64, RO-68
YOKOSUKA NAVAL DISTRICT	RO-31

These Type A midget submarines, each capable of carrying two 18-inch torpedoes, were brought to Kiska to help repulse expected U.S. landings. They were not used, and when the Japanese withdrew, they were scuttled by internal demolition charges. (U.S. Navy)

conditions in the Aleutians were extremely hazardous. Japanese submarines were not equipped for cold weather service, and the RO boats lacked radar needed for navigation and combat, a device that was widely used by the U.S. forces to great advantage. The submarines attempted to resupply the beleaguered garrisons and evacuate troops if necessary; and, of course, they sought out U.S. shipping targets. From 21 May to late June the Japanese submarines made fifteen successful supply and evacuation runs to Attu and Kiska. They landed 125 tons of supplies and removed 820 men from both islands to the Japanese base at Paramushiro at the northern end of the Kurile Islands. They were able to remove all troops from Kiska some three weeks before the Americans assaulted the island.

There were several losses in the Aleutians campaign: the submarines I-2 and I-157 ran aground and were damaged; the I-155 was put out of action after suffering damage in a storm; the I-7 and I-31 were sunk by U.S. destroyers (the I-31 after almost torpedoing the battleship PENNSYLVANIA); and the I-9 was sunk by a U.S. submarine chaser. The I-24 was sunk by a U.S. submarine chaser after the craft attacked and rammed the submarine some fifty miles off Attu.

In this period the I-17 was sunk by a New Zealand trawler, the TUI, and U.S. naval aircraft 40 miles off Noumea Bay on 19 August. The TUI had also participated in sinking the I-1 earlier in the year. With these losses the submarine supply operation in the Aleutians came to an end.

On 19 November 1943 the U.S. Navy began the Central Pacific campaign with attacks against Japanese air bases in the Gilbert and Marshall island groups. The U.S. task forces included six fleet carriers and five light carriers—the largest concentration of aircraft carriers that had ever been assembled by any navy. Of these carriers, only the venerable SARATOGA had been in commission when the war started two years earlier. In addition, there were eight smaller escort or "jeep" carriers to provide direct support to the landing operations. The carrier strikes marked the beginning of assaults against the Tarawa and Makin atolls in the Gilbert Islands.

The American offensive began shortly after Vice Admiral Takeo Takagi became commander of the Sixth Fleet, relieving Vice Admiral Teruhisa Komatsu in November 1943.

FRUITLESS COUNTERATTACKS

In response to the U.S. landings, Vice Admiral Takagi ordered nine submarines into the Gilberts to break up the American assault. There were no Japanese surface or air forces available for a counterattack at Tarawa. The submarines were the I-19, I-21, I-35, I-39, I-40, I-169, I-174, I-175, and RO-38. Their task was formidable and, in view of the quantity and quality of U.S. antisubmarine forces, impossible.

Admiral Takagi issued confusing and contradictory orders in an effort to make the Americans think he had more submarines than were available. The result was a continuous and almost chaotic redeployment of submarines to meet changing conditions. He ordered some boats to cruise on the surface and send radio messages in an effort to confuse U.S. intelligence. Three different sentry lines were formed, one after another—one north of Makin on 26 November, and a second and third the following day.

Addressing these changes in orders, Lieutenant Commander Nobukiyo Nambu, captain of the I-174, was quoted as saying:

> On December 1, I was not more than 3 miles off Makin, waiting for that [U.S.] convoy, but no enemy ships appeared. In the meantime, other submarines were dashing back and forth between various stations assigned to them by Sixth Fleet. First an order would say "move." Then it would be changed to "move, navigating on the surface." Still later it would become "wait, remaining on the surface." These orders ignored completely the strong and weak features of a submarine. I'm positive that most of our submarines that were lost went down during this hectic and confused period.[1]

Six of the nine submarines dispatched to the Gilbert and Marshall islands were sunk in 1943: The I-19, I-35, I-39, and probably RO-38 were sunk by U.S. destroyers and destroyer escorts; the I-21 was sunk by aircraft from the escort carrier CHENANGO; and the I-40 was apparently sunk by land-based naval aircraft. Two men from the I-35 are believed the only survivors from these six boats.

The only success of these submarines was the sinking of a U.S. escort carrier by the I-175 under Lieutenant Commander Sunao Tabata. On patrol northeast of the Marshalls when the U.S. assault began, Tabata headed south toward Makin. On the morning of 24 November he sighted the LISCOME BAY. Shortly after 5 A.M. he fired a salvo of torpedoes at the carrier. At 5:13 one torpedo struck the ship. The carrier had no warning of the attack. There was an explosion as the torpedo hit—some sources say two hit—and a few seconds later there was a huge detonation from within the ship as her bomb magazines exploded. Twenty-three minutes after the I-175's torpedo struck, the flaming LISCOME BAY slid under the water, taking with her the rear admiral commanding the task group, her captain, and 642 other men. The I-175 escaped, although she suffered heavy damage from U.S. escort ships.

The loss of the LISCOME BAY did not affect the American thrust into the Japanese-controlled areas. The American amphibious assault on the Gilberts and Marshalls continued, with Kwajalein, late headquarters for the Sixth Fleet, being stormed by U.S. Marines on 31 January 1944.

During this operation, the U.S. submarine CORVINA was assigned to patrol off the Japanese naval base of Truk to intercept Japanese warships that sortied in response to the American landings. The CORVINA, on her first war patrol, was torpedoed on 16 November by the I-176. The Japanese submarine claimed two hits for three torpedoes fired. The CORVINA sank without survivors, the only American submarine sunk by Japanese submarines in the war (which also sank one Soviet and one Dutch submarine).

COOPERATION BETWEEN GERMANY AND JAPAN

Also during 1943 large-scale German U-boat activities were conducted in the Indian Ocean and to a lesser extent in the Far East. These operations are of significance to this review of Japanese submarine activities, as these U-boat cruises and the several cruises by German merchant raiders in cooperation with Japanese submarines mark the only operational cooperation by the military forces of Germany and Japan throughout the entire war.

Germany, which had gone to war with Britain in September 1939, sent the pocket battleship ADMIRAL GRAF SPEE into the Indian Ocean late that year; in early 1941 her sister ship ADMIRAL SCHEER had rounded the Cape of Good Hope to prey on Allied merchantmen in the Indian Ocean. In addition, several surface raiders—disguised as merchant ships—entered the Indian Ocean beginning in the spring of 1940. Because of the limited British and Commonwealth naval forces available in that theater, these ships had many successes. The merchant raiders continued intermittent operations into the Indian Ocean and Far Eastern waters up until October 1943, when the U.S. submarine TARPON torpedoed and sank the raider MICHEL south of Yokohama. The MICHEL had sailed from Japan in May of 1943 for the Indian Ocean and was returning to Yokosuka when she was sunk, the last of eleven German merchant raiders at sea from 1940 to 1943.

Germany declared war on the United States on 11 December 1941, four days after the Japanese attack on Pearl Harbor. The earlier military pacts between Germany, Japan, and Italy did not clarify naval cooperation in the event of war. A few days after Pearl Harbor—probably on 16 December—an agreement was drawn up between Germany and Japan outlining their respective submarine operations in the Indian Ocean. Commodore Karl Doenitz, head of the U-boat arm when the war began, had envisioned submarine operations in the Indian Ocean from the outset of the conflict. In December 1941 he reportedly phoned Rear Admiral Otto Schniewind, the chief of staff to the commander in chief of the Navy, "Ah, Schniewind, I want to talk to you about the U-Boat construction program. . . . And we also want to go ahead with the Type X-B minelayer boats for use *outside* European waters, namely around the Cape of Good Hope, Simonstown, Colombo, Singapore."[2] At the

1. Zenji Orita and Joseph D. Harrington, *I-Boat Captain* (Canoga Park, Calif.: Major Books, 1976), pp. 185–86.

2. Quoted in Allison W. Saville, "German Submarines in the Far East," *U.S. Naval Institute Proceedings* (August 1961), p. 80.

time, however, the successes of the merchant raiders in the Indian Ocean, the periodic successes of blockade runners bringing critical raw materials from the East into Germany, and the conditions in the Atlantic vis-a-vis submarine warfare gave no need for U-boats to enter the Indian Ocean.

The first U-boat operation in the Indian Ocean began in November 1942 when the Germans sent five U-boats around the Cape of Good Hope and into the southern approaches of the Mozambique Channel. These U-boats sank twenty-four ships that month and then withdrew back into the Atlantic. According to the official British naval history, "A crisis, which might have assumed serious proportions had the enemy been able to reinforce the attackers, thus subsided. Though the U-boat's foray into these distant waters had been short, it had been very fruitful."[3]

The defeat of the U-boats in the Atlantic in the spring of 1943 led to large-scale Indian Ocean operations as Doenitz sought areas with less-defended Allied merchant shipping. In June of 1943 nine attack boats and two supply submarines departed French and German ports for the Indian Ocean. These submarines were subjected to intensive U.S. and British antisubmarine attacks while in the Atlantic, six U-boats being sunk before they reached the Cape Town area. The surviving submarines refueled from German tankers in the Indian Ocean and enjoyed many successes. Also, on occasion, Japanese submarines refueled U-boats in the region.

After their Indian Ocean cruises, the U-boats returned to their French or German bases until, in August 1943, the U-178 reached the Japanese submarine base at Penang off the coast of Malaya. From that time on, U-boats regularly used the Japanese naval bases of Penang and Singapore to replenish their fuel, torpedoes, and supplies. The Germans established their own support facilities at these bases, and from June 1944—because of the crowded conditions at Singapore—opened a new submarine base at Surabaja, Java. One German historian wrote:

> The German U-boat bases in the Far East were largely self-supporting, and the German staff had to struggle continually against the opposition of the lower Japanese officialdom. Most of the latter were men of peasant origin, rooted in the ideas and customs of their island country. Only among the senior officials who were descended from the ancient Samurai could the necessary understanding be found to bridge the gulf between European and Oriental conceptions and ways of thought.
>
> Thus the Germans were left to shift for themselves. They acquired the great 4,400-acre plantation of Tjikopoe [Java] and, cultivating it with the assistance of Japanese workers, grew the vegetables which are so necessary to the comfort of German stomachs. They made a variety of preserved foods, including bread, which were packed and sealed in containers of pure tin. These were then loaded on to the U-boats returning to Germany, so providing food for the crew and a valuable raw material for German industry.[4]

At the U-boat bases there were recreational areas for the crews, with sports fields, swimming pools, and beaches, and ample supplies of German schnapps, French whiskey, and Japanese beer. Japanese women were also available for the pleasure of the crews. Still, the U-boat sailors were bored, frustrated, homesick, and suffered a high incidence of malaria—often running as high as 25 percent—despite the availability of quinine.

The U-boat operational areas were pushed farther east in the Indian Ocean, in part because of the shortage of Japanese submarines for such deployments and because of improving Allied antisubmarine efforts. The German naval attaché in Tokyo, Admiral Paul Wenneker, directed all German naval activities in the Indian Ocean and Far East, with the actual U-boat operations run by U-boat headquarters in France.[5]

Despite U.S. forces being on the offensive in the Solomons and then in the Central Pacific, the Japanese were able to deploy eight submarines in the Indian Ocean in the fall of 1943 to collaborate with German U-boats in attacking Allied shipping. During 1943 the number of U-boats in the Indian Ocean reached a peak of seven, making a total of fifteen Axis submarines preying on the numerous merchant ships on that broad sea. From September to December 1943 the I-10, I-26, I-27, I-37, RO-110, and RO-111 scored a large number of successes there. And Japanese submarines would make additional forays into the Indian Ocean in 1944 (see chapter 4).

But the tide of battle was shifting toward the Allies. U-boats sank eleven ships in the Indian Ocean in March 1944. Only twelve other Allied merchant ships were sunk by enemy forces in all other ocean areas that month, an indication of the effectiveness of Allied countermeasures. Several U-boats were essentially based in the Far East by the last year of the war: Penang was their principal operating base; Kobe and Singapore were used for repairs and heavy maintenance; Djakarta and Surabaja were used for loading raw materials in U-boats, with the last also serving as a repair base. The desperate German need for metals and chemicals caused U-boats attempting the return to Europe to be loaded with up to 150 tons of cargo.

The loss of submarines and the long delays in maintenance and repairs at the Far East bases led to only two U-boats being fully operational at the start of 1945. Eight others were undergoing repair, and two were loading cargo. One of the operational boats, the U-862, which had a Japanese flag painted on her conning tower, apparently to help identify her to Japanese forces, made the last successful German patrol in the Far East in February. She sank one merchant ship. In April the U-183 set off to attack U.S. shipping near the Philippines, but was torpedoed on the 23rd by the U.S. submarine BESUGO in the Java Sea—one of two U-boats sunk by American submarines, the other having occurred in European waters in 1943. There was one survivor from the U-183.

A total of fifty-seven U-boats (plus five Italian submarines) operated in the Indian Ocean-Far East during the war. Of these, thirty-two were sunk and two were captured by the Allies en route back to Germany. Six were interned by the Japanese when the war ended in Europe in early May 1945: the attack submarines U-181 and U-862; two cargo submarines, the U-195 and U-219; and two ex-Italian boats, the UIT-24 and UIT-25. Four of the U-boats had made two patrols into the Indian

3. S. W. Roskill, *The War At Sea 1939–1945,* vol. 2 (London: Her Majesty's Stationery Office, 1956), p. 271.

4. Harald Busch, *U-boats at War* (New York: Ballantine Books, 1955), p. 156.

5. Details of the U-boat command structure in the Far East are provided in Saville, op. cit.

Ocean, and the U-181 had come out three times. The highest number of German submarines on patrol at any given time was eleven. In all, these submarines sank 151 merchant ships. The U-boats are also credited with having carried almost one thousand tons of cargo from the Far East to Europe, but this was only a fraction of the cargo of a single merchant ship. Returning to France the U-boats carried up to 155 tons of rubber, tin, tungsten, quinine, and opium. None of the ten specialized-cargo U-boats sent to the Far East ever returned to Germany.

The German submarines in the Indian Ocean did inflict significant damage on the Allies, and the U-boats forced the Allies to divert anti-submarine forces from other regions, making a significant contribution to the Axis war effort. The U-boats may have made a greater effort, however, had they sailed *eastward* from their Far East bases, operating against the U.S. naval and merchant ships in the South Pacific.

THE ITALIAN EXPERIENCE

While the German submarines were deployed to the Indian Ocean and the Far East as commerce raiders, the Italian boats were strictly cargo carriers, ordered to break through the Allied blockade of Europe to deliver raw materials and chemicals from the Far East. Working under German direction, the Italian submarine command at Bordeaux had seven submarines no longer suitable for commerce raiding; the Italians proposed to transfer their crews to new German-built craft. Admiral Doenitz agreed, with the stipulation that the Italian boats then be employed as blockade runners to the Far East.

Accordingly, five heavily laden Italian submarines sailed from France for the Far East during May and June 1943.[6] Only three reached their destination; two were lost at sea to unknown causes, although there are indications one was sunk by British air attacks in the Bay of Biscay the day after she left port. The three surviving boats—also subjected to Allied attack—successfully made the voyage to the Far East, carrying alloy-steel, bottled mercury, and special munitions.

The two other Italian cargo boats were ready to depart France in September 1943 when the Fascist Italian government fell, and they did not sail. At the same time the three submarines at Singapore were taken over by the Japanese and their crews interned. The boats were then turned over to the Germans and were recommissioned with UIT designations for U-boat(Italian). The two ex-Italian boats remaining in German service were retroceded to Japan when Germany capitulated in May 1945. These were the COMMANDANTE ALFREDO CAPPELLINI, becoming the German UIT-24 and then I-503, and the LUIGI TORELLI, becoming the UIT-25 and then the I-504.[7]

During 1943 Italian submarines used the Japanese port of Sabang in Sumatra. An Italian sloop served as a headquarters and base ship for the Italian boats when they arrived in the Far East.

I-BOATS TO EUROPE

The Japanese I-30, after operating in the Indian Ocean during 1942, travelled on to Germany. She was sunk by a mine en route back to Japan (as described in chapter 2).

The next submarine to sail for Germany was the I-8, which was ordered to carry an extra crew to the German-held port of Brest, France, to man a new German submarine that was to be handed over to the Japanese Government, the U-1224. The I-8 sailed from Penang on 6

These photos show the I-30 arriving at Lorient, France, in 1942, the first Japanese submarine to travel to German-occupied Europe. Submarines marked the only area of operational cooperation between the Axis powers in World War II. (Anthony J. Watts and K.R. MacPherson)

---

6. These boats had their torpedoes and one section of batteries removed; there were also other changes during their conversion to the cargo role. When loaded, they were difficult to dive, trim, and maneuver.

7. The German UIT-23, formerly the Italian REGINALDO GIULIANI, was torpedoed by the British submarine TALLY HO in the Malacca Strait in February 1944.

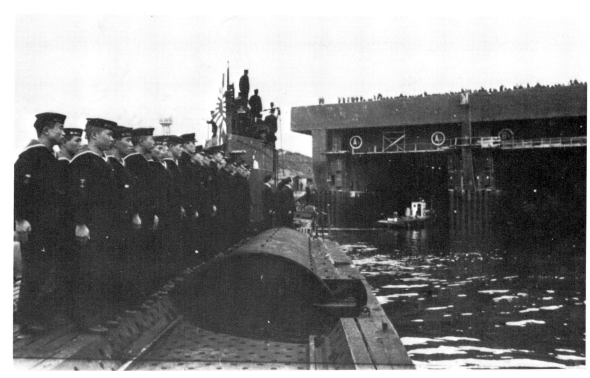

The crew of the I-8 stands at attention on deck as the submarine enters the bomb-proof U-boat "pens" at Brest, France. She was the only Japanese submarine to sail from a Japanese port to Europe and return safely to Japan. (*Ships of the World*)

The crew of the I-8 relaxing at a French chateau: A German U-boat officer playing the accordion leads a conga line of Japanese submariners. (Courtesy of Royal Navy Submarine Museum)

July 1943, accompanied by the I-10, which served as a tanker to refuel her in the Indian Ocean. The I-8 carried a cargo of much-needed quinine for the Germans. The trip across the Indian Ocean was uneventful, but the I-8 was badly battered by gales as she rounded the Cape of Good Hope, sailing far to the south to avoid British patrols.

Off the Azores the I-8 rendezvoused with a U-boat and, with rubber boats transferring men between the submarines, the Germans fitted the Japanese craft with a radar warning receiver to detect Allied search radars when the I-boat was surfaced to recharge her batteries. The I-8 was able to proceed safely to Brest, with German aircraft and surface ships escorting her into port on 5 September 1943, completing a voyage of sixty-one days.

After being refueled and provisioned, the I-8 set out for the return trip to the Far East. Special weapons and other equipment needed by Japan were carried as cargo. She passed through the Bay of Biscay, but as she crossed the equator, the I-8 was attacked by an Allied aircraft. The submarine survived and continued the trip, reaching Singapore in early December after sixty-four days at sea. The submarine then went on to Japan, the only I-boat to successfully complete the almost 30,000-mile round trip between Japan and France.

The third Japanese submarine ordered to Germany was the I-29. In April of 1943 while in the Indian Ocean she had rendezvoused with the U-180 south of Madagascar where the I-29 took on board Mr. Chandra Bose. Leader of an Indian independence movement, he had been Hitler's guest in Germany and was now being used to fight against the British in India. An officer en route to Germany was transferred to the U-boat, after which the I-29 carried Bose and a companion safely to Penang, arriving there in early May.

Early in November 1943 the I-29 again departed Penang en route to Germany. Following the same route as the I-8 and I-30, she reached a French port, exchanged cargoes, and returned safely to the Far East. After leaving Singapore for Japan, however, the I-29 was passing through the Bashi Channel south of Formosa when the U.S. submarine SAWFISH torpedoed and sank her on 26 July 1944.

A few days after the I-29 had departed for France in November 1943, the I-34 left Singapore for the same destination. As she neared Penang Island, the I-34 was torpedoed by the British submarine TAURUS on 13 November.

The fifth and last submarine to attempt the passage, the I-52 was returning from Europe to Japan when she was caught by aircraft from the U.S. escort carrier BOGUE in the Atlantic. She was sunk on 24 June 1944.[8]

U-BOATS FOR JAPAN

The Germans offered the Japanese several U-boats during the war as a means of providing their allies with advanced submarine technology. The U-511 (completed in 1941) left Germany in early April 1943 for the Indian Ocean. En route, the U-boat sank two merchant ships. Upon

8. The BOGUE was the top-scoring Allied escort carrier of the war, also sinking seven German submarines, with two others—one of them the Japanese RO-501—being sunk by a combination of BOGUE aircraft and other surface ships.

The crew of the I-29 returning the cheers from German submarines as the I-boat arrives at Lorient. This photo, taken from the German U-190, shows the radio aerial strung from the after end of the conning tower to the stern, a common feature of large Japanese submarines. (Royal Canadian Navy)

arrival in Japan in July 1943, the U-511 was transferred to the Japanese Navy as a personal gift from Hitler to Emperor Hirohito, being renamed RO-500. The RO-500 was used as a test ship and training ship at Kure. She survived the war.

A Japanese crew took over the new U-1224 in Kiel in February 1944 and sailed her for Japan as the RO-501. While en route to Japan, the RO-501 was caught in the mid-Atlantic on 13 May by the BOGUE hunter-killer group and sunk by a destroyer escort. (Of the four U-boats taken

The German U-511 at sea prior to her transfer to Japan. Upon transfer to Japan she was initially named *Satsuki No. 1*, with the U-1224 being named *Satsuki No. 2;* however, they were quickly changed to RO-500 and RO-501, respectively.

German officers and ratings at Kure in August 1943 during transfer of the U-511 to Japan. At left, the submarine has the Japanese designation RO-500, but still flies the German naval ensign. These men remained in the Far East to help service German and Italian submarines using Japanese bases.

over in May 1945, the U-181 became the I-501, the U-862 became the I-502, the U-219 became the I-505, and the U-195 became the I-506.)

This aspect of German-Japanese naval cooperation paid few benefits to the Japanese; however, the I-boats that did reach Germany, as well as several merchant ships that reached Nazi-held Europe early in the war, carried raw materials badly needed in Germany, albeit the quantity was small.

In addition to the transfer of the U-511 and U-1224 to Japan, with the former boat being carefully examined by Japanese engineers, the German Navy provided certain submarine equipment (especially periscopes) as well as design drawings to the Japanese. Also, the head of the Japanese military delegation in Berlin, Vice Admiral Katsuo Abe, was given access to considerable U-boat material, was able to visit submarines under construction, and had discussions of future U-boat programs with Admiral Doenitz. Admiral Abe sent lengthy, coded messages about German U-boat programs to Japan that were intercepted and decrypted by British intelligence, providing valuable information for the Allies.[9] As the official British intelligence history noted, the decrypt of one of Abe's meetings with Doenitz, his chief of the operational staff, and the chief constructor of U-boats "was of inestimable value" to the Allies from both an operational and technical viewpoint.[10]

BALANCE SHEET

In addition to the six submarines sunk in the Gilberts and Marshalls area during November 1943, two other Japanese submarines were sunk that month: the I-34, torpedoed off Penang, and the RO-100, bombed

9. This was a separate activity from the Japanese naval and military attache's in Berlin. The Axis Pact had provided for a military commission to be established in Berlin. Vice Admiral Abe was head of the Japanese delegation to the commission in 1943-1945.

10. F. H. Hinsley, et al., *British Intelligence in the Second World War,* volume 3 part 1 (London: Her Majesty's Stationery Office, 1984), p. 245. Appendix 11 of the volume is a detailed intelligence report on two of the decrypts.

by U.S. Army aircraft off Bougainville in the Solomons. Significant among the year's losses was the I-19, which had sunk the USS WASP a year earlier; now under Lieutenant Commander Shigeo Kobayashi, the I-19 had carried out a floatplane reconnaissance of Pearl Harbor on 17 November 1943, and was then ordered to the Gilberts and her rendezvous with a U.S. destroyer's depth charges.

There were two unusual I-boat losses in 1943. The I-179 submerged during a training evolution in the Inland Sea on 14 July and sank with all hands. A hatch had been left open. There were no survivors.

A total of twenty-nine submarines were lost to all causes in 1943. During 1943 the number of Japanese submarines in commission increased despite the high losses. That year Japanese shipyards completed thirty-seven boats, providing a net increase of eight submarines for a year-end force of seventy boats. Although submarines continued to be the Navy Ministry's No. 2 priority (air strength was No. 1), major production resources were still being allocated to submarine production.

Nevertheless, the effectiveness of the total submarine force had begun to decline, the result of several factors: many boats were being assigned to supply operations, they had no radar, and U.S. antisubmarine capabilities were increasing. Also, the quality of their crews declined as existing, peacetime-trained and combat-experienced crews were being lost faster than they could be replaced by even inexperienced crews.

In return for the loss of twenty-nine submarines in 1943, Japanese undersea craft sank only fifty-six Allied merchant ships—almost half of them in the Indian Ocean, including one a marked hospital ship, sunk by the I-177. The most significant submarine success was the I-175 torpedoing the escort carrier LISCOME BAY, a sinking that had absolutely no impact on U.S. naval operations. The I-boats also sank one U.S. submarine, two PT-boats lying alongside a torpedoed freighter, and an LST. And, the I-11 scored a single torpedo hit on the Australian light cruiser HOBART in July of 1943, putting her out of service for seventeen months, again testimony to the excellence of Japanese torpedoes.

4 Strategy and Operations, 1944

Japan began 1944 with a larger submarine force than she had at the outset of the war. But into the spring of 1944, Japanese submarines were still engaged in Phases II and III of the wartime operational concepts—attacks on merchant ships and supplying bypassed island garrisons. The submarine force had not been trained for either of these roles.

By the spring of 1944, U.S. Marines had captured the key Japanese atolls in the Marshall archipelago and Eniwetok, several hundred miles farther west. U.S. carriers were ranging across the Central Pacific at will, launching air strikes against the major Japanese base at Rabaul on New Britain and the several islands that comprise the Marianas— the latter only 1,200 miles from Tokyo.

The U.S. carrier forces encountered virtually no opposition from the Japanese fleet, whose commander in chief sought to conserve his slowly rebuilding forces for a major engagement. He expected that battle to be fought when the American carriers had penetrated even more deeply into Japanese territory, where his ships, carrier aircraft, and land-based aircraft could give Japan its long-sought victory. The Japanese submarine force, which might have been employed to attack these U.S. warships as they steamed across the Pacific, was engaged mainly in resupply operations, although there were some sorties against the U.S. naval forces in the Marshalls.

In the Southwest Pacific, following the Japanese withdrawal from Guadalcanal in early 1943, U.S. forces continued to climb the Solomons chain. (Here, too, U.S. carrier raids gave support to Allied ground troops.) Japanese submarines did sink one U.S. Navy fleet oiler and a smaller harbor tanker in the Southwest Pacific; most of their efforts, however, were spent in supply and evacuation operations. On the night of 8 January the I-177 came into the small port of Sio on the southeast coast of New Guinea to take off the commanding general of Japanese forces on the island and carry him up the coast to Madang, 110 miles to the north. The submarine was driven off by U.S. torpedo boats the first and second nights; late in the afternoon of the third day, the general was able to come on board, but the I-177 was again attacked by PT-boats, and she was stalked again during the cruise up the coast. On 11 January the general and his staff were landed at Madang.

By that time Rabaul was no longer safe for Japanese ships or submarines. The I-181 was able to leave Rabaul a few days later, but she was apparently sunk by the U.S. destroyers on 16 January; the RO-37,

TABLE 5. SUBMARINE FORCE, 1 JANUARY 1944

FIFTH FLEET	
7th Submarine Division	I-2, I-5, I-6
SIXTH FLEET/SUBMARINE FLEET flagship: Katori tender: Yasukuni Maru	
12th Submarine Division	I-169, I-171, I-174, I-175, I-176
22nd Submarine Division	I-177, I-180, I-181, I-185
34th Submarine Division	RO-36, RO-37, RO-38, RO-39, RO-42, RO-44
1st Submarine Squadron flagship: I-11 tender: Heian Maru	
2nd Submarine Division	I-16, I-19, I-21, I-39, I-40
15th Submarine Division	I-32, I-35, I-36, I-38, I-41
8th Submarine Squadron	I-8, I-26, I-27, I-29, I-37
30th Submarine Division	I-162, I-165, I-166, RO-110, RO-111, RO-112
11th Submarine Squadron flagship: Chogei tender: Tsukushi Maru	I-42, I-43, I-45, I-52, I-183, I-184, RO-40, RO-41, RO-43, RO-113, RO-114, RO-115
SOUTHWEST AREA FLEET	
7th Submarine Squadron	
51st Submarine Division	RO-104, RO-105, RO-106, RO-108, RO-109
KURE NAVAL DISTRICT	
Kure Submarine Squadron tender: Jingei	RO-31, RO-500
18th Submarine Division	I-121, I-122, I-153, I-154, I-155
19th Submarine Division	I-156, I-157, I-158, I-159
33rd Submarine Division	RO-62, RO-63, RO-64, RO-67, RO-68
YOKOSUKA NAVAL DISTRICT	
6th Submarine Division	RO-57, RO-58, RO-59

which had sunk the U.S. oiler earlier in the month, was sunk on 22 January. The I-11 was also sunk in the South Pacific, en route to the Ellice Islands after patrolling off Samoa on 11 January. She was either the victim of a U.S. destroyer attack or an operational loss.

February began with the loss of the I-171 off Buka Island, just north of Bougainville in the Solomons.

Another Japanese base, that of Penang off the Malay coast, the principal support facility for Japanese and German boats operating in the Indian Ocean, also became vulnerable in early 1944. British submarines operating from Ceylon were patrolling off Malaya, while there was increased British naval activity in the eastern Indian Ocean. The I-27, the most successful Japanese submarine in Indian Ocean operations (fourteen ships sunk), left Penang on 4 February 1944. She is believed to have sunk a British merchant ship on the 12th, but was herself sunk by British destroyers that same day. A few days after the I-27 loss, the RO-110 left Penang for the Bay of Bengal only to be sunk a few days after that by an Indian sloop and a pair of Australian minesweepers. A short time later the British submarine Tally Ho sank the German UIT-23 off Penang.

A few Japanese submarines did make successful patrols into the Indian Ocean in 1944, including the I-8, which had earlier made the round-trip voyage to Europe. Under Commander Tatsunoke Ariizumi, the I-8 had several successes. On 26 March she torpedoed the Dutch merchant ship Tjisalak south of Colombo. The ninety-eight survivors were murdered. On 2 July the I-8 sank the American freighter Jean

Nicolet. About ninety-five survivors were taken onto the submarine's deck. One was shot outright and many others tortured before being thrown overboard; the submarine then dived with the other merchant seamen left tied up on deck. There were survivors of the crime, and after the war several Japanese officers were tried and executed. Ariizumi shot himself when his submarine was returning to Japan at the end of the war.

Several Japanese submarines were kept in the Central Pacific, primarily to provide warning of U.S. carrier forces moving westward. These submarines, however, failed to give warning in mid-February 1944 as the U.S. carriers approached Truk—sometimes called the Gibraltar of the Pacific. Planes from nine U.S. carriers struck Truk on 17–18 February. An earlier U.S. reconnaissance flight had given the Japanese command some warning of the Truk raid, and all major warships had departed. But the base and many merchant ships and submarines there were taken by surprise when the nine U.S. carriers struck.

Those submarines moored inside the harbor at Truk were able to submerge, and all survived the raid, but a destroyer and two dozen auxiliary and merchant ships were sunk and many more damaged. One of the ships sunk at Truk was the ex-submarine tender Rio de Janeiro Maru, which had been converted to a transport the previous fall. Two days before the attack the light cruiser Katori, long the flagship of the Sixth (Submarine) Fleet, was transferred to the Kure training squadron. She was caught north of Truk during the raid by U.S. surface warships and along with two Japanese destroyers sunk in the uneven gun duel.

The Katori was one of three similar, cruiser-type ships designed for the role of training ships. They served mainly as flagships in the war, with the 5,890-ton Katori employed as flagship for the Sixth (Submarine) Fleet until immediately before being sunk by U.S. surface ships in February 1944. The Katori carried a main battery of only four 5.5-inch guns.

Vice Admiral Takagi, commander of the Sixth Fleet with headquarters at Truk, was present when the carrier planes struck. His flagship, the tender HEIAN MARU, heavily laden with supplies and spare parts, was sunk. With Truk now vulnerable to U.S. carrier strikes, Takagi would have to withdraw his submarines from Truk, all the way back to Japan.

Several Japanese submarines were sunk by the intensive U.S. antisubmarine operations in the Central Pacific during this period: destroyers and destroyer escorts killed the I-175, RO-39, and RO-40; the U.S. submarine ASPRO sank the I-43 off Truk with a radar-directed salvo of four torpedoes on 15 February. The I-175, which had sunk the LISCOME BAY, had the unfortunate distinction of being the first Japanese submarine to fall victim to the hedgehog, a new shipboard antisubmarine weapon that fired a pattern of small depth charges ahead of the attacking ship. These weapons, which detonated only when they struck a sub, did not deafen a ship's sonar as did depth charges that exploded at a pre-set depth. The RO-39 was sunk off Wotje by a U.S. destroyer, while the I-132 was lost the following month in the same area. She was making a supply run to that isolated garrison and ran afoul of a U.S. destroyer escort and submarine chaser. The I-171 was lost to unknown causes while en route from Rabaul to Buka, probably in February.

The February U.S. carrier strike on Truk was followed, in March, by the carriers sailing still farther westward, to strike the Palau Islands at the western end of the Carolines group. Part of the Japanese fleet had fled there after the strikes against Truk, but the main fleet units had again departed before the American planes struck; the carrier planes were successful against the second-rate naval ships, merchantmen, and aircraft that were still there. There was essentially no Japanese opposition. The Japanese naval high command was still hoarding what forces it could to attack the American fleet when it steamed into the Carolines, or even farther west.

U.S. forces sank two Japanese submarines in March. Surface ships caught the I-32 off Wotje Island, and the submarine TUNNY sank the I-42 off Angaur Island near Palau.

The U.S. carriers returned to strike Truk on 4 April, and in that raid the I-169 dived in the lagoon to escape American bombs, a compartment was flooded, and several crewmen drowned. A salvage attempt was made, but the lift cables failed and the submarine was abandoned.

Other submarine losses in April were the I-2, sunk by a U.S. destroyer while on a supply run near New Ireland; the I-174 en route to Truk, probably an operational casualty; the I-180 by a destroyer escort in the Aleutians; the I-183 in Japanese home waters by the U.S. submarine POGY, and the RO-45 by destroyers and aircraft from the light carrier MONTEREY south of Truk.

RADAR MAKES THE DIFFERENCE

The first operational Japanese submarine fitted with radar, the I-15, departed Kure for a patrol station on 15 May. Despite her radar, which suffered breakdowns, she was attacked by U.S. forces, damaged, and forced to return to base.

Of all the technical developments in submarine warfare in World War II, radar, because of its proliferation in Allied naval forces and the lack of it in Japanese submarines, was the most significant. Until almost the

Radar in Allied ships and aircraft, and the lack of it in Japanese submarines, was a decisive factor in the Pacific War. This photo shows the Type 3 Mark 1 Mod 3 air-search radar fitted in the RO-43, installed just before the submarine departed on her last voyage in February 1945. At right is a radio direction loop. (*Ships of the World*)

end of the war, when some submarines were fitted with snorkel devices, Japanese submarines had to surface to use their diesels to recharge their batteries, the source of power for underwater propulsion. Submarines generally ran at high speed on the surface at night, using the cloak of darkness while they recharged their batteries. The radar fitted in Allied aircraft, surface ships, and submarines changed the situation. The captain of the RO-64, Lieutenant Commander Kennosuke Torisu, wrote of the events following his first successful torpedo attack:

> When I surfaced the ship after dark, we were suddenly lighted up by flares dropped from a plane. I dove. Terrifying indeed was the ensuing struggle between the hunters and the hunted. Only a few hours were left before dawn, when I managed to shake off the two or three enemy destroyers.
>
> This experience in my first encounter with an enemy radar brought home to me the fact that because of radar, the cloak of darkness was no longer sufficient protection to the submarine.[1]

The Japanese belatedly provided radar (and radar warning devices) to their submarines. Two types of radar became available to them in 1944: the Type 3 Mark 1 Mod 3, a two-meter air-search radar adapted from a land-based radar, and the Mark 2 Mod 2, a ten-centimeter, surface-search radar, designed specifically for shipboard use. The Type 3 Mark 1, a relatively simple, easy-to-use set, was fitted in the I-1, I-10, RO-100, and I-400 classes, with two sets being provided in the large I-400 submarines. The Mark 2, not a reliable set, was installed in submarines of the I-10, I-14, and I-400 classes. In addition, all five of these

1. Kennosuke Torisu and Masataka Chihaya, "Japanese Submarine Tactics," U.S. Naval Institute *Proceedings* (February 1961), p. 78.

submarine classes were fitted with radar warning receivers in an effort to intercept Allied radar transmissions before the submarines were detected.

THE ENGLAND SINKS SIX

Japanese fleet rebuilding efforts—especially the building of new carriers and the production of naval aircraft—were to provide carrier forces to challenge the U.S. Pacific Fleet by May or June of 1944. While there were major problems in exercising the Japanese carriers and in training pilots, the forces were being assembled. At the same time U.S. submarines were extracting a toll of Japanese ships. (One U.S. submarine, the BONEFISH, scored two hits on a Japanese light carrier on 22 May 1944, but the torpedoes failed to explode and the flattop escaped. Two and a half years after the start of the war, U.S. ships were still suffering torpedo detonator problems.) Thus, the scene was set for Operation A-Go, the Japanese counter to the U.S. Navy-Marine Corps drive across the Central Pacific.

In preparation for the forthcoming battle, in May 1944 Vice Admiral Takagi set up new submarine sentry lines to determine the direction of the next U.S. offensive. The I-10, I-38, and RO-42 were stationed east of the Admiralty Islands, off the northern coast of New Guinea and west of Rabaul. Ten more submarines were assigned to an area to the north of the Admiralty Islands, the I-41, I-44, I-53, RO-104, RO-105, RO-106, RO-108, RO-109, RO-112, and RO-116. These submarines were to provide warning of an American approach to the Admiralty Islands or to the Philippines. The seven RO-boats were new, medium-size boats with inexperienced crews. The original intent of the Sixth Fleet staff had been to first send them into the Indian Ocean to gain experience against relatively easy targets and limited antisubmarine forces before having to face the U.S. Navy.

Sailors load projectiles on the spigots of a hedgehog. The ahead-throwing weapon had a range of about 250 yards, firing a roughly circular pattern of twenty-four projectiles fuzed to explode only on impact with a submarine. Originally developed by the British, the hedgehog permitted a surface ship to maintain sonar contact with a target, while using depth charges forced the ship to overrun the target and thus lose contact for the last few minutes. (U.S. National Archives)

The destroyer escort ENGLAND was the top-scoring antisubmarine ship of any navy in World War II, being responsible for the destruction of six Japanese submarines. Several hundreds of these DEs were produced for the submarine wars in the Atlantic and Pacific. Her ASW weapons are barely visible—a single hedgehog just behind the foremost 3-inch gun, and depth-charge racks and throwers aft. (U.S. Navy)

These Central Pacific deployments by Vice Admiral Takagi—who had no submarine experience prior to taking command of the Sixth Fleet—would result in the worst losses for the Japanese submarine force of any period in the war. U.S. antisubmarine forces were dispatched to the Japanese patrol areas, which had been detected by intelligence decryption of Japanese radio traffic.[2] Three U.S. destroyer escorts were vectored to the Admiralty patrol line, including the USS ENGLAND, named for a young ensign killed in the battleship OKLAHOMA at Pearl Harbor on 7 December 1941. On 19 May they found, and the ENGLAND sank, the I-16, which had just departed Truk with a cargo of supplies to be taken to Bougainville.

The three U.S. warships—all armed with hedgehogs as well as depth charges—began to overrun the picket line on the 22nd. That day the ENGLAND sank the RO-106, and the next day she sank the RO-104. The three escorts were encountering a Japanese submarine at roughly thirty-mile intervals. The trio then missed the next boat in line, the RO-105, but the ENGLAND sank the RO-116 on 24 May and the RO-108 on 26 May. On 31 May the escorts GEORGE and RABY located and took on the RO-105, but not until the ENGLAND joined the attack was that submarine sunk. The U.S. ships reported their successes, and some of these messages, reportedly intercepted and decoded by the Japanese, caused the other submarines on the Admiralty picket line to change positions and thus escape the ENGLAND. By sinking six submarines in twelve days, she was the top-scoring antisubmarine ship of any navy in either world war.

Three other submarines were lost in May: the RO-501 (ex-U-1224), sunk in the Atlantic while en route from Germany to Japan; the RO-45, sunk by U.S. destroyers and aircraft just twenty miles off Truk; and the I-176, which was downed by depth charges from U.S. destroyers while carrying supplies to troops on Buka. (Tanabe, who had commanded the I-176 when she sank the YORKTOWN, had been given command of a newer submarine; he would survive the war.) The total number of Japanese submarines lost in May was thus nine, the worst month of the war so far. But June 1944 would be even worse, for the Japanese surface fleet as well as for submarines.

THE BATTLE OF THE PHILIPPINE SEA

On 6 June 1944, as Allied troops landed at Normandy halfway around the world, ships of the U.S. Navy's carrier force passed out from Majuro Atoll in the Marshalls and set course for the Marianas. The carrier striking force consisted of seven fleet and eight light fleet carriers, seven fast battleships, and numerous supporting ships. Behind the carriers was an armada of amphibious transports and landing ships, accompanied by eleven escort carriers to provide close air support for the assault troops.

Air attacks against the Marianas began on the afternoon of 11 June. The Japanese carrier fleet was based at Tawi Tawi, an island base in the Sulu Sea in the southern Philippines. This base was close to the oil fields in Borneo, reducing the need for tankers to run the gauntlet of

2. Such intercepts were widely used by U.S. submarines; this was the first time major use was made by antisubmarine forces. See W.J. Holmes, *Double-Edged Secrets* (Annapolis, Md.: Naval Institute Press, 1979), p. 172.

American submarines that were interdicting merchant ships travelling from the East Indies to Japan. Even before the carriers went to sea, U.S. submarines operating in the Tawi Tawi area—to keep watch on the Japanese ships—sank four destroyers and three of the invaluable oilers, with the USS DARTER torpedoing three of those destroyers in four days.

The Japanese First Mobile Fleet, which sortied from Tawi Tawi in response to the U.S. carriers approaching the Marianas, consisted of five large and four light carriers, five battleships, and their screen; some 440 aircraft were on the carrier decks (compared to just over 900 on the fifteen U.S. carrier decks). As the carriers departed Tawi Tawi on the morning of 13 June, they were observed by a U.S. submarine, one of *twenty-eight* U.S. submarines supporting the Marianas operation.

U.S. submarines continued to track the progress of the Japanese fleet, and as the carrier-versus-carrier battle was joined on 19 June, the USS ALBACORE found the Japanese carrier force steaming into her torpedo range. One of a spread of six torpedoes struck the brand-new 29,300-ton carrier TAIHO. Gasoline lines were sprung in the carrier and there was other damage, but the ship soon returned to full operational status. Later in the day, however, an inexperienced officer tried to vent the gasoline fumes; this and other improper practices led to a violent detonation that afternoon. The TAIHO exploded and was wrapped in flames. She sank a short time later. Also that morning the U.S. submarine CAVALLA torpedoed the carrier SHOKAKU, a veteran of the Pearl Harbor attack. Three hits destroyed her. U.S. carrier-based aircraft sank a third Japanese carrier, and some 400 Japanese carrier planes were lost that day in what was known as the "Marianas Turkey Shoot." Damage to U.S. ships was minimal, as were U.S. aircraft losses.

On the next day, 20 June, the U.S. carriers flew strikes against the remaining Japanese carriers. The U.S. planes sank another Japanese carrier and damaged several others, but were forced to land back on board their ships after dark and with the fuel dials of many aircraft registering empty. At 10:45 P.M. the U.S. carrier force commander, Vice Admiral Marc Mitscher, ordered his carriers to turn on their lights, and the flagship of each of the four task groups pointed a searchlight skyward as a homing beacon for the aircraft.

The carrier force was thus illuminated and "sitting ducks" for a Japanese submarine attack. But none of the Japanese submarines in the area was in a position to sight or attack the U.S. warships.

For the first time in the Pacific War submarines performed in the fleet role for which they had trained and exercised in the 1930s—locating and damaging the enemy main force before the fleet action began. The American submarines performed well. Only three Japanese submarines, the RO-36, RO-43, and RO-114, were initially dispatched to operate east of the Marianas; by the time the Japanese naval leadership realized that the U.S. approach to the Marianas was not a diversion for an assault against the Philippines, it was too late to dispatch more submarines. Other submarines were later ordered into the area. Even the dispatched submarines had problems of command because Vice Admiral Takagi was on Saipan when the Americans struck; Rear Admiral Noboru Owada, commander of Submarine Squadron 7 at Truk, took temporary command of submarine operations.

As things sorted out by mid-June, three parallel lines of Japanese sentry submarines were established out to 300 miles to the east of the Marianas, consisting of:

I-5	I-53	RO-42	RO-112
I-6	I-184	RO-43	RO-113
I-10	I-185	RO-47	RO-114
I-38	RO-36	RO-109	RO-115
I-41	RO-41	RO-111	RO-117

Thus, twenty submarines were arrayed, belatedly, and even then they were placed too far east to affect the carrier battle. While these submarines made no contribution to the Philippine Sea battle, several were sunk during the following two weeks: the RO-36, RO-42, RO-44, RO-111, I-6, I-185, and probably the RO-114 by U.S. destroyers and destroyer escorts; the I-184 by aircraft from a U.S. escort carrier; and the RO-117 by a Navy B-24 (PB4Y-1) land-based patrol bomber.

The I-10 was directed to Saipan to take off Admiral Takagi and his staff, while the I-41 was dispatched to Guam to retrieve stranded pilots who had lost their planes. The I-10 was sunk before she could carry out her assignment, and the I-38 was then directed to take off Admiral Takagi, but could not carry out her assignment either. The I-41 successfully completed her mission, delivering 106 passengers to Japan.

(The I-10 was apparently sunk on 4 July by the destroyer DAVID W. TAYLOR and the escort RIDDLE. They pummeled the submarine with depth charges and hedgehogs for an hour before their sonars detected a huge underwater explosion. The U.S. ships were screening a group of ubiquitous escort carriers and fleet oilers that were supporting the Marianas operation. However, there is a possibility that the I-10 was sunk earlier by U.S. aircraft.)

While the Japanese submarines failed to have any influence on the long-awaited carrier battle, their losses in the period were considerable. After losing fifteen submarines in the first three months of the year, in April the Japanese lost seven submarines, in May nine were lost, and in June—the worst month of the war for Japanese submariners—eleven boats were sunk, including the I-52 in the Atlantic by planes from the USS BOGUE and the I-33, which had been bombed and sunk at Truk in 1942, salvaged, and towed back to Japan. She had been repaired and was recommissioned on 1 June only to be lost on trials on the 13th.

AFTERMATH OF THE BATTLE

In July 1944 Rear Admiral Owada passed command of the Sixth Fleet to Vice Admiral Shigeyoshi Miwa at Kure. Vice Admiral Takagi died on Saipan on 7 July in a *banzai* attack against American troops. Two days later Japanese resistance on Saipan ceased. Just before the fighting ended, Vice Admiral Nagumo, who had commanded the carrrier force at Pearl Harbor and at Midway, committed *seppuku* on Saipan.

Vice Admiral Miwa had earlier commanded Submarine Squadron 3. This was the fourth change of command of the submarine fleet since the war began (not including Owada's brief turn at command).

As U.S. naval forces continued to operate in the Marianas, and B-29 bomber bases were being built on the main islands of Guam, Saipan, and Tinian, large amounts of shipping were required, making the area

of major interest to Sixth Fleet planners. But U.S. destroyer escorts succeeded in sinking four of the submarines sent into the Marianas during July—the I-5, I-6, I-55, and RO-48.

Two more submarines were lost in July, both to Allied undersea craft: the I-166 departed Penang on 16 July for the Indian Ocean; the following night the British TELEMACHUS torpedoed her. Her captain and the bridge watch survived the sinking. The I-29 had just returned from a successful cruise to Europe; after a stopover at Singapore, she departed for Japan on 26 July. Four days later she was torpedoed south of Formosa by the USS SAWFISH. A few sailors survived.

The following month the first Japanese submarine without torpedo tubes departed on an operational mission. She was the I-362, the second of the D1-type cargo submarines. The medium-size submarine departed Yokosuka on 21 August carrying eighty tons of provisions for the isolated island of Nauru, west of the Gilberts. The supply run was successful, after which the submarine ran into Truk to pick up eighty-three stranded fliers and return them to Japan. Two days after the I-362 departed from Japan, the lead ship of the class, the I-361, left for Wake, carrying out eight tons of food and bringing back thirty passengers. The third boat of the class to go to sea, the I-364, was sunk outside of Tokyo Bay by the U.S. submarine SEA DEVIL on 14 September.

The I-364 was the latest loss on the list of naval and merchant ships now being sunk on an almost daily basis off the Japanese coasts. In all, U.S. submarines would sink twenty-one Japanese submarines and two U-boats during the war.[3] In the last year of the war, U.S. submarines would continuously ply the waters off the Japanese homeland with virtual immunity from the impotent Japanese antisubmarine forces.

Meanwhile, as almost a conclusion to the Central Pacific campaign, in mid-September the Americans landed on Peleliu and Ulithi in the Carolines. While the fighting on Peleliu was savage, the Japanese had almost entirely withdrawn from Ulithi, and that island quickly became the major U.S. fleet staging base west of Hawaii. Again Japanese submarines were directed to attack the U.S. warships and transports offshore. The I-177 was sunk by a destroyer escort off Peleliu. Three RO-class submarines survived and returned to Japan, but they sank no ships. And on 26 September the RO-47 was sunk in the Marianas by a destroyer escort.

ON TO THE PHILIPPINES

Beginning in early September 1944, U.S. carriers struck at Japanese positions in the Philippines almost continuously, the prelude to the invasion that would begin the following month.

The U.S. naval forces assembled for the assault on the Philippines included twelve fleet and light carriers, plus eighteen escort carriers, the latter to provide close support for the assault troops. Hundreds of screening ships, transports, and landing ships also steamed toward the

---

3. British submarines would sink two I-boats as well as 16 U-boats and 18 Italian submarines during the war—a total of 36; other Allied submarines sank four U-boats and one Italian submarine. Japanese submarines sank one British, one Dutch, and one U.S. submarine. All submarines sunk were destroyed while on the surface or in the act of surfacing/diving except for the German U-864, detected and sunk by HMS/m VENTURER off the coast of Norway while both submarines were completely submerged.

Philippines. Against this massive assembly of naval power, the Japanese sent three task forces—two composed of battleships, cruisers, and destroyers sailing from north of Borneo, and a force of one large and three light carriers, plus two battleships fitted with flight decks aft, sailing from Japan. The carrier force was a decoy; there were only a few aircraft on the carrier decks. The decoys, however, succeeded in luring the main U.S. carrier-battleship force away from Leyte Gulf, permitting one of the Japanese surface action groups to attack the U.S. escort carrier groups. But that Japanese force, as well as the other surface group, was devastated by U.S. warships and aircraft. (All four of the Japanese carriers in the decoy force were sunk, including the ZUIKAKU, the last of the six carriers that had struck Pearl Harbor. In this second battle of the Philippines Sea, the United States lost one light carrier and two escort carriers, and other ships were damaged.

Once more the Japanese naval high command dispatched submarines to turn away the invaders, and once more they failed. By the time of the carrier-versus-decoy battle on 25 October, fourteen submarines were at sea:

I-26	I-44	I-53	RO-41	RO-109
I-38	I-45	I-54	RO-43	RO-112
I-41	I-46	I-56	RO-46	

As the submarines sought positions to attack the U.S. armada, the I-26 was sunk, probably by a U.S. destroyer escort (although there is some question about the cause of her loss), and the I-54 was sunk by a pair of destroyers on 23 October. The same day the I-45 sank a U.S. destroyer escort off Leyte, but before the day was over one of the escort's sister ships found and destroyed the I-boat. The only other U.S. ship struck by submarine torpedoes that day was an LST, which survived. Another submarine sunk off the Philippines was the I-46 on 28 October, apparently detected by a radar-equipped aircraft that called in a destroyer for the kill.

The submarines continued to attack. On the 24th the I-56 put a torpedo into the U.S. escort carrier SANTEE, which had just been struck by a suicide plane in the first organized kamikaze air attack of the war. Despite the thin-skinned flattop being a converted oiler, without the subdivision and other damage-control features of a true warship, the SANTEE survived the double attack. There were sixteen dead and more wounded in the carrier, but her crew was able to extinguish the fires, make emergency repairs, and the ship was soon steaming away at 16½ knots, about one knot short of her top speed.

No other U.S. ships were hit by submarine torpedoes off the Philippines, despite the many launched, until 3 November, when the I-41 torpedoed the USS RENO. The antiaircraft cruiser survived the hit and was successfully towed the 1,500 miles to the newly established U.S. advance base at Ulithi. The I-41 escaped the area and survived only until 18 November, when planes from the escort carrier ANZIO and a destroyer escort teamed up to sink her.

The I-37 was sunk the following day by U.S. destroyer escorts while on the first human-torpedo or kaiten mission (see below). Also, on 12 November a U.S. destroyer sank the I-38 twenty-five miles south of Yap Island in the Western Carolines.

The final I-boat loss of November and for 1944 was another of the specialized cargo submarines, the I-365. The U.S. submarine SCABBARDFISH torpedoed her off the coast of Japan on 28 November while she was returning from a supply run to Truk. One survivor was taken on board the American submarine. More successful were the cargo boats I-366 and I-367, which made resupply runs from Japan to Pagan Island and Wake, respectively, in early December.

The only other major Japanese submarine success against U.S. warships in the fall was by the RO-41, which torpedoed a destroyer escort north of New Guinea on 3 October. The ship was heavily damaged, and after a sister ship took off most of her crew, she capsized and was lost. Other ships and planes from an escort carrier took up the hunt for the I-boat. One of the planes sighted a submarine submerging in an area that was designated as a safety zone, in which U.S. submarines operated and hence no submarines were to be attacked. The plane still dropped two bombs and dye markers; an escort followed up with hedgehogs. The target was the U.S. submarine SEAWOLF, and she sank with all hands, an indirect victim of the RO-41.

ENTER THE KAITEN

The failure of conventional air, surface, and submarine forces to stop the American drives in the Central and Southwest Pacific led the Japanese to adopt unconventional or suicide forces. The first attack by organized suicide planes or kamikazes occurred on 24 October when Manila-based planes struck at the U.S. escort carriers off the Philippine coast. The suiciders struck several escort carriers, with one, the SANTEE, being hit a short time later by a torpedo from the I-56. Two of the "jeep" carriers were sunk, with the others—including the SANTEE—forced to withdraw for repairs. Soon the kamikazes began falling out of the skies off Leyte to strike the fleet carriers. The U.S. Navy now faced the most effective weapon yet developed by the Japanese armed forces.

Meanwhile, another kamikaze weapon was being prepared for use against the American fleet, the "human torpedo" or kaiten. This weapon was also born out of desperation during the defeats of 1944. Beginning in November 1944 this became the primary operational concept of the Japanese submarine force—Phase IV: submarine-launched kaiten attacking U.S. ships at anchor at forward bases. The initial kaiten was a 24-inch-diameter Type 93 torpedo—the surface-launched "Long Lance"—cut in half with a cockpit section inserted for a pilot and controls (see chapter 11). The kaiten was to be carried to the proximity of a U.S. ship or naval anchorage by a submerged submarine, released, and propelled at high speed by its oxygen-fueled engine to smash into the enemy. With a speed of forty knots for one hour, the kaiten could outrun any American warship. There was no provision for the kaiten to be recovered by the launching submarine, and although the Japanese Naval General Staff had insisted that a means be provided for the pilot to be ejected from the kaiten about 150 feet from impact, no pilot is known to have attempted to escape from his speeding torpedo as it approached its target.

The first group of kaiten pilots had begun training in August 1944, and three submarines were taken in hand for modification to carry the submersibles. These were the I-36, I-37, and I-38, all B1-type submarines built as long-range scouts with a floatplane hangar and flush-deck catapult forward of the conning tower and a 5.5-inch gun aft. The aircraft equipment and gun were removed and fittings installed for carrying four *kaiten*, two forward and two aft. (The I-36 was refitted in early 1945 to carry six.)

Experimental launchings were conducted from the I-36, after which four *kaiten* were lowered onto the racks of each of the three I-boats. The pilots in this first group—called the *Kikusui* mission—were all officers, the senior pilot on each submarine being a graduate of the Etajima Naval Academy. Training of the *kaiten* pilots was initially conducted at a secret base established at Otsujima, an island off the town of Tokuyama on Honshu. Some thirty *kaiten* pilots began training in August 1944, followed soon after by a class consisting of 200 prospective aircraft pilots, all unmarried, all volunteers, selected from student aircraft pilots.[4] In *kaiten* with their warheads removed and ballast fitted in their place, the pilots trained extensively in bays and inlets of the Inland Sea; several fatalities were suffered in this arduous training.

Prior to the departure of the first *kaiten* force, Vice Admiral Miwa, commander of the Sixth Fleet, visited the pilots. There was a formal ceremony to honor the pilots, Miwa presenting each with a new ceremonial sword, while all available officers and men were paraded in dress uniform. A farewell dinner, also attended by Miwa, feted the soon-to-be heroes.

The following morning, 8 November, the pilots participated in religious ceremonies and then, while observers cheered, they boarded the three waiting I-boats. Their *kaiten* were already mounted on the mother submarines. The senior *kaiten* pilot on the *Kikusui* mission was Lieutenant

4. One pilot was allowed to marry while in training.

Kaiten pilots about to embark in the submarine I-36 (for the *Todoroki* group) pose for a last photograph. There are three officers and three enlisted *kaiten* pilots. All wear the *hamachi* headband, with words of encouragement inscribed.

A pair of *kaiten* forward of the conning tower of a C2-type submarine. Note the *kaiten* tie-down arrangement; in the early operations, the tie-downs had to be released while the submarine was on the surface with the *kaiten* floating free as she submerged. The arrangement was rapidly changed to permit release while submerged. (Courtesy of Royal Navy Submarine Museum)

Lieutenant Hiroshi Kuroki (left) and Lieutenant (junior grade) Sekio Nishina were co-inventors of the *kaiten* human torpedo. Both men died at the controls of *kaiten*.

The I-47 going to sea late in the war with *kaiten* embarked abaft the conning tower. Under Lieutenant Commander Zenji Orita, the I-47 was one of the few fleet submarines to survive the war. Her forward 5.5-inch gun was later deleted to permit carrying four *kaiten* aft and two more forward.

(junior grade) Sekio Nishina, co-inventor of the device, who, after instructing other pilots, had sought the honor of going out on the first *kaiten* attack mission.[5] Maintenance specialists also embarked in the submarines to repair any problems detected in the *kaiten* during the twelve-day transit to the objectives. The submarines, each carrying four *kaiten*, slipped out to sea, the I-36 and I-47 en route to the U.S. fleet base at Ulithi in the western Carolines, and the I-37 for the nearby Kossol Strait, an anchorage for U.S. ships. All three submarines also had a load of Type 95 torpedoes to use in attacks against U.S. ships after the *kaiten* had been launched. A reconnaissance plane had earlier reported that the Ulithi lagoon, capable of accommodating some eight hundred ships, was filled with warships, auxiliaries, and transports of all sizes and types.

The I-36 and I-47 successfully approached Ulithi and stood close in by the entrance to the broad lagoon, preparing to launch their *kaiten*.

5. Nishina's co-inventor was Lieutenant Hiroshi Kuroki; he drowned during a *kaiten* trial run on 6 September 1944.

In the mother submarines ceremonies were again held, with the pilots wearing dress white uniforms and carrying their short swords as they climbed into their *kaiten*. In these submarines two of the *kaiten* could be reached only from the submarine deck, and those pilots climbed aboard and the submarines submerged, entrapping their pilots for the approximately three hours until launch. The other two pilots in each submarine could climb through tubes connecting the submarines' pressure hulls and a lower entry hatch to two of the *kaiten*. (Later all submarines would have internal access tubes.) A telephone connection permitted the submarines' navigators to provide the pilots with last-minute navigation data.

Shortly after 4 A.M. on 20 November, the four I-47 *kaiten* were cast off, one by one. All were successfully launched. But on board the I-36 there were difficulties; two *kaiten* would not launch after their engines were started, and the third failed to start because of water leakage into the craft. The fourth manned torpedo departed on schedule. The I-36 withdrew despite the pleas of the three remaining pilots for the submarine to surface and attempt to repair their craft.

Shortly after five A.M.—on schedule—there was an explosion in the Ulithi lagoon, followed a few minutes later by a second detected by the I-47. At 5:45 A.M. and again at 6:05 the I-36 reported hearing detonations. Both submarines then turned back toward Japan. Three days later a Japanese reconnaissance aircraft overflew Ulithi and, based on the explosions detected by the submarines and this flight, the Japanese Navy credited the five *kaiten* pilots with sinking three U.S. aircraft carriers and two battleships!

Kaiten pilot Yutaka Yokota wrote that after the pilots still in training were told of the first mission's results:

> The meeting broke up in bedlam, everyone shouting, congratulating and cheering the *kaiten* plan. This was repeated at Otsujima, and again at Hikari. There nearly two hundred *kaiten* pilots, instructors and trainees were gathered, for a detachment from Nara had finally arrived to join my group. Three aircraft carriers! And two battleships! That ought to give the enemy something to worry about!
>
> I said a short prayer, giving thanks for the success of Nishina and the others. The *kaiten* was now a proven weapon. It had shown what it could do. If luck smiled on me, I too would strike such a blow at our nation's enemy. I, too, would send a carrier to the bottom of the sea![6]

6. Yutaka Yokota and Joseph D. Harrington, *The Kaiten Weapon* (New York: Ballantine Books, 1962), p. 53.

But the actual damage inflicted by this new form of submarine warfare at Ulithi was much less: the *kaiten* believed to be piloted by Lieutenant Nishina struck the large fleet oiler MISSISSINEWA. That auxiliary, loaded with more than 400,000 gallons of aviation gas, blew up and sank with the loss of fifty of her crew, the first ship to fall victim to the human torpedoes. Most, if not all, of the four other *kaiten* entered the lagoon. They attacked two cruisers, but gunfire from the cruisers, a ramming by a destroyer, and depth charges dropped by a U.S. Marine aircraft destroyed them all. Like most other Japanese submarine operations, the evaluation of the *kaiten*'s success was greatly exaggerated.

The I-37 and her four *kaiten* never reached the Kossul Strait. She was detected by destroyer escorts on the 19th and sunk. Thus, for the expenditure of one fleet submarine and nine *kaiten*, the first human torpedo operation had destroyed one American oiler.

THE PENULTIMATE BALANCE SHEET

The Japanese Navy lost fifty-eight submarines in 1944—more than in the first two years of the war combined, and more than the U.S. Navy lost in the entire conflict. Radar, hedgehogs, and simply the vast numbers of U.S. warships and aircraft made it virtually impossible for the

A Type C midget submarine lies on the shore of Cebu in the Philippines. The Japanese used these two-man submarines from bases in the Philippines in an effort to ward off the U.S. invasion. They had no successes. (Imperial War Museum)

submarines to operate in any waters that U.S. or British naval or air forces could reach. And U.S. submarines demonstrated that not even Japanese submarines off the home islands were impervious to attack.

Against those losses Japanese shipyards delivered thirty-five new submarines in 1944, resulting in a net numerical loss of twenty-three boats. But the new submarines, mostly without radar and largely manned by inexperienced crews, coupled with poor deployments, could neither be effective nor even survive. Many boats were still employed in supply operations.

Although the completion of thirty-five submarines was similar to the rate of 1943, the Navy Ministry's emphasis on building during 1944 had shifted to priorities of, in order, land-based aircraft, escort ships, submarine chasers, *submarines*, and transports. With the demand for these types of ships becoming increasingly urgent, the construction of major warships, including aircraft carriers, was slowed down or suspended.

By 1944 there were severe problems in the shipbuilding industry: there was a shortage of steel and of skilled workers. Also affecting shipbuilding were the shortages of oxygen, which hampered steel cutting and steel repairing, and precision tools. And beginning in late 1944, U.S. long-range B-29 bombers from the Marianas began to bomb the

Japanese homeland, and would soon interfere with all forms of industrial activity.

At the highest levels of government there were discussions about shifting all available ship and aircraft production to suicide weapons. Based in large part on the exaggerated claims of the *kaiten* supporters and the actual damage being inflicted by *kamikaze* air attacks, the Navy Ministry established the following production priorities for the coming year: First: special attack (*kamikaze*) aircraft; Second: special attack underwater and surface forces—including suicide boats and midget submarines as well as human torpedoes; other aircraft; other small naval vessels; and the conversion of existing naval craft for special attack missions.

SUPPLY SUBMERSIBLES

The Japanese began employing submarines to supply troops ashore, beginning with the Guadalcanal campaign of 1942 and continuing until the end of the war. Many innovative devices and tactics were used to carry out supply missions, including the *unpoto* and *unkato* supply submersibles. These devices were rarely successful in delivering supplies (see page 30).

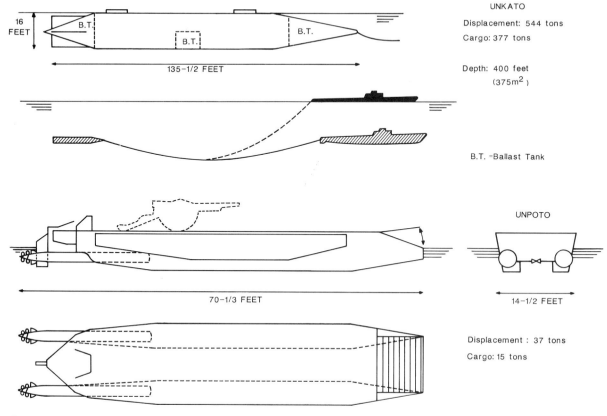

16 FEET

B.T.

B.T.

B.T.

135-1/2 FEET

UNKATO

Displacement: 544 tons

Cargo: 377 tons

Depth: 400 feet
(375m^2)

B.T. =Ballast Tank

70-1/3 FEET

UNPOTO

14-1/2 FEET

Displacement : 37 tons

Cargo: 15 tons

Submarine towing devices.

5 Strategy and Operations, 1945

In the winter of 1944–1945 American troops continued their drive to recapture the Philippines. A force of escort aircraft carriers, with a screen of destroyers and destroyer escorts, remained off the Philippines to provide continuous air support to the troops ashore. The fast carrier force, after resting at Ulithi, returned to sea in early 1945, spearheaded by fifteen fast carriers. These carriers began the new year with strikes against Formosa, then swung south to fly raids against Japanese installations in Indochina, after which they turned back north to strike the Philippines. After a brief respite at Ulithi, sixteen fast carriers attacked the main Japanese island of Honshu on 16 February. Their primary target was Tokyo with its surrounding airfields.

TABLE 6. SUBMARINE FORCE, 1 JANUARY 1945

SIXTH FLEET/SUBMARINE FLEET*	
flagship/tender: Tsukushi Maru†	I-8, I-12
1st Submarine Division	I-13, I-400
15th Submarine Division	*I-36, I-38, *I-44, *I-47, *I-48, *I-53, I-54, *I-56, *I-58
34th Submarine Division	I-177
	RO-41, RO-43, RO-46, RO-47, RO-49, RO-50, RO-109, RO-112
7th Submarine Squadron	*I-361, I-362, *I-363, *I-366, *I-367, *I-368, *I-369, *I-370, I-371
8th Submarine Squadron	RO-113, RO-115
11th Submarine Squadron	
flagship: Chogei	I-372
	RO-55, RO-56
	HA-101, HA-102, HA-104‡
KURE NAVAL DISTRICT	RO-62, RO-68, RO-500
19th Submarine Division	I-121, I-122, I-155, *I-156, *I-157, *I-158, *I-159, *I-162, *I-165
33rd Submarine Division	RO-63, RO-64, RO-67
YOKOSUKA NAVAL DISTRICT	
6th Submarine Divison	RO-57, RO-58, RO-59
ESCORT COMMAND	HA-106

*Submarines modified to carry *kaiten* human torpedoes.
†The Tsukushi Maru was transferred from the Sixth Fleet to the Kure Naval District, and the tender Nachi Maru was assigned to Kure on 20 January 1945.
‡HA indicates third-class or coastal submarines.

The Tokyo raids were the opening moves for the invasion of Iwo Jima, which began three days later. Iwo Jima, located midway between the Marianas and Tokyo, would permit U.S. fighters to escort the B-29 bombers over Japan and provide a refuge for damaged B-29s after strikes against Japan. While the carrier raid on Japan was a surprise to the Japanese high command and there was little response, the Iwo Jima assault brought massive attacks by aerial *kamikazes* against the U.S. carrier force and the vast numbers of supporting ships, transports, and landing ships.

The Japanese submarine force was engaged in Phase III (supply) and Phase IV (*kaiten*) operations at the start of 1945. On 18 January the Japanese Supreme Council for the Direction of the War made suicide attacks the official government policy. The council decided to "concentrate on converting all armament production to special attack weapons of a few major types."

On the naval side production was concentrated on four weapons: the *kaiten* human torpedoes, *kairyu* two-man midget submarines, *koryu* five-man midget submarines, and *shinyo* wooden suicide boats. In addition, the Navy Ministry drew up plans to train six thousand men who, with SCUBA-type swimming gear, would carry small mines at the end of poles to explode them against approaching landing craft. This *fukuryu* force would be the final layer of naval defense for the Japanese homeland.

The first layer would be the surviving I-boats, which would carry *kaiten* against U.S. warships and transports being readied at forward bases.

THE SIXTH FLEET IN TRANSITION

At the start of 1945 there were forty-seven submarines in commission, sixteen less than the number available at the start of the conflict with the United States. But of the 1945 submarines, ten were of the I-361/D1 supply type, without torpedo tubes, and another four were of the smaller HA-101/SS supply type, also sans torpedo tubes and armed only with small-caliber deck guns. Suitable only for training were six RO-boats, including one former German U-boat, the surviving minelaying boats I-121 and I-122, and several other older boats.

This left some twenty relatively modern attack submarines in service, including the brand-new I-400, the first of the aircraft-carrying STo type. This submarine was the largest undersea craft yet built, dwarfing all previous efforts by any navy. The STo design was built specifically to launch floatplane raids against New York and other major American cities; subsequently, as the war moved closer to Japan, the mission for the I-400s was revised. The first priority target was to be the Panama Canal to slow the shifting of Allied forces from the Atlantic to the Pacific theaters. There was a large hangar that could accommodate three fully assembled aircraft (with wings folded) and parts for a fourth. The aircraft developed specifically for the I-400 was the Aichi M6A1 *Seiran,* a high-performance monoplane with twin floats. Maximum speed was almost 300 mph, and two 550-pound bombs or one 1,760-pound weapon could be carried when the aircraft was catapulted from a submarine's deck. The floats could be released in flight to facilitate the plane being used in a *kamikaze* attack. Planning for a strike against the Panama Canal in place of American city targets began while awaiting the completion of additional submarines of this type.

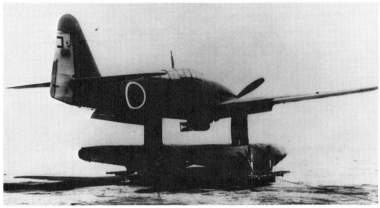

The Aichi M6A1 *Seiran* was developed specifically for operation from the STo/I-400-class submarines for air strikes against American cities. Bombs or a torpedo could be carried; the planned, forward-firing, fixed machine guns were not fitted, but a flexible 13-mm machine gun was fired by the second crewman. The *M* designation prefix indicates a special-purpose seaplane; it was used only for the M6A1. Their first air strike was planned against the U.S. forward base at Ulithi.

Another factor in submarine force consideration was that Japanese submarine captains and crews were totally inexperienced, while the level of competence of the U.S. antisubmarine forces was increasing even with the large buildup of air, surface, and submarine forces.

Most of the remaining attack submarines as well as most of the D1-type cargo submarines were being modified to serve as mother ships for *kaiten,* as were several of the older I-boats. Racks were installed on their decks to carry from two to six human torpedoes, with tubes permitting the *kaiten* pilots to climb directly from the submarine's pressure hull up into the torpedoes while the submarine remained submerged. In most cases the main deck gun and, in the case of those fitted to carry aircraft, also the hangars were deleted. (See table 6 for a list of submarines converted to carry *kaiten.*)

THE SECOND KAITEN MISSION

Jubilant over the imagined success of the first *kaiten* mission against Ulithi, the Sixth Fleet staff drew up plans for more ambitious missions. The *kaiten* program had been expanded rapidly, with the training base at Otsujima soon supplemented by other training centers as *kaiten* production was increased (see chapter 11). Several hundred volunteers, including many in air pilot training for whom aircraft were not available, were assigned to the *kaiten* program. Thus, all *kaiten* pilots—officers and enlisted alike—would be volunteers (and unmarried, except for the one who was given permission to marry while in training).

The second *kaiten* mission—called *Kongo*—would be a simultaneous strike against several U.S. bases, with twenty-four human torpedoes being launched from six submarines. Twenty-four *kaiten* would mean twenty-four American warships and transports sunk, based on Japanese assessment of the first mission. All *kaiten* were to be launched against their targets on 11 January except for the I-48, which would make the second strike of the *Kongo* mission against Ulithi nine days later.

TABLE 7. *KONGO* MISSION

Submarine	Kaiten	Target
I-36	4	Ulithi
I-47	4	Hollandia, New Guinea
I-48	4	Ulithi
I-53	4	Kossol Strait
I-56	4	Admiralty Islands
I-58	4	Apra Harbor, Guam

Again with formal and religious ceremonies, the *kaiten* pilots prepared for departure. Their chariots were loaded onto the submarines, and with *kaiten* pilots and maintenance men embarked, the I-boats departed for the *Kongo* mission.

All six I-boats are believed to have successfully reached their objectives despite the gauntlet of U.S. antisubmarine forces through which they had to pass. Three submarines were able to launch all of their *kaiten:* the I-36 at Ulithi, the I-47 at Humboldt Bay off Hollandia, and the I-58 off Guam. The I-53 reach the Kossol Strait and began launching her four *kaiten;* one failed to launch, and the second exploded immediately after leaving the submarine, but the two others got away successfully.

The I-56 approached the Manus anchorage in the Admiralty Islands, but the heavy defenses, including antisubmarine nets, prevented her from coming close enough to launch her *kaiten*. The submarine, with her four frustrated *kaiten* pilots, returned to Japan. The I-48 was sunk by U.S. destroyer escorts near Ulithi on 23 January. Because that was after the date scheduled for her attack, the Japanese assumed that she had launched her four *kaiten*. Thus, fourteen *kaiten* were apparently launched against U.S. anchorages.

When the five surviving submarines returned to Japan and their officers were debriefed, the Sixth Fleet staff estimated that more than a dozen U.S. ships had been sunk—possibly as many as eighteen, including a battleship at Ulithi. In reality, for the loss of one I-boat and the nineteen *kaiten,* no U.S. ships were sunk or damaged in the *Kongo* mission.

A CHANGE OF DIRECTION

Although the Sixth Fleet staff believed that the *kaiten* attacks against ports were very effective, they were not stopping the American advance.

Also, the defenses against submarines off the forward bases were being increased, as evidenced by the abortive attempt by the I-56 to launch her *kaiten* into the Manus anchorage.

Accordingly, the *kaiten* targets were changed from warships and transports in harbor to ships in the open sea, especially transports and tankers beyond the invasion area where there would be fewer escorting warships. The third *kaiten* operation—designated the *Chihaya* group—would have three submarines to launch sixteen human torpedoes against U.S. ships along the supply routes to Iwo Jima. The ex-transport submarines I-368 and I-370 could each embark five *kaiten,* while the I-44 could carry six of the craft. With appropriate ceremonies and honors, the *kaiten* pilots embarked on the mother submarines.

Two of the *Chihaya* submarines left port on 20 February (the day after U.S. Marines landed on Iwo Jima), and the I-44 departed on 23 February. Both of the ex-supply submarines were detected and attacked by U.S. forces; Japanese sources indicate that the I-370 managed to launch her *kaiten,* and hits against U.S. ships were reported. The I-370 was sunk by a destroyer escort and the I-368 by aircraft from an escort carrier, both off Iwo Jima. The I-44 ran into alerted antisubmarine patrols, and her captain was unable to reach suitable targets. According to one account:

The I-370 departs for the *Chihaya* mission with her officers and *kaiten* pilots (standing atop their torpedoes) waving to those ashore. The submarine and all five *kaiten* were lost without scoring any successes. Note the small conning tower of the I-370, built specifically for the transport role. (*Maru* magazine)

[The I-44] returned on March 9, all *kaiten* unfired. Patrols were so thick after I-368 and I-370 were sunk that they couldn't get near Iwo Jima, although many targets were there. I-44, in fact, was detected every time she tried to surface and take a look around. She could not even recharge her batteries. Enemy planes and ships kept her under the waves for forty-six and one-half hours, and the air inside her hull was slowly being poisoned. The I-44's captain, Lieutenant Commander Genbei Kawaguchi, finally had to call off his operation because his crew and *kaiten* pilots were too exhausted after their ordeal to be effective. He decided to live and fight another day.[1]

Upon the I-44's return to base, her captain was relieved of command by an infuriated Admiral Miwa. Again, despite the loss of two submarines and the destruction of ten *kaiten,* no U.S. ships were sunk or damaged. The six *kaiten* pilots who returned with the I-44, as well as those who failed to launch from other submarines—and some would come back several times—returned to the living after saying their personal and ceremonial farewells and drinking the last toast of a Japanese warrior about to face death. It was a most difficult situation for those men, and certainly affected the morale of other pilots in training as well as their own.

The fourth *kaiten* mission—named *Shimbu*—was to be carried out by the I-36 and I-58, which left port in late February carrying six and four human torpedoes, respectively. The I-36 experienced engine trouble while still in the Bungo Strait and returned to port on 9 March. The I-58 was ordered to move into the Ryukyu Islands and serve as a radio beacon for a *kamikaze* air attack to be flown against U.S. ships anchored at Ulithi on 11 March. She jettisoned her *kaiten* and made her best possible speed to the beacon position, returning to base on the 16th. Again, it was a traumatic experience for the pilots who had gone to sea in these submarines and returned. The *kamikaze* air attack against U.S. ships anchored at Ulithi on 11 March did inflict damage on the aircraft carrier Randolph.

SUBMARINE LOSSES

The submarine force was suffering other losses, beyond those sunk in the *kaiten* operations, as the smaller RO-boats were being sent out for torpedo attacks against U.S. ships. During January the large I-12 disappeared in the Central Pacific, probably an operational loss. Through March, six submarines were sunk by U.S. destroyers and destroyer escorts—the already cited I-48 and I-370 as well as the I-8, I-362, RO-41, and RO-115; aircraft from the escort carrier Anzio sank the RO-43 and I-368; and submarines sank the RO-55, RO-112, RO-113, and I-371. The I-371 was sunk by the USS Lagarto while engaged in supply runs via Truk. The USS Batfish sank the three other submarines.

The Batfish was operating off the northern Philippine island of Luzon on 9 February 1945 when she fired at a surfaced Japanese submarine and sank the RO-55. On the 11th the Batfish detected and sank the RO-112 off Camiguin Island, and two days later the U.S. submarine sank the RO-113 off Babuyan Island. Although the escort Thomason reported attacking the surfaced RO-55 late on the night of 7 February, and was initially given credit for sinking the submarine, it appears more likely that the Batfish in fact destroyed the RO-55, making her the only submarine of any nation to sink three of her own kind.

All three Batfish successes came through the detection of radar emissions from the Japanese submarines. Intercepts of Japanese radio communications indicated that four submarines had been ordered to Luzon to evacuate stranded pilots to Japan, where trained pilots were desperately needed. The Batfish was one of four submarines ordered to form a barrier to intercept the Japanese undersea craft.

Late on the night of 9 October the Batfish's AN/APR-1 intercept receiver detected nearby radar emissions. The receiver's antenna was a fixed dipole, and the submarine had to be turned for the operators to locate the precise direction of the radar emissions. Periodically the Batfish used her own surface radar to search for the target. The Batfish made a high-speed surface run toward the target, about 14 miles away.

The Japanese submarine, the RO-55, appears to have used her air-search radar continuously, apprehensive of a surprise air attack. Those emissions and periodic use of the Batfish's own SJ radar put the U.S. submarine in an attack position just before midnight. Four torpedoes were fired, and all four missed. Although all exploded at the end of their runs, the Japanese submarine continued on the surface, using her radar. The Batfish patrol report stated, "We would never have operated our radar like that. We put our set on only sporadically. We thought it insane of them to be running with their radar blaring away, and we were even more surprised when the [Japanese] boat took no action after our torpedoes went past it."

At two minutes after midnight the Batfish fired three more torpedoes. The first failed to launch; the second struck the RO-55, and the third passed over the rapidly sinking Japanese submarine. There were no survivors.

Late on the night of the 11th the Batfish again detected radar emissions. After approaching her target, the hapless RO-112, on the surface the Batfish submerged to periscope depth and made a radar approach. Four torpedoes were fired at the RO-112 and three struck, sinking the submarine with her entire crew.

The detection of the RO-113 by the Batfish came early on the 13th. Again, the Japanese submarine was using her air-search radar. The Batfish used her passive AN/APR-1 and, judiciously, her SJ search radar to close; from a submerged position, she fired three torpedoes, one of which struck and sank the submarine. Again, there were no survivors.

(The Batfish had sunk a Japanese destroyer the previous August and would also be credited with five Japanese merchant ships.)

U.S. carrier raids against Japanese ports on 19 March scored hits on several Japanese ships, among them the new submarines I-205, I-400, and RO-67.

The principal torpedo success by Japanese submarines was a single hit on the destroyer Renshaw by the ill-fated RO-43. The U.S. ship survived the hit.

THE FUTILE KAITEN MISSIONS

Following the conquest of Iwo Jima, the next target of that American drive was the island of Okinawa, only 340 miles south of the Japanese

1. Yutaka Yokota and Joseph D. Harrington, *The Kaiten Weapon* (New York: Ballantine Books, 1962), p. 91.

home island of Kyushu. Okinawa was to have been the final stepping stone before the Allied assault landed on the beaches of the Japanese home islands in the fall of 1945. Again led by the fast carriers, an armada of warships, auxiliaries, transports, and landing ships was assembled and sailed for Okinawa. D-day for the Okinawa landings would be 1 April.

The Sixth Fleet staff and Japanese naval high command continued to believe that each *kaiten* mission was destroying one U.S. ship per human torpedo launched. Therefore, they felt that only the aerial *kamikazes* and underwater *kaiten* could halt or delay the American drive to the Japanese home islands. Large *kamikaze* air attacks were to be sent against the warships. The Sixth Fleet sent out the fifth *kaiten* mission to attack the shipping en route to Okinawa. This *Tatara* group consisted of the I-44 (four *kaiten*), I-47 (six), I-56 (six), and I-58 (four). This group would attack the U.S. shipping anchored off Okinawa, shipping that would be heavily defended. The submarines departed the *kaiten* bases between 29 March and 3 April.

The submarines confronted U.S. antisubmarine forces almost immediately upon exiting the Inland Sea. Day and night they played hide-and-seek with U.S. antisubmarine ships and aircraft. The I-56 was found and sunk on 18 April by a combination of carrier planes, destroyers, and escorts; the I-44 survived this deadly game until 29 April when planes from an escort carrier found and sank her. The I-47 was attacked

several times until, leaking oil and with the *kaiten* on her deck damaged, she returned to port. The I-58 was directed to rendezvous with a *surface* group for a joint *kamikaze* attack on the U.S. shipping off Okinawa.

The surface group was led by the YAMATO, the largest battleship ever built. Steaming toward Okinawa with a light cruiser and eight destroyers, the dreadnought had only enough fuel for a one-way trip. Once in the invasion area her 18.1-inch guns and the guns and torpedoes of her consorts were to devastate the transports and landing ships. Several hundred aerial *kamikazes* were to coordinate with the surface ships as was the *kaiten*-carrying I-58.

But U.S. carrier planes found the surface group before it rendezvoused with the I-58. Bombs and aerial torpedoes sent the YAMATO to the bottom along with the light cruiser and four of the destroyers. This was the last sortie of Japanese surface ships in World War II.

The I-58 then steamed south, attempting to outflank the antisubmarine defenses, but was unsuccessful and finally was directed to return to Japan. Her *kaiten* remained on her deck. None of the twenty *kaiten* on this, the fifth mission with the human torpedoes, was launched against U.S. ships.

In addition to the *kaiten*-carrying I-44 and I-56, six other submarines were lost in April. Three boats were sunk by destroyers and destroyer escorts, the RO-49, RO-56, and RO-109; the RO-46 went down to torpedoes from the U.S. submarine SEA OWL; and the RO-64 and

A pair of U.S. Navy auxiliary ships lift a midget submarine from the shallows off Okinawa. The craft was attacked and sunk by U.S. naval aircraft during the assault on Okinawa. (U.S. Navy)

RO-67 were lost in Japanese home waters after striking mines laid by U.S. aircraft. (U.S. Navy records credit the destroyer HAGGARD with sinking the I-371 by depth charges and ramming on the night of 22–23 March. But that I-boat was sunk earlier by the submarine LAGARTO, and the HAGGARD apparently killed the smaller RO-49.)

An effort to operate *kaiten* from Okinawa against the landing ships also failed. Eight of the human torpedoes, their pilots and mechanics, were sent out to Okinawa by ship, but the ship was sunk. The *kaiten* failures at Okinawa were in stark contrast to the aerial suiciders, who sank thirteen U.S. destroyers and twenty other ships and damaged more than one hundred, among them ten U.S. and British aircraft carriers and three escort carriers. While these losses failed to halt or even delay the assault on Okinawa, they demonstrated the relative effectiveness of aerial *kamikazes*.

FURTHER KAITEN EFFORTS AND FAILURES

The severe submarine losses and the failure of the *kaiten* efforts led to a rethinking of submarine strategy at Sixth Fleet headquarters. And in May, Vice Admiral Miwa was succeeded as fleet commander by Vice Admiral Tadashige Daigo.

The decision was made to have the *kaiten*-carrying submarines operate farther away from the main combat areas, attacking the supply lines in the rear areas, where there would be fewer antisubmarine escorts. A sixth *kaiten* mission was ordered for the I-36 and I-47, each carrying six human torpedoes. These two boats, forming the *Tembu* group, departed Japan on 20 and 22 April, respectively.

The I-36 sighted a convoy and released four of her six human torpedoes; the two others had mechanical problems and could not launch. The submariners heard four detonations and reported that four U.S. transports or cargo ships had been sunk. A U.S. escort ship with the convoy on 27 April sighted two *kaiten*, one of which was sunk and the other exploded. The explosions may also have been depth charges. No U.S. ships were reported sunk on that date. The I-36 returned safely to base.

The I-47 also made contact with a convoy. The submarine captain, the veteran Lieutenant Commander Zenji Orita, decided to attack with torpedoes and fired a salvo of four at the convoy. Although three explosions were heard, no ships were sunk in this 1 May attack. The next day the I-47 launched four of her human torpedoes against U.S. shipping, but the only known result was slight damage to one cargo ship. The I-47 returned to port with two *kaiten* that she had been unable to launch.[2]

A seventh *kaiten* mission was launched on 5 May with one submarine, the I-367, carrying five human torpedoes. This *Shimbu* mission operated

2. The commanding officer of the I-47 was the author of *I-Boat Captain;* one of the two surviving *kaiten* pilots was Yutaka Yokota, author of *The Kaiten Weapon*.

Vice Admiral Tadashige Daigo, seated in blue uniform, was the last commander of the Sixth (Submarine) Fleet. Here he poses with members of his staff and officers and *kaiten* pilots (with bandanas) of the I-36 before a mission. *Kaiten* pilots were sent off with formal ceremonies, presents, and prayers.

off Okinawa, with four of the *kaiten* suffering mechanical failures. One *kaiten* was launched and a ship sinking was reported, but there was no U.S. loss on that day and the I-367 returned to base.

The eighth *kaiten* mission was composed of the *Todoroki* group—the attack submarines I-36 and I-165, and the ex-supply submarines I-361 and I-363. The I-36 carried six *kaiten,* the I-165 two, and the ex-supply boats five each, a total effort of four submarines and eighteen human torpedoes. The submarines departed from Japan at intervals from 23 May through 16 June.

Only the I-36 was able to launch her *kaiten,* and only three of those could be launched, in two separate attacks, the others falling victim to mechanical problems and then to damage from depth-charge attacks. Two ships were claimed for those three *kaiten,* but in fact there were no U.S. losses to the *Todoroki* group. Only two of the submarines returned to port, the I-36 heavily damaged, leaking oil and narrowly avoiding a four-torpedo salvo from a U.S. submarine as she entered the Inland Sea.

In return for the failure of the *Todoroki* group, the I-361 was sunk on 30 May by aircraft from the escort carrier ANZIO some 400 miles southeast of Okinawa. (The ANZIO's aircraft sank the RO-43, I-361, and I-368; twice teaming up with the destroyer escort LAWRENCE C. TAYLOR, her planes helped to sink the I-13 and I-41, making the ANZIO the most effective antisubmarine carrier in the Pacific theater; the USS BOGUE, which sank two Japanese submarines, was the top-scoring "jeep" carrier in the Atlantic.) The I-165 survived until 27 June when, 450 miles east of Saipan and searching for U.S. transports, she was pounced upon and sunk by Tinian-based Navy PV Ventura bombers.

There was one more submarine loss in June (the I-361 was the only loss in May). The former minelayer I-122, relegated to training duties, was sunk in an inlet of the Sea of Japan on the 10th by the U.S. submarine SKATE. Two unfinished submarines at the Kure Navy Yard, the high-speed I-204 and the seaplane support ship I-352, were smashed by bombs from U.S. Army B-29s flying from the Marianas.

THE SUBMARINE CARRIERS

In July 1945 the submarine force initiated the Phase VI tactical concept, the use of submarine-launched aircraft to strike U.S. targets. Early in the war the Japanese had used submarine-launched floatplanes for reconnaissance, with two token fire-bomb raids being flown against the United States from the I-25. The large I-400 submarine carriers had been developed for the mission of striking New York and other American cities. While they were being completed, this was changed to attacks on Panama Canal locks in an effort to slow the transfer of warships and troop ships from the Atlantic to join the war against Japan.

Five of the I-400s were laid down in 1943–1944, the lead ship being completed at the end of 1944. Two hulls were abandoned in March 1945 as available construction capability was being shifted to suicide weapons. The I-402 was modified before completion to permit her to carry petroleum from the East Indies to the Japanese home islands. She did not, however, undertake a tanker trip before the war ended.

Thus, only the I-400 and I-401 were completed as aircraft carriers, being able to carry three assembled floatplanes plus parts for a fourth.

The submarines of the D1/I-361 class were built for the transport role, having no torpedo tubes, but were pressed into combat service as *kaiten* carriers. The I-361 was sunk on a *kaiten* mission to Okinawa.

Two slightly smaller submarine carriers, the I-13 and I-14 of the AM type, were completed in 1944–1945. These submarines could carry two floatplanes each.

By May of 1945 the I-400 and I-401 were ready for operations and were formed with the I-13 and I-14 into the 1st Submarine Division under Captain Tatsunoke Ariizumi. The four submarines could carry a total of ten planes. For the strike on the Panama Canal, six planes would carry torpedoes to attack the canal's locks, and four planes would carry bombs. However, the *Seiran* floatplane bombers were not yet available.

The aircraft-carrying submarine I-400 at sea. These undersea craft, the largest built by any nation up to that time, could carry three assembled high-performance M6A floatplanes and parts for a fourth. Two of these submarines and the slightly smaller aircraft-carrying I-14 were en route to strike Ulithi when the war ended. (U.S. National Archives)

Production of the planes had been delayed by U.S. bombings of the Aichi aircraft factory at Nagoya, and there was a severe shortage of aviation gasoline. The latter problem was solved in early June with the return of the submarine tanker I-351 from Singapore with 132,000 gallons of aviation fuel. The 901st Air Group was formed to train pilots for the submarine carriers as the aircraft were belatedly delivered.

With diesel fuel oil also in short supply in Japan, the submarines were to go to Dairen, Manchuria, to take on a full load. The I-401, however, struck a magnetic mine laid a few days earlier by U.S. B-29s and had to return to Kure for repairs. Her dummy funnels (to help disguise the ship when on the surface) were transferred to the I-400, which succeeded in reaching Dairen and returned with a full load of fuel and other supplies. During this period the four submarines had snorkels installed to alleviate the need to surface to recharge their batteries.

Intensive workup with the aircraft finally began at Nanao Bay on the western coast of Honshu. Models of the Panama Canal locks were used for target practice. Two aircraft were lost in this workup. The I-400 and I-401 were able to surface, ready their three planes, and catapult them into the air in forty-five minutes. While the submarines and aircraft were training, the Naval General Staff made the decision to attack the Ulithi anchorage instead of the Panama Canal; this could have a more immediate effect on the war, hopefully destroying some of the U.S. aircraft carriers while they were at rest.

The revised Ulithi attack plan called for the I-400 and I-401 to each launch three planes in suicide attacks against Ulithi. The I-13 and I-14 would each carry two partially assembled high-speed reconnaissance planes to Truk. There the planes would be assembled and fly over Ulithi to choose targets for the attack planes. Submarine-delivered *kaiten* would make a coordinated attack, if possible.

The I-13 and 1-14 sortied on 2 July and the I-400 and I-401 on 26 July, with Captain Ariizumi riding the I-401. On the 16th the I-13 was sunk. The I-14 arrived at Truk with her reconnaissance planes on 4 August, and the six-plane raid on Ulithi by the I-400 and I-401 was scheduled for 17 August. The planes would be launched in the predawn darkness, with luminous paint used on the aircrafts' assembly points to permit the fitting of wings and other equipment in the dark.

THE FINAL KAITEN MISSION

The ninth and final *kaiten* mission—carried out by the *Tamon* group—began on 14 July when the attack submarine I-53 left port with six *kaiten*. She was followed through August 8 by the remaining five submarines of the group, the I-47 and I-58 also with six *kaiten* each, and the ex-supply submarines I-363, I-366, and I-367, each with five human torpedoes. This was the largest *kaiten* effort, six submarines carrying thirty-three *kaiten,* albeit with the departures being drawn out over more than three weeks.

Mechanical problems plagued the *kaiten,* and three submarines were forced to return to base without making attacks—the I-47, I-363, and I-367. Still, this was the most successful mission of the entire *kaiten* effort.

On 22 July either the I-47 or I-367 damaged a transport off Okinawa with a conventional torpedo, although some sources contend the damage was inflicted by a *kaiten* from the I-53. The next success was definitely that of a *kaiten* from that submarine. On the 24th the I-53 launched two *kaiten* against a convoy of LSTs transiting from Okinawa to Leyte with the destroyer escort UNDERHILL. That afternoon the escort sighted what was believed to be a mine. It was apparently one of the two *kaiten* from the I-53. A submarine chaser and the UNDERHILL attacked, probably sinking one *kaiten* with depth charges, but the second human torpedo struck the destroyer escort. The explosion broke the UNDERHILL in two parts. Only 125 of the 238 men on board the escort survived the sinking.

Three days later, on 27 July, the I-58 launched a pair of *kaiten* to attack a tanker. Two explosions were heard; no U.S. ships were hit. But on the 30th the I-58, using her Type 95 torpedoes, scored one of the major successes of Japanese submarines in the war. Late that night Lieutenant Commander Mochitsura Hashimoto, captain of the I-58, detected what he believed to be a battleship of the NEW MEXICO class. The ship was the heavy cruiser INDIANAPOLIS, which had just carried components for an atomic bomb to Tinian. The cruiser was steaming, unescorted, from Guam to Okinawa.

Hashimoto decided to attack with torpedoes rather than *kaiten* and, with minimum maneuvering, fired a salvo of six torpedoes. Seventy-five seconds later two torpedoes hit the U.S. warship; the violent explosions ripped out portions of the ship's bottom and, without being able to send a radio signal, and perhaps a quarter of an hour after being hit, the INDIANAPOLIS slid beneath the waves. Of 1,199 men on board when the INDIANAPOLIS was hit, several hundred were killed outright. The survivors spent eighty-four hours in the open sea until they were found. When the rescue operation was over, there were only 316 survivors.[3]

The *Tamon* boats I-53, I-58, and I-366 stayed at sea into August. Four of their sister ships were sunk during July. The I-351, on another tanker trip from Singapore to Japan, was sunk by the U.S. submarine BLUEFISH on 14 July; the BLUEFISH rescued three survivors. The I-13 went down to aircraft from the carrier ANZIO. On the 18th the I-372, having just been converted to a submarine tanker, was sunk during a carrier air strike on Yokosuka, and on the 28th the unfinished submarine carrier I-404 was sunk by carrier aircraft at Kure. Another supply boat, the I-373, would be the last Japanese submarine sunk during the war, being torpedoed by the U.S. submarine SPIKEFISH on 14 August.

3. The commanding officer of the INDIANAPOLIS was subjected to a court-martial, which sat in December 1945. He was found guilty of hazarding his ship's safety through failure to zigzag. Lieutenant Commander Hashimoto was a witness at the court-martial.

The I-53 launched the *kaiten* on their last operational mission, which damaged one U.S. Navy transport and sank a destroyer escort. Note the flag and submarine number sewn to the conning tower. (K.R. MacPherson)

On 7 August the Japanese submarines at sea received a radio news bulletin announcing that Hiroshima had been destroyed by a single bomb. Two days later another atomic bomb devastated Nagasaki.

The I-58 launched another pair of *kaiten* against a convoy north of Luzon on 10 August, and the I-366 sent three *kaiten* against a convoy north of Palau the following day. None of the human torpedoes scored hits. The final *kaiten* attack came on the 12th, when the I-58 sent her last two *kaiten* against what was thought to be a seaplane carrier between Leyte and Okinawa. Her target was actually a dock landing ship, which was apparently scraped by a *kaiten* but escaped damage. That human torpedo was sunk by depth charges from a destroyer escort, which, in turn, was also scraped by a *kaiten* that passed on and exploded clear of the warship.

Claiming up to seven ships destroyed on the cruise, the I-58 headed back to Kure. According to her commanding officer:

> On the evening of August 15, I-58, her crew elated, was running on the surface looking for targets on passage from the vicinity of Okinawa to the Bungo Channel. I was standing on the bridge scanning the horizon in the direction of the setting sun when I was suddenly called to the hatch by the senior wireless rating. I thought I had never seen a man so sad. He looked ready to burst into tears at any minute. "Please come down a minute," he said. Reluctantly, I followed him down, and drawing me to a corner of the wardroom, he said, "Look what's come." It was a communique announcing the end of hostilities. I felt stunned, but after considering for a moment I decided it could only be some newspaper stunt, not an official signal. Taking a grip on myself, I said, "This may be a broadcast for the purpose of a *démarche*. Destroy it and throw it away."[4]

4. Mochitsura Hashimoto, *Sunk!* (New York: Henry Holt and Company, 1954), p. 152.

A *kaiten* Type 2 is launched off the stern of the cruiser KITAKAMI during February 1945 trials of surface-launching the craft. At the end of the war, it was planned to launch them from shore bases as well as from submarines against the U.S. invasion forces. (Shizuo Fukui)

But upon arrival of the I-58 in Japan on 17 August there was no question of the validity of the dispatch. It had been broadcast on 15 August to all forces—the Emperor's order for immediate surrender.

Thus the *kaiten* effort and the war were ended. The *kaiten* had failed, as had the overall submarine effort. While approximately forty Allied warships, transports, and auxiliaries were claimed as *kaiten* victims, in fact the only sinkings to human torpedoes were the oiler MISSISSINEWA (on the first *kaiten* mission) and the destroyer escort UNDERHILL (on the last mission). A few other ships were damaged. In return, eight submarines and almost nine hundred Japanese lives were lost in the human-torpedo program.

A U.S. flag officer wrote what might be considered the epitaph for the *kaiten* effort: ". . .the Imperial Navy did a lot better with its torpedoes *before* the human guidance system was added."[5]

THE FINAL PHASE

A final tactical phase being considered when the war ended was the use of the new high-speed I-201/ST-class submarines for attacks against U.S. warships. These submarines, with an underwater speed of up to seventeen knots, were comparable in some respects to the advanced German Type XXI U-boats. U.S. antisubmarine forces would be hard-pressed to cope with the I-201s armed with Type 95 torpedoes if the submarines were astutely handled.

Other submarine-related programs were being developed when the war ended. For example, to help the fuel-starved military forces in the home islands, seven I-boats and four of the new HA-class submarines

5. Rear Admiral Bruce McCandless, USN (Ret.), Commentary on "*Kaiten*—Japan's Human Torpedoes," U.S. Naval Institute *Proceedings* (July 1962), p. 120.

TABLE 8. SUBMARINE FORCE, 15 AUGUST 1945

COMBINED FLEET	
10th Special Attack Squadron	HA-109, HA-111
SIXTH FLEET/SUBMARINE FLEET	
1st Submarine Division	I-14, I-400, I-401, I-402
15th Submarine Division	I-36, I-47, I-53, I-58, I-156, I-157, I-158, I-159, I-162, I-201, I-202, I-363, I-366, I-367, RO-50, HA-103, HA-105
16th Submarine Division	I-369, HA-101, HA-102, HA-104
52nd Submarine Division	HA-201, HA-202, HA-205, HA-207, HA-208, HA-209, HA-210
11th Submarine Squadron flagship: CHOGEI	I-203
FIRST SOUTHERN EXPEDITIONARY FLEET	I-501, I-502
SECOND SOUTHERN EXPEDITIONARY FLEET	I-505, I-506
KURE NAVAL DISTRICT	
Kure Submarine Squadron	
33rd Submarine Division	I-121, RO-62, RO-63, HA-106, HA-107, HA-108, HA-203, HA-204

were being prepared to serve as submarine tankers to carry fuel from Singapore to Japan (the largest being the I-402). This fuel was to permit thousands of *kamikazes*—aircraft, motor boats, midget submarines, and human torpedoes—to attack the assaulting hordes of U.S. troops that were scheduled to begin landing on Japanese beaches in the fall of 1945.

There were some one hundred *kaiten* and four hundred midget submarines available when the war ended. (There were also two thousand small motor boats with explosive charges and several thousand aircraft being readied for suicide missions.) The submarines HA-109 and HA-111 were designated as tenders for the midgets, and the older submarines I-156, I-157, I-158, I-159, and I-162 were planned to deliver *kaiten* to various coastal locations where the human torpedoes were to operate frcm land bases. These submarines then would carry out *kaiten* attack missions against the invasion fleet along with the I-37, I-44, and I-48, the effective remnants of the Japanese submarine fleet.

POST MORTEM

When the war ended, the submarine carriers I-400 and I-401 were at sea; they returned to Japan, on the surface, flying the black flag of surrender. The submarines were to return unarmed. All torpedoes were fired and the planes catapulted from the I-401 and smashed and pushed over the side from the I-400. The giants had never fired a shot in anger. The few other submarines at sea also returned to port, marking the end of Japanese submarine operations.

After these submarines and those that had been surrendered in Japanese ports were examined by U.S. and British submarine specialists, they were to be disposed of by sinking. Escorted by U.S. ships, 24 of the surviving submarines got underway on their own power with minimum crews before dawn on 1 April 1946 in Operation Road's End. Nine others remained in port for various reasons. The largest of those making this last voyage was the I-402. Her aircraft-carrying sister ships I-400 and I-401 and the slightly smaller I-14 were to be disposed of after further examination at Pearl Harbor.

Sailing in two columns with accompanying U.S. ships, the Japanese submarines moved out of Sasebo Bay to a point 60 miles offshore, just beyond the 100-fathom line (32°37′ North latitude, 129°17′ East longitude). According to one observer, "The Japanese crewmen, as a parting gesture, had fastened sprigs of cherry blossoms to the conning towers of their ships, creating a curiously festive note, though touched with melancholy for them. One crew had painted his conning tower bright green, a striking contrast to the gray-brown hues of their companions."*

At the objective, small boats took the Japanese crews off the submarines and U.S. demolition experts affixed fuzes to the previously installed explosive charges. Shortly after 1 P.M. on 1 April, explosions racked the I-157, and a few moments later the I-367's charges detonated

*Roderick D. Sage, "Operation Road's End," *Shipmate*, September 1985, p. 32.

The Japanese I-400 as she surrendered off Honshu to the smaller U.S. destroyer escort WEAVER on 28 August 1945. The submarines had destroyed all of their offensive weapons, including aircraft, when they surrendered. (U.S. Navy)

and both submarines rapidly sank. One after another the other submarines followed. The I-402 and the small HA-201, lashed together, were used as target practice for destroyers' 5-inch guns before they were scuttled. By 4:30, when the operation was halted, 24 submarines had been sunk.

On 5 April the remaining nine submarines were towed to sea and were similarly scuttled in Operation Dead Duck.

Japanese submarine losses from December 1941 through August 1945 totaled 136, including the hapless I-33, which was counted twice as a loss. The I-33 was sunk by U.S. Army aircraft at Truk in 1943, raised and repaired only to be lost through accident shortly after being recommissioned in 1944. In comparison, the U.S. Navy lost only fifty-two submarines from all causes during the war. Beyond these losses, many of the Japanese submarines afloat in August 1945 were unable to go to sea because of damage suffered from U.S. antisubmarine forces at sea or from U.S. bombers—naval and Army Air Forces—that struck Japanese bases and shipyards almost continuously during the last months. As indicated above, perhaps a score of Navy submarines were fully operational at the end of the war, as were a large number of Army transport submarines.

The Japanese submarine effort failed, and failed badly in World War II. Despite several successes in 1942, notably against U.S. aircraft carriers, the submarines failed to influence the outcome of any of the major naval engagements or, of course, the war.

The Japanese Naval General Staff believed, however, that submarines did have some influence on the conflict, and that they caused

The vanquished: From left, the aircraft-carrying I-400, I-401, and I-14 alongside the U.S. submarine tender PROTEUS (AS 19) at Yokosuka on 7 September 1945. All three submarines have their collapsible aircraft cranes in the raised position (mounted forward, on the port side of the catapult track). In the background is the battleship NAGATO, which survived the war to become a target at the Bikini atomic bomb tests in July 1946. (U.S. Navy)

After the war the aircraft-carrying I-400, I-401, and I-14 travelled from Japan to Guam and then to Pearl Harbor (above) for examination by U.S. submarine specialists. Several U.S. fleet boats are moored at left, beyond the submarine escape tank at the Pearl Harbor Submarine Base. The Japanese submarines were subsequently scuttled. (U.S. National Archives)

The captain of the I-400, Commander Toshiwo Kusaka, listens to an interpreter during an interrogation. (U.S. National Archives)

major casualties. The official postwar claims by the Japanese Navy list seven U.S. aircraft carriers sunk by submarine torpedoes and one carrier plus one seaplane carrier sunk by *kaiten.* In reality, two U.S. large carriers and one escort carrier were lost to Japanese submarines. Similarly, the Japanese Navy listed one U.S. battleship sunk at Pearl Harbor by midgets, two battleships sunk by submarine torpedoes, and three by *kaiten* (the last three at Ulithi with human torpedoes launched from the I-47). No U.S. battleships were sunk by the Japanese submarine force. Other estimates of Allied ships sunk as well as damaged were also widely inaccurate.

After the war the U.S. Navy, with assistance from the Royal Navy, made an extensive survey of the Japanese Navy, based on an examination of ships and weapons, interrogations, and review of documents. Most of the blame for the failures of the submarine force appears to fall on the shoulders of the officer corps—submarine commanding officers, division and squadron commanders, the commanders of the Sixth Fleet, and to a lesser degree, the naval high command. Discussing these shortcomings, the survey report states: "Not only were the submarines unduly restricted as to what they were permitted to attack while on individual patrol, but during large operations each was frequently restricted to an ambush station with orders not to leave it even though a valuable target appeared outside his limits, or even though the enemy he was "ambushing" had passed him by."[6]

Closely related to this lack of flexibility was the doctrine of radio silence imposed on most submarine operations: "Blind adherence to radio si-

6. U.S. Naval Technical Mission to Japan, Ship and Related Targets, Japanese Submarine Operations (S-17), February 1946, p. 8.

Japanese cruisers, destroyers, and submarines at Kure after the surrender. (U.S. Naval Historical Center)

A Japanese submarine sinks after being scuttled off Goto Island, near Sasebo, on 1 April 1946. Another stands by while a U.S. Navy PBM Mariner patrol bomber circles overhead. (U.S. Navy)

lence was quite puzzling. Although there were many lengthy transmissions when there seemed to be no justification (as on our West Coast during the early stages), there were times when radio silence was a fatal error. There are two outstanding examples. In the Solomons episode, the contacting submarine did not immediately report, but waited until he could pull well clear of the scouting line. Also when our antisubmarine forces discovered and 'rolled' their 'NA' Ambush line . . . [the USS ENGLAND's attacks] one submarine after another was sunk without a single effort to warn others."[7]

The results of the above attitudes were reported in these words: "This investigator endeavored to form an unbiased opinion of the attack audacity of Japanese submariners. The conviction grew, through conversations, interrogations and study, that the percentage of overly discreet was large. It was frankly impossible to believe that submarines could spend weeks on the U.S. west coast 'without contacts,' or spend more than 40 days running among the Solomons during the Guadalcanal campaign 'without seeing any targets.' Even the Japanese commanding officers could not disguise their embarrassment when recounting these tales. Further enlightenment is found in the extremely large number of times the target was 'too far away to attack.'"[8]

There were, of course, several notable exceptions to this attitude on the part of Japanese submarine commanders and of more senior offi-

cers. And, of course, at all levels of the submarine forces there were unquestioned dedication and tenacity.

In summary, the official report reads: "Hampered by shortages of all kinds, assigned to a minor role with its forces dispersed in a losing war against a well-equipped enemy, the Japanese submarine force should be given credit for effort. However, in addition to its handicaps, there were several shortcomings of its own which prevented creditable performance. Among these shortcomings were vacillating policies in building, false economy in withholding submarines for future use, failure to correct known mistakes, confusion of tactical command, poor communications, and a lack of individual caliber in many of the commanding officers. Briefly, in no particular could it be said that the Japanese submarine force excelled, while examples are many of its deficiency in strategical, tactical, research and personnel performance."[9]

Although highly critical, this assessment is in agreement with statements by many knowledgeable Japanese officers. Admiral Fukudome concluded his own review of Japanese submarines in the war with: "The Japanese Navy expected much from its submarines, and for this reason alone both officers and men were carefully selected and put through the most rigorous training. They considered themselves superior in technique in the field of submarine warfare to any in other navies. But when it came to the test of actual warfare, the results were deplorable."[10]

7. *Ibid.*, p. 9.
8. *Ibid.*

9. *Ibid.*, p. 1.
10. Vice Admiral Fukudome in *Sunk!,* p. 160.

6 Submarines and Submarine Classes

Japanese submarines were originally numbered in a simple, sequential order. However, as indicated below, there was some duplication of numbers. In 1924 three separate classes were established, based on the first three letters of the Japanese alphabet: I (written as the Greek lambda) was assigned for first-class or large submarines, RO to second-class or medium submarines, and HA to third-class or coastal boats. This post-1924 numbering system also suffered from omissions and redundancies. The confusion was so great that on 20 May 1942 the twenty-seven submarines numbered between I-52 through I-85 were renumbered from I-152 through I-185.

Midget submarines were listed in the coastal HA-series.

The following is a chronological listing of all Japanese submarines. The ship order numbers were begun with the Third Fleet Replenishment Program of 1937. The former U-boats received by Japan in 1919 were given O-series names and are listed at the end of chapter 7 of this volume. The former German U-boats and Italian submarines acquired by Japan during World War II are listed at the end of chapter 8 or chapter 9, under their I or RO designations, respectively.

Ship Order Number	Ship Name/ Number	Type/ Notes		Lead Ship Completed
1904 Program				
	1, 2, 3, 4, 5		Holland	1905
	6, 7		modified Holland	1906
1907 Program				
	8,9	later HA-1	C1 Vickers	1909
	10, 11, 12	later HA-3	C2 Vickers	1911
	13	later HA-6	modified Vickers	1912
1910 Program				
	14,15	later HA-10	S Schneider-Laubeuf	1917
	14 (II)	later HA-9	S2 Schneider-Laubeuf	
1915 Program				
	16, 17	later HA-7	C3 Vickers	1916
	18	later RO-1	F1 Fiat-Laurenti	1919
1916 Program				
	19, 20	later RO-11	K1 medium	1919
	21	(RO-1 class)	F1 Fiat-Laurenti	
1917 Program				
	22, 23, 24	later RO-13	K2 medium	1920
	25, 26	later RO-51	L1 medium	1920

Ship Order Number	Ship Name/ Number	Type/ Notes		Lead Ship Completed
1918 Program				
	27 to 30	later RO-53	L2 medium	1921
	31, 32, 33	later RO-3	F2 medium	1922
	34 to 43	later RO-16	K3 medium	1922
1919 Program				
	44	later I-51	KD1 large	1924
	45	later RO-26	K4 medium	1924
	46, 47	later RO-57	L3 medium	1922
	48, 49, 50	later I-21/121	KRS large	1927
1920 Program				
	51	later I-52/152	KD2 large	1925
	(I-52 to 56)		KD2 large cancelled	(1922)
	57	(RO-57 class)	L3 medium	
	58	(RO-26 class)	K4 medium	
	59	later RO-60	L4 medium	1924
1921 Program				
	62	(RO-26 class)	K4 medium	
	64	later I-53/153	KD3A large	
1922 Program				
	68 to 71	later RO-29	KT medium	1923
	71		small, high-speed	1938
	72, 73	(RO-60 class)	L4 medium	
	74, 75, 76	later I-1	J1 scouting	1926
	77,78	(I-53/153 class)	KD3A large	
	84	(RO-60 class)	L4 medium	
	RO-64 to 68	(RO-60 class)	L4 medium	
	I-4	(I-1 class)	J1 scouting	
	I-5		J1M scouting	1932
	I-24		KRS large	
	I-56 to 60	later I-156	KD3B large	1927
	I-61, I-62	later I-162*	KD4 large	1929
	I-63	(I-56/156 class)	KD3B large	
	I-64	(I-62/162 class)	KD4 large	
	I-65 to 67	later I-165	KD5 large	1932
1st Replenishment Program (1931)				
	I-6		J2 scouting	1935
	I-68 to 73	later I-168	KD6A large	1934
	RO-33, RO-34		K5 medium	1935
2nd Replenishment Program (1934)				
	I-7, I-8		J3 scouting	1937
	I-74, I-75	later I-174	KD6B large	1938

Ship Order Number	Ship Name/ Number	Type/ Notes		Lead Ship Completed
3rd Fleet Replenishment Programaam (1937)				
	No. 71	experimental		1938
35	I-9	A1	headquarters	1941
36	I-10	A1	headquarters	
37 to 42	I-15	B1	scouting	1940
44 to 48	I-16	C1	attack	
4th Fleet Replenishment Program (1940)				
138	(I-9 class)	A1	headquarters	
139 to 152	(I-15 class)	B1	scouting	
154 to 163	I-76	KD7	large	1942
1940 Urgent War Program (1941)				
201 to 209	RO-35	K6	medium	
210 to 213	RO-100	KS	medium	1942
1941 Emergency Program				
370 to 375	I-40	B2	scouting	1943
376 to 381	I-46	C2	attack	
385 to 396	(RO-35)	K6	medium	1943
400 to 408	(RO-100)	KS	medium	
1941 Additional Program				
620	I-12	A2	headquarters	
621	I-13	AM	(begun as A2)	
625	I-52	C3	attack	
626	(I-52)	C3	attack	
627	I-54	B3	scouting	
628	(I-52)	C3	attack	
629	(I-54)	B3	scouting	
630	(I-52)	C3	attack	
631	(I-54)	B3	scouting	
632	(I-52)	C3	attack	
633 to 636	(I-54)	B3	scouting	
640 to 654	RO-35	K6	medium	
655 to 657	I-351	SH	aircraft support	1945

Ship Order Number	Ship Name/ Number	Type/ Notes		Lead Ship Completed
5th Fleet Replenishment Program (1942)				
700	(I-9)	A1	headquarters	
701	(I-9)	A1	headquarters	
702 to 709	(I-15)	B1	scouting	
710 to 713	(I-46)	C2	attack	
714	I-400	STo	aircraft carrier	1945
715 to 723	(RO-35)	K6	medium	
730 to 732	(I-351)	SH	aircraft support	
Modified 5th Fleet Replenishment Program (1942)				
5101 to 5114	(I-54)	B3	scouting	
5115 to 5132	modified I-54			
5141 to 5155	(I-52)	C3	attack	
5156 to 5180	modified I-52	C3	attack	
5181 to 5223	(RO-35)	K6	medium	
5231 to 5248	(I-400)	Sto	aircraft carrier	
Additional Program (1942)				
5461 to 5471	(I-361)	D1	transport	
1943 to 1944 War Program				
2961	(I-372)	D1	transport	
2962 to 2967	I-373	D2	transport	1945
4501 to 4532	I-201	ST	high-speed	1945
4601 to 4612	HA-101	SS	transport	1944
4911 to 4989	HA-201	STS	attack	1945
1944 to 1945 War Program†				
(88 ships)	(HA-201)	STS	attack	
(10 ships)	(HA-201)	STS	attack	
(76 ships)	(I-201)	ST	high-speed	
(13 ships)	(I-351)	SH	aircraft support	
(92 ships)	(I-361)	D1	transport	
(140 ships)	(I-373)	D2	transport	

*I-61 lost before 1942 reclassification.
†None of these ships was ordered.

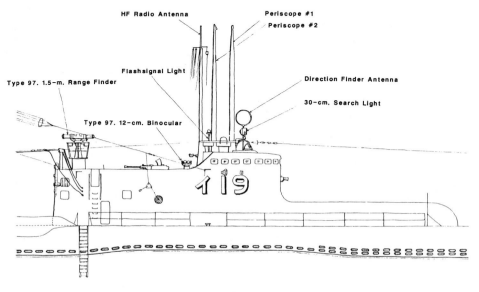

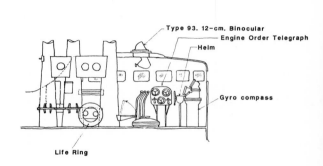

Details of the bridge arrangement of the B1-type submarine I-15 at the time of completion in 1940.

7 Early Submarines

Japanese interest in submarines can be traced to the 1890s when a U.S. Navy board of inspection was examining the HOLLAND VI, the latest submarine design of immigrant Irish school teacher John P. Holland. This Holland underwater craft would, in 1900, be accepted as the first official U.S. Navy submarine (later designated SS-1).

The HOLLAND VI was built at the Crescent Shipyard in Elizabethport, New Jersey, in 1896–1897. In July of 1897 two Japanese officers visited the yard and climbed through the craft. The following year, after the submarine had been moved to the Atlantic Yacht Basin in Brooklyn, New York, the HOLLAND VI was visited by Count Kosuke Kizaki. Subsequently, during underway trials Count Lieutenant Takashi Sasaki went down in the HOLLAND VI in October 1898, and Lieutenant Kenji Ide, assigned to the embassy in Washington, submerged in the craft during a demonstration in the Potomac River in April 1900.

With the start of hostilities between Russia and Japan in 1904, the Japanese government ordered five boats of the basic Holland design to be built by the Electric Boat Company at the Fore River shipyard in Massachusetts. These submarines were built and shipped in sections to Japan on board merchant ships for reassembly at the Gokaska dockyard in Yokosuka. A short time later the Japanese also decided to construct two much-improved Holland-design submarines, and the director of the Kawasaki shipyard at Kobe came to the United States to discuss submarine building procedures with John Holland. These latter submarines, Nos. 6 and 7, were experimental designs. (During this period tsarist Russia purchased submarines from Simon Lake, Holland's principal competitor in the United States, and from Germany.)

The first Holland submarines for Japan were completed in mid-1905, by which time a Japanese squadron under Vice Admiral Heiharchiro Togo had decisively defeated a Russian fleet in the Tsushima Straits. Thus, the Japanese effort to obtain submarines for the conflict, like the similar Russian submarine program, was too late to have an impact on the war. The Japanese were also reported to have taken a small Russian submersible, which was referred to as the PETR KOTCHKA type, at Port Arthur, but that craft was rendered useless before the port's surrender to the Japanese.

Following the procurement of these U.S. designs, the Japanese Navy sought out designs from Britain, France, and Italy. Submarines No. 8 through 12 were built by the British firm of Vickers, with the latter three assembled in Japan. These were followed by several Japanese-built submarines based on the Vickers design—Nos. 13, 16, and 17.

Submarines No. 14 and 15 were ordered from Creusot in France to a Schneider-Laubeuf design, but the No. 14 was taken over by France in 1916 and placed in service as the ARMIDE. Japanese-built derivatives of this type were a second submarine No. 14 and Nos. 19, 20, and 22 through 24. Later submarines derived from these were Nos. 34 through 43, 45, 58, 62, and 68 through 70.

The plans for the Italian Fiat-Laurenti design were acquired by Japan, and submarines No. 18 and 21 were built in Kobe. Subsequent Japanese submarines developed from this design were Nos. 31 through 33.

The Japanese participated in the 1914–1918 war on the Allied side, with a small Japanese antisubmarine squadron serving in the Mediterranean, while other Japanese naval forces operated against German interests in the Pacific. Late in the war the Japanese acquired the British L-class design from Vickers, and submarines No. 25 through 30, 46, 47, 57, 59, 72, 73, 84, and RO-64 through -68 were derived from this design.[1]

After the war the Japanese acquired several former U-boats, and numbered them in an O-series. Of the 176 German submarines surrendered in 1918, Britain was allocated 105, France 46, Italy 10, Japan 7, the United States 6, and Belgium 2. The Japanese took over the seven U-boats from the British with the understanding that they would be used only for research and experimental work, and would be rendered incapable of military service by 1 July 1921. Further, engines, armament, and equipment from these U-boats could not be used for new submarines. Studies of these U-boats led to two series of Japanese designs, the I-21/I-121 class, based on the minelaying U-125, and the I-52/I-152, developed from the U-139.

1. The Soviet Navy also built derivatives of this design, based on the British L-55 that had sunk in the Gulf of Riga (off Kronshtadt) in 1919 and was refloated and repaired by the Soviets in 1928.

5 SUBMARINES: HOLLAND TYPE

Number	Builder	Launched	Completed	Notes
1	Fore River, Quincy, Mass.	30 Mar 1905	1 Aug 1905	stricken 1922
2	Fore River, Quincy, Mass.	2 May 1905	5 Sep 1905	stricken 1922
3	Fore River, Quincy, Mass.	16 May 1905	5 Sep 1905	stricken 1922
4	Fore River, Quincy, Mass.	27 May 1905	1 Oct 1905	sunk in Inland Sea 14 Nov 1916; refloated; stricken 1922
5	Fore River, Quincy, Mass.	13 May 1905	1 Oct 1905	stricken 1922

Displacement:	105 tons surfaced
	130 tons submerged
Length:	67 feet (20.4 m) oa
Beam:	11¾ feet (3.63 m)
Draft:	10¼ feet (3.12 m)
Propulsion:	gasoline engine; 180 hp
	electric motor; 70 hp; 1 shaft
Speed:	9 knots surfaced
	7 knots submerged
Range:	185 n.miles at 8 knots surfaced
Depth:	125 feet
Complement:	13 officers and men
Torpedo tubes:	1 18-inch (457-mm) bow
Torpedoes:	2

Japan's first submarine, No. 1, at Yokosuka in 1905. These early Holland craft had tear-drop hulls, similar to the designs that would much later be used for high-speed undersea craft. (Shizuo Fukui)

These submarines were fabricated in the United States, the No. 1 being laid down in November 1904. They were shipped to Japan by merchant ship, arriving at Yokohama on 12 December 1904 and assembled and fitted out at the Yokosuka (Gokaska) Navy Yard.

The No. 4 sank at Kure on 14 November 1916 after a gasoline explosion; she was raised and repaired.

The submarine No. 6 with officers and men around her diminutive conning tower. Japan acquired Holland-built submarines for the war with Russia, but neither side was able to employ submarines before the 1904–1905 war ended. (*Ships of the World*)

EXPERIMENTAL SUBMARINE: MODIFIED HOLLAND TYPE

Number	Builder	Launched	Completed	Notes
6	Kawasaki Shipbuilding, Kobe	28 Sep 1905	30 Mar 1906	sunk at Kure 15 April 1910; refloated and stricken 1923

Displacement: 57 tons surfaced
 63 tons submerged
Length: 73¾ feet (22.5 m) oa
Beam: 7 feet (2.1 m)
Draft: 6½ feet (2.0 m)
Propulsion: gasoline engine; 250 hp
 electric motor; 22 hp; 1 shaft
Speed: 8.5 knots surfaced
 4 knots submerged
Range: 185 n.miles at 8 knots surfaced
 12 n.miles at 4 knots submerged
Depth:
Complement: 14–16 officers and men
Torpedo tubes: 1 18-inch (457-mm) bow
Torpedoes: 1

Submarines No. 6 and 7 (see below) were built specifically for experimental purposes, being based on a modified Holland design. They were the first submarines built from the keel up in Japan, both being laid down in November 1904. Note their small size in comparison with the previous Holland design.

The No. 6 sank accidently during a training mission; all 16 men on board were lost. At the time the boat was using a snorkel-like breathing tube to permit underwater operation of the gasoline engine. The boat apparently dipped and the tube flooded, stopping the engine, and she sank.

Submarine No. 6 was the first submarine built from the keel up in Japan. She accidently sank in Hiroshima Bay in April 1910, killing her crew of sixteen. The submarine was raised and returned to service. The craft is now preserved as a memorial at the Kure Naval Station. (*Ships of the World*)

1 EXPERIMENTAL SUBMARINE: MODIFIED HOLLAND TYPE

Number	Builder	Launched	Completed	Notes
7	Kawasaki Shipbuilding, Kobe	28 Sep 1906	30 Mar 1906	stricken 1923

Displacement:	78 tons surfaced
	95 tons submerged
Length:	84½ feet (25.7 m) oa
Beam:	8 feet (2.4 m)
Draft:	7½ feet (2.3 m)
Propulsion:	gasoline engine; 250 hp
	electric motor; 22 hp; 1 shaft
Speed:	8.5 knots surfaced
	4 knots submerged
Range:	185 n.miles at 8 knots surfaced
	12 n.miles at 4 knots submerged
Depth:	
Complement:	14 officers and men
Torpedo tubes:	1 18-inch (457-mm) bow
Torpedoes:	1

Submarines No. 6 and 7, the latter shown here at Kure on 5 February 1916, were two of the many one-of-a-kind experimental submarines built by the Japanese as they sought optimum designs during almost every period of pre−World
War II development. (K.R. MacPherson)

5 SUBMARINES: VICKERS C1/C2 TYPE

Number	Builder	Launched	Completed	Notes
8	Vickers, Barrow-in-Furness	19 May 1908	26 Feb 1909	changed to HA-1 in 1924; stricken 1929
9	Vickers, Barrow-in-Furness	19 May 1908	9 Mar 1909	changed to HA-2 in 1924; stricken 1929
10	Vickers, Barrow-in-Furness	4 Mar 1911	12 Aug 1911	changed to HA-3 in 1924; stricken 1929
11	Vickers, Barrow-in-Furness	18 Mar 1911	26 Aug 1911	changed to HA-4 in 1924; stricken 1929
12	Vickers, Barrow-in-Furness	27 Mar 1911	3 Aug 1911	changed to HA-5 in 1924; stricken 1929

Displacement:	No. 8, 9	286 tons surfaced
		321 tons submerged
	No. 10 to 12	291 tons surfaced
		326 tons submerged
Length:	142 feet (43.3 m) oa	
Beam:	13½ feet (4.1 m)	
Draft:	11¼ feet (3.4 m)	
Propulsion:	gasoline engine; 600 hp	
	electric motor; 300 hp; 1 shaft	
Speed:	12 knots surfaced	
	8.5 knots submerged	
Range:	660 n.miles at 12 knots surfaced	
	60 n.miles at 4 knots submerged	
Depth:		
Complement:	26 officers and men	
Torpedo tubes:	2 18-inch (457-mm) bow	
Torpedoes:	2	

These were British-built submarines, the first two (C1 type) being built at Vickers and shipped to Japan; the three later submarines (C2 type) were shipped to Japan in sections, being assembled and fitted out at the Kure Navy Yard. The lead ship was laid down in August 1907.

Submarine No. 8 (later HA-1) at Kure on 26 December 1916. (K.R. Mac-Pherson)

The Vickers-design submarines No. 10 (foreground) and No. 11. Later redesignated HA-3 and HA-4, respectively, these submarines were built in sections in England and shipped to Kure for assembly. (*Ships of the World*)

1 EXPERIMENTAL SUBMARINE: MODIFIED VICKERS TYPE

Number	Builder	Launched	Completed	Notes
13	Kawasaki, Kobe	18 July 1912	30 Sep 1912	changed to HA-6 in 1924; stricken 1929

Displacement:	304 tons surfaced
	340 tons submerged
Length:	126¾ feet (38.6 m) oa
Beam:	12½ feet (3.8 m)
Draft:	9¾ feet (3.0 m)
Propulsion:	gasoline engine; 1,160 hp
	electric motor; 300 hp; 1 shaft
Speed:	10 knots surfaced
	8 knots submerged
Range:	
Depth:	
Complement:	26 officers and men
Torpedo tubes:	2 18-inch (457-mm) bow
Torpedoes:	2

Submarine No. 13 was an experimental craft based on the Vickers C1/C2 design with more-powerful surface propulsion. The craft was laid down in March 1910.

Submarine No. 13 (later HA-6) was a Japanese copy of the original Vickers design. A steering wheel can be seen on the conning tower as a sailor works on the radio mast; an officer stands in front of the conning tower. (*Ships of the World*)

2 SUBMARINES: SCHNEIDER-LAUBEUF S TYPE

Number	Builder	Launched	Completed	Notes
14	Creusot, Chalon-sur-Saone	July 1915	(1916)	taken over by French Navy
15	Creusot, Chalon-sur-Saone	7 Apr 1916	20 July 1917	changed to HA-10 in 1924; stricken 1929

Displacement:	457 tons surfaced
	665 tons submerged
Length:	186¼ feet (56.7 m) oa
Beam:	17 feet (5.2 m)
Draft:	9¾ feet (3.0 m)
Propulsion:	2 diesels; 2,000 hp
	electric motor; 850 hp; 2 shafts
Speed:	17 knots surfaced
	10 knots submergedu
Range:	2,050 n.miles at 10 knots surfaced
	60 n.miles at 4 knots submerged
Depth:	
Complement:	approx. 30 officers and men
Torpedo tubes:	6 18-inch (457-mm) 2 bow + 4 superstructure
Torpedoes:	8
Guns:	1 MG (see notes)

These submarines were built in France for the Japanese Navy, but No. 14 was taken over by the French Navy in 1915 and placed in commission as the ARMIDE. The similar AMAZONE and ANTIGONE of this design were begun for the Greek Navy, but were similarly taken over by the French Navy. Submarine No. 15 was laid down in November 1913.

This was the first Japanese submarine to have a deck gun, originally a machine gun; after World War I, the Japanese unit was fitted with a 3-inch deck gun forward of the conning tower.

The French-built submarine No. 15 (later HA-10) photographed on trials in April 1917. Note her bow configuration, deck structure, and vertical rudder. Her sister ship No. 14 was taken over by the French Navy in June 1915, just prior to launching. (K.R. MacPherson)

1 SUBMARINE: MODIFIED SCHNEIDER-LAUBEUF S2 TYPE

Number	Builder	Launched	Completed	Notes
14 (II)	Kure Navy Yard	1918	Apr 1920	changed to HA-9 in 1924; stricken 1929

Displacement:	480 tons standard
	529 tons surfaced
	737 tons submerged
Length:	192¼ feet (58.6 m) oa
Beam:	17 feet (5.2 m)
Draft:	10¾ feet (3.2 m)
Propulsion:	2 diesels; 2,000 hp
	electric motor; 850 hp; 2 shafts
Speed:	16.5 knots surfaced
	10 knots submerged
Range:	2,050 n.miles at 10 knots surfaced
	60 n.miles at 4 knots submerged
Depth:	
Complement:	approx. 30 officers and men
Torpedo tubes:	4 18-inch (457-mm) 2 bow + 2 superstructure
Torpedoes:	8
Guns:	1 MG

This was built to a modified Schneider-Laubeuf design to replace the original French-built submarine No. 14. She was laid down in March 1918, being built under license from the French firm.

2 SUBMARINES: IMPROVED VICKERS C3 TYPE

Number	Builder	Launched	Completed	Notes
16	Kure Navy Yard	15 Mar 1916	1 Nov 1916	changed to HA-7 in 1924; stricken 1929
17	Kure Navy Yard	15 Mar 1916	2 Feb 1917	changed to HA-8 in 1924; stricken 1929

Displacement:	290 tons surfaced
	326 tons submerged
Length:	143½ feet (43.7 m) oa
Beam:	13½ feet (4.1 m)
Draft:	11¼ feet (3.4 m)
Propulsion:	2 diesels; 600 hp
	electric motor; 300 hp; 1 shaft
Speed:	12 knots surfaced
	8.5 knots submerged
Range:	660 n.miles at 12 knots surfaced
	60 n.miles at 4 knots submerged
Depth:	
Complement:	26 officers and men
Torpedo tubes:	4 18-inch (457-mm) 2 bow + 2 superstructure
Torpedoes:	4

These submarines were essentially copies of the British-built Vickers submarines, being given the Japanese design designation C3.

The Vickers-design submarine No. 16 (later HA-7) presents an unusual configuration when on the surface. There is a ladder rigged to the forward edge of the conning tower. (*Ships of the World*)

2 SUBMARINES: FIAT-LAURENTI F1 TYPE

Number	Builder	Launched	Completed	Notes
18	Kawasaki, Kobe	28 July 1919	31 Mar 1920	changed to RO-1 in 1924; stricken 1930
21	Kawasaki, Kobe	22 Nov 1919	20 Apr 1920	changed to RO-2 in 1924; stricken 1932

Displacement:	689 tons standard
	717 tons surfaced
	1,047 tons submerged
Length:	215¼ feet (65.6 m) oa
Beam:	20 feet (6.0 m)
Draft:	13¾ feet (4.2 m)
Propulsion:	2 diesels; 2,600 hp
	electric motor; 1,200 hp; 2 shafts
Speed:	13 knots surfaced
	8 knots submerged
Range:	3,500 n.miles at 10 knots surfaced
	75 n.miles at 4 knots submerged
Depth:	130 feet (40 m)
Complement:	43 officers and men
Torpedo tubes:	5 18-inch (457-mm) 3 bow + 2 stern
Torpedoes:	8
Guns:	(see notes)

These submarines were built to Italian plans. They were Japan's first oceangoing submarines. Design designation was F1. All of the reload torpedoes were stowed forward. In the early 1920s a 3-inch deck gun was installed forward of the conning tower.

Submarine No. 18 (later RO-1) was of the Italian Fiat-Laurenti design. The No. 18 and her sister ship No. 21 were Japan's first oceangoing submarines. (Dave Meeriman)

2 SUBMARINES: K1 TYPE

Number	Builder	Launched	Completed	Notes
19	Kure Navy Yard	15 Oct 1917	31 July 1919	changed to RO-11 in 1924; stricken 1931
20	Kure Navy Yard	1 Dec 1917	18 Sep 1919	changed to RO-12 in 1924; stricken 1931

Displacement: 720 tons standard
                  735 tons surfaced
                  1,030 tons submerged
Length: 227 feet (69.2 m) oa
Beam: 20¾ feet (6.3 m)
Draft: 11¼ feet (3.4 m)
Propulsion: 2 diesels; 2,600 hp
                  electric motors; 1,200 hp; 2 shafts
Speed: 18 knots surfaced
                  9 knots submerged
Range: 4,000 n.miles at 10 knots surfaced
                  85 n.miles at 4 knots submerged

Depth:
Complement: 44 officers and men
Torpedo tubes: 6 18-inch (457-mm) 4 bow + 2 stern amidships
Torpedoes: 10
Guns: 1 3-inch (76-mm)

These comparatively large submarines were the first fitted with a major deck gun (installed forward of the conning tower).

Submarine No. 19 with her starboard amidships torpedo tube visible in the deck structure, just forward of the conning tower. No gun is fitted in this view.

3 SUBMARINES: K2 TYPE

Number	Builder	Launched	Completed	Notes
22	Kure Navy Yard	31 Mar 1919	17 Feb 1921	changed to RO-14 in 1924; decommissioned in 1931; scrapped 1948
23	Kure Navy Yard	26 Aug 1919	30 Sep 1920	changed to RO-13 in 1924; stricken 1932
24	Kure Navy Yard	14 Oct 1920	30 June 1921	changed to RO-15 in 1924; stricken 1931

Displacement: 755 tons surfaced
                  1,050 tons submerged
Length: 230 feet (70.1 m) oa
Beam: 20 feet (6.1 m)
Draft: 12¼ feet (3.6 m)
Propulsion: 2 diesels; 2,600 hp
                  electric motors; 1,200 hp; 2 shafts
Speed: 17 knots surfaced
                  8 knots submerged
Range: 6,000 n.miles at 10 knots surfaced
                  85 n.miles at 4 knots submerged

Depth:
Complement: 45 officers and men
Torpedo tubes: 6 18-inch (457-mm) 4 bow + 2 stern
Torpedoes: 10
Guns: 1 3-inch (76-mm)
                  1 MG

These were further improvements of the K1 design with a significantly greater range. No. 22 was laid down in September 1918.
RO-14 was employed as training hulk from 1931 to 1940.

6 SUBMARINES: L1/L2 TYPE

Number	Builder	Launched	Completed	Notes
25	Mitsubishi, Kobe	25 Oct 1919	30 June 1920	changed to RO-51 in 1924; stricken 1940
26	Mitsubishi, Kobe	9 Mar 1919	30 Nov 1920	changed to RO-52 in 1924; stricken 1932
27	Mitsubishi, Kobe	6 July 1920	10 Mar 1921	changed to RO-53 in 1924; stricken 1938
28	Mitsubishi, Kobe	13 Oct 1920	10 Sep 1921	changed to RO-54 in 1924; stricken 1939
29	Mitsubishi, Kobe	10 Feb 1921	15 Nov 1922	changed to RO-55 in 1924; sunk off Kobe 1923; refloated and stricken 1939
30	Mitsubishi, Kobe	11 May 1921	16 Jan 1922	changed to RO-56 in 1924; stricken 1940

Displacement:	893 tons standard	Complement:	48 officers and men
	902 tons surfaced	Torpedo tubes:	No. 25, 26: 6 18-inch (457-mm) 4 bow + 2 amidships
	1,195 tons submerged		No. 27 to 30: 4 18-inch (457-mm) 4 bow
Length:	231½ feet (70.6 m) oa	Torpedoes:	10
Beam:	23½ feet (7.1 m)	Guns:	1 3-inch (76-mm)
Draft:	12¾ feet (3.9 m)		1 MG
Propulsion:	2 diesels; 2,400 hp		
	electric motors; 1,600 hp; 2 shafts		
Speed:	17 knots surfaced		
	8 knots submerged		
Range:	5,500 n.miles at 10 knots surfaced		
	80 n.miles at 4 knots submerged		
Depth:	200 feet (60 m)		

These submarines were a refinement of the British L-class built with plans developed by Vickers. The first two submarines (L1 type) had two amidships torpedo tubes fitted to fire broadside torpedoes; these were deleted in the last four boats (L2 type). No. 26 sank at Kure through flooding on 29 October 1923; raised and returned to service.

3 SUBMARINES: F2 TYPE

Number	Builder	Launched	Completed	Notes
31	Kawasaki, Kobe	10 May 1921	17 July 1922	changed to RO-3 in 1924; stricken 1932
32	Kawasaki, Kobe	22 June 1921	5 May 1922	changed to RO-4 in 1924; stricken 1930
33	Kawasaki, Kobe	17 Sep 1921	9 Mar 1922	changed to RO-5 in 1924; stricken 1930

Displacement:	740 tons surfaced	Depth:	130 feet (40 m)
	1,047 tons submerged	Complement:	43 officers and men
Length:	215¼ feet (65.5 m) oa	Torpedo tubes:	5 18-inch (457-mm) bow
Beam:	20 feet (6.0 m)	Torpedoes:	8
Draft:	13¼ feet (4.0 m)	Guns:	1 MG
Propulsion:	2 diesels; 2,600 hp		
	electric motors; 1,200 hp; 2 shafts		
Speed:	18 knots surfaced		
	8 knots submerged		
Range:	3,500 n.miles at 10 knots surfaced		
	75 n.miles at 4 knots submerged		

This was a further modification of the Fiat-Laurenti/F1 design. These submarines were not popular and had a brief service life.

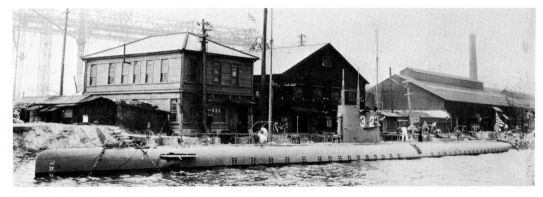

Submarine No. 32 (later RO-4). Note her rounded bow.

Submarine No. 31 (later RO-3) in peacetime pose, with awnings spread and crew mustered on deck. Note the rounded bow; ship-like prows were more effective in larger submarines for long-range surface transits. (*Ships of the World*)

10 SUBMARINES: K3 TYPE

Number	Builder	Launched	Completed	Notes
34	Kure Navy Yard	24 Feb 1921	20 Oct 1921	changed to RO-16 in 1924; stricken 1932
35	Kure Navy Yard	25 Mar 1921	15 Dec 1921	changed to RO-17 in 1924; stricken 1936
36	Kure Navy Yard	28 Dec 1921	15 Mar 1922	changed to RO-18 in 1924; stricken 1936
37	Kure Navy Yard	22 Apr 1921	29 Apr 1922	changed to RO-19 in 1924; stricken 1936
38	Yokosuka Navy Yard	26 Oct 1920	1 Feb 1922	changed to RO-20 in 1924; stricken 1932
39	Yokosuka Navy Yard	26 Oct 1920	1 Feb 1922	changed to RO-21 in 1924; stricken 1932
40	Yokosuka Navy Yard	15 Oct 1920	10 Oct 1922	changed to RO-22 in 1924; stricken 1932
41	Yokosuka Navy Yard	25 Oct 1921	28 Apr 1923	changed to RO-23 in 1924; stricken 1932
42	Sasebo Navy Yard	8 Dec 1919	30 Nov 1920	changed to RO-24 in 1924; stricken 1932
43	Sasebo Navy Yard	17 July 1920	25 Oct 1921	changed to RO-25 in 1924; sunk in collision with cruiser TATSUTA off Sasebo 19 March 1924; refloated and employed as test ship; stricken 1936

Displacement:	736 tons standard	Depth:	
	755 tons surfaced	Complement:	45 officers and men
	1,050 tons submerged	Torpedo tubes:	6 18-inch (457-mm) 4 bow + 2 stern
Length:	230 feet (70.1 m) oa	Torpedoes:	10
Beam:	20 feet (6.1 m)	Guns:	1 3-inch (76-mm)
Draft:	12¼ feet (3.7 m)		1 MG
Propulsion:	2 diesels; 2,600 hp		
	electric motors; 1,200 hp; 2 shafts		
Speed:	17 knots surfaced		
	8 knots submerged		
Range:	6,000 n.miles at 10 knots surfaced		
	85 n.miles at 4 knots submerged		

This class was developed from the Schneider-Laubeuf/K2 design. It was the largest class of submarines built by the Japanese Navy prior to World War II, with two additional naval shipyards being introduced to submarine construction.

Submarine No. 42 moored to a buoy. Later renumbered RO-24, this class, developed originally from a French design, had a very short service life. (*Ships of the World*)

3 SUBMARINES: K4 TYPE

Number	Builder	Launched		Completed		Notes
45	Sasebo Navy Yard	18 Oct	1921	25 Jan	1923	changed to RO-26 in 1924; stricken 1940
58	Yokosuka Navy Yard	22 July	1922	13 July	1924	changed to RO-27 in 1924; stricken 1940
62	Sasebo Navy Yard	13 Apr	1922	30 Nov	1923	changed to RO-28 in 1924; stricken 1940

Displacement:	770 tons surfaced	Depth:	
	1,070 tons submerged	Complement:	45 officers and men
Length:	243 feet (74.2 m) oa	Torpedo tubes:	4 21-inch (533-mm) bow
Beam:	20 feet (6.1 m)	Torpedoes:	8
Draft:	12¼ feet (3.7 m)	Guns:	1 3-inch (76-mm)
Propulsion:	2 diesels; 2,600 hp		1 MG
	electric motors; 1,200 hp; 2 shafts		
Speed:	16 knots surfaced		
	8 knots submerged		
Range:	6,000 n.miles at 10 knots surfaced		
	85 n.miles at 4 knots submerged		

These were similar to the K3 class; however, they introduced 21-inch torpedo tubes to Japanese submarines. They were scrapped in 1947-1948.

Photographed after 1924 with the number RO-27 on her conning tower, submarine No. 58 and her sister ships spent most of their careers in the training role. (*Ships of the World*)

3 SUBMARINES: L3 TYPE

Number	Builder	Launched	Completed	Notes
46	Mitsubishi, Kobe	3 Dec 1921	30 July 1922	changed to RO-57 in 1924; surrendered Aug 1945; scrapped 1946
47	Mitsubishi, Kobe	2 Mar 1922	25 Nov 1922	changed to RO-58 in 1924; surrendered Aug 1945; scrapped 1946
57	Mitsubishi, Kobe	28 June 1922	20 Mar 1923	changed to RO-59 in 1924; surrendered Aug 1945; scrapped 1946

Displacement:	889 tons standard
	897 tons surfaced
	1,195 tons submerged
Length:	250 feet (76.1 m) oa
Beam:	23⅓ feet (7.1 m)
Draft:	13 feet (3.9 m)
Propulsion:	2 diesels; 2,400 hp
	electric motors; 1,600 hp; 2 shafts
Speed:	17 knots surfaced
	8 knots submerged
Range:	5,500 n.miles at 10 knots surfaced
	80 n.miles at 4 knots submerged
Depth:	195 feet (58.5 m)
Complement:	48 officers and men
Torpedo tubes:	4 18-inch (457-mm) bow
Torpedoes:	10
Guns:	1 3-inch (76-mm)
	1 MG

These submarines were similar to the Royal Navy's L-class design. Endurance was 20 days at sea. The lead ship was laid down in November 1920. Plans for additional submarines of this class (No. 48–50) were cancelled because of the Washington naval treaty of 1922.

All three submarines were assigned to training duties at Kure in 1941 and shifted to Yokosuka in April of 1943. In May 1945 they were taken out of service and stripped.

Later RO-series submarines are listed in chapter 9.

The RO-57 (formerly No. 46) survived into World War II as a training ship; from May 1945, after being stricken from the fleet, she was employed to train midget submarine crews.

The newly completed submarine No. 47 (later RO-58), on 4 November 1922, shortly before her official completion. The RO-58 served as a training ship during World War II. (Imperial War Museum)

4 SUBMARINES: KT TYPE

Number	Builder	Launched	Completed	Notes
68	Kawasaki, Kobe	5 Dec 1922	15 Sep 1923	changed to RO-29 in 1924; stricken from fleet list 1 Apr 1936
69	Kawasaki, Kobe	18 Jan 1923	29 Apr 1924	changed to RO-30 in 1924; surrendered Aug 1945; scrapped
70	Kawasaki, Kobe	Feb 1923	10 May 1927	changed to RO-31 in 1924; surrendered Aug 1945; scuttled off Kongo Point 5 Apr 1946
71	Kawasaki, Kobe	19 Mar 1923	31 May 1924	changed to RO-32 in 1924; surrendered Aug 1945; scrapped

Displacement:	665 tons standard
	1,000 tons submerged
Length:	243½ feet (74.2 m) oa
Beam:	20 feet (6.1 m)
Draft:	12¼ feet (3.7 m)
Propulsion:	2 diesels; 1,200 hp
	electric motors; 1,200 hp; 2 shafts
Speed:	13 knots surfaced
	8 knots submerged
Range:	6,600 n.miles at 10 knots surfaced
	85 n.miles at 4 knots submerged
Depth:	200 feet (60 m)
Complement:	
Torpedo tubes:	4 18-inch (457-mm) bow
Torpedoes:	10
Guns:	1 4.7-inch (120-mm)
	1 MG

Less-powerful diesel engines were fitted in these submarines, resulting in a lower surface speed. As built, a fifth 18-inch torpedo tube was fitted; it was subsequently removed.

The No. 68 was laid down in June 1921.

The No. 70 sank during diving trials in Kobe Harbor on 21 August 1923. She was raised and refitted at Kawasaki from November 1924, but moved to the Kure Navy Yard for completion because of financial difficulties at Kawasaki; returned to service 25 September 1926. The RO-30 and RO-32 were stricken from the fleet list on 1 April 1942 and moored as training submarines at the submarine school at Otake.

Later RO-series submarines are listed in chapter 9.

Submarine No. 69 at sea with her battle flag flying. A short time later she was renumbered RO-30. She has her two periscopes and two radio masts raised; the 4.7-inch gun is forward. (U.S. Naval Historical Center)

The RO-30 began service as submarine No. 69. Outdated when World War II began, she was employed as a training ship until 1942 when she was stricken from the Navy List and employed as a training hulk at the Otake submarine school. (*Ships of the World*)

1 MINELAYING SUBMARINE: EX-GERMAN UE II TYPE

Number (former)	Builder	Launched	Completed	Notes
O-1 (U-125)	Blohm & Voss, Hamburg	26 May 1918	4 Sep 1918	acquired 26 Nov 1918; scrapped 1922

Displacement:	1,164 tons surfaced 1,512 tons submerged	Torpedo tubes:	4 19.7-inch (500-mm) bow
Length:	269 feet (81.5 m) oa	Torpedoes:	12 + 42 mines
Beam:	24¼ feet (7.4 m)	Guns:	1 5.9-inch (152-mm)
Draft:	13¾ feet (4.2 m)		
Propulsion:	2 diesels; 2,400 bhp electric motors; 1,200 hp; 2 shafts		
Speed:	14.75 knots surfaced 7 knots submerged		
Range:	12,500 n.miles at 8 knots surfaced 35 n.miles at 4.5 knots submerged		
Depth:	245 feet (75 m)		
Complement:	40 officers and men		

This was one of seven former German U-boats surrendered to the British at the end of World War I that were retransferred to Japan. The submarines were to be used only for experimental purposes by the Japanese.

The U-125 was a large, minelaying craft, designed specifically to lay mines off the U.S. coast. The design was German project No. 45. Two horizontal mine tubes were fitted in the stern.

1 SUBMARINE: EX-GERMAN U-43 CLASS

Number (former)	Builder	Launched	Completed	Notes
O-2 (U-46)	Danzig Werft	18 May 1915	17 Dec 1915	acquired 26 Nov 1918; scrapped 1922

Displacement:	725 tons surfaced 940 tons submerged	Depth:	165 feet (50 m)
Length:	213¼ feet (65.0 m) oa	Complement:	36 officers and men
Beam:	20⅓ feet (6.2 m)	Torpedo tubes:	6 19.7-inch (500-mm) 4 bow + 2 stern
Draft:	12 feet (3.7 m)	Torpedoes:	8
Propulsion:	2 diesels; 2,000 bhp electric motors; 1,200 hp; 2 shafts	Guns:	2 3.5-inch (88-mm)
Speed:	15.25 knots surfaced 9.75 knots submerged		
Range:	11,400 n.miles at 8 knots surfaced 51 n.miles at 5 knots submerged		

German submarine project No. 25. The U-43 was assigned to Japan after the war, but was not taken; no Japanese designation assigned.

The submarine O-1, formerly the U-46, at Tokyo in April 1919. Note the saw-teeth forward to help her cut through antisubmarine nets; the forward 3.5-inch gun is visible under the awning. (Shizuo Fukui)

1 SUBMARINE: EX-GERMAN U-51 CLASS

Number (former)	Builder	Launched	Completed	Notes
O-3 (U-55)	Germania Werft, Kiel	18 Mar 1916	8 June 1916	acquired 26 Nov 1918; scrapped 1922

Displacement:	715 tons surfaced	Range:	9,400 n.miles at 8 knots surfaced
	902 tons submerged		55 n.miles at 5 knots submerged
Length:	214 feet (65.2 m) oa	Depth:	165 feet (50 m)
Beam:	21 feet (6.4 m)	Complement:	39 officers and men
Draft:	11¾ feet (3.6 m)	Torpedo tubes:	4 19.7-inch (500-mm) 2 bow + 2 stern
Propulsion:	2 diesels; 2,400 bhp	Torpedoes:	8
	electric motors; 1,200 hp; 2 shafts	Guns:	2 3.5-inch (88-mm)
Speed:	17 knots surfaced		
	9 knots submerged		

2 COASTAL SUBMARINES: EX-GERMAN UC III TYPE

Number (former)	Builder	Launched	Completed	Notes
O-4 (UC-90)	Blohm & Voss, Hamburg	19 Jan 1918	15 July 1918	acquired 1 Dec 1918; scrapped 1921
O-5 (UC-99)	Blohm & Voss, Hamburg	17 Mar 1918	20 Sep 1918	acquired 22 Nov 1918; scrapped 1921

Displacement:	474 tons surfaced	Depth:	245 feet (75 m)
	560 tons submerged	Complement:	32 officers and men
Length:	185 feet (56.1 m) oa	Torpedo tubes:	3 19.7-inch (500-mm) 2 side + 1 stern
Beam:	18 feet (5.5 m)	Torpedoes:	7 + 18 mines
Draft:	12½ feet (3.8 m)	Guns:	1 4.1-inch (105-mm)
Propulsion:	2 diesels; 600 bhp		
	electric motors; 770 hp; 2 shafts		
Speed:	11.5 knots surfaced		
	6.5 knots submerged		
Range:	9,430 n.miles at 7 knots surfaced		
	40 n.miles at 4.5 knots submerged		

These were minelaying submarines with six vertical mine tubes installed in the forward portion of the hull. Note that two torpedo tubes were amidships, external to the pressure hull, outboard of the conning tower, and one in the stern. Project No. 45a.

The former German minelaying submarine UC-99, still flying the German flag about 1917. She became the Japanese O-5 in 1918, one of several U-boats the Japanese scrutinized. (Drüppel)

2 COASTAL SUBMARINES: EX-GERMAN UB III TYPE

Number (former)		Builder	Launched	Completed	Notes
O-6	(UB-125)	Weser AG, Bremen	16 Apr 1918	18 May 1918	acquired 20 Nov 1918; scrapped 1921
O-7	(UB-143)	Weser AG, Bremen	21 Aug 1918	3 Oct 1918	acquired 26 Nov 1918; scrapped 1921

Displacement:	516 tons surfaced
	651 tons submerged
Length:	182½ feet (55.3 m) oa
Beam:	19 feet (5.8 m)
Draft:	12 feet (3.7 m)
Propulsion:	2 diesels; 1,100 bhp
	electric motors; 788 hp; 2 shafts
Speed:	13.6 knots surfaced
	8 knots submerged
Range:	8,580 n.miles at 6 knots surfaced
	55 n.miles at 4 knots submerged

Depth:	165 feet (50 m)
Complement:	34 officers and men
Torpedo tubes:	5 19.7-inch (500-mm) 4 bow + 1 stern
Torpedoes:	10
Guns:	1 3.3-inch (88-mm)

These UB-type submarines were considered coastal craft by the Germans. Project No. 44.

The submarine O-6 at Yokosuka on 23 June 1919. She still has her German U-boat number on the conning tower. (Shizuo Fukui)

8   I-Series Large Submarines

Beginning with the 1919 shipbuilding program, the Japanese constructed large, oceangoing fleet submarines, based initially on German submarine designs. In addition to their large size, these submarines were characterized by long cruising ranges and large torpedo and gun batteries.

I-series designations were assigned to these submarines from 1924 on. Their type designations were initially based on the words *kaidai* (large) and *junsen* (cruiser).

One non-I-series submarine is listed in this chapter, the No. 71, an experimental high-speed submarine built in the late 1930s. That craft, in several respects the most advanced submarine of her time, was the prototype for a later I-boat design and is listed below in chronological order. Three submarine classes in the I-series built specifically for the cargo/transport role are listed in chapter 12.

Also given I-series designations, and listed below, are six former German and two former Italian submarines, all taken over by the Japanese Navy during World War II.

Sources differ on the causes, locations, and dates of many of the submarine losses. The information provided here, while depending primarily on Japanese data, reflects some degree of judgment on the authors' part.

1 LARGE SUBMARINE: KD1 TYPE

Number	Builder	Launched	Completed	Notes
44	Kure Navy Yard	29 Nov 1921	20 June 1924	changed to I-51 in 1924; stricken in 1941

Displacement:	1,390 tons standard		Complement:	60 officers and men
	1,500 tons surfaced		Torpedo tubes:	8 21-inch (533-mm) bow
	2,430 tons submerged		Torpedoes:	24
Length:	300 feet (91.4 m) oa		Guns:	1 4-inch (120-mm)
Beam:	29 feet (8.8 m)			1 3-inch (76-mm)
Draft:	15 feet (4.57 m)			
Propulsion:	4 diesels; 5,200 hp			
	electric motors; 2,000 hp; 4 shafts (see notes)			
Speed:	20 knots surfaced			
	10 knots submerged			
Range:	20,000 n.miles at 10 knots surfaced			
	100 n.miles at 4 knots submerged			
Depth:	200 feet (60 m)			

This was by a significant margin the largest submarine yet built in Japan and served as a prototype for future long-range submarines. Laid down in February 1922. The I-51 was re-engined in 1932 with two diesels geared to two shafts; also the 3-inch gun was removed. Note the high surface speed and range. She was used as a training boat from 1930 to 1939.

Submarine No. 44 (later I-51) was, in many respects, the first modern Japanese fleet submarine. Although smaller than contemporary U.S. submarines, by most criteria she was comparable or superior in performance. (National Archives)

4 MINELAYING SUBMARINES: KRS TYPE

Number	Builder	Launched	Completed	Notes
48	Kawasaki, Kobe	30 Mar 1926	31 Mar 1927	changed to I-21 in 1924; changed to I-121 in 1939; surrendered Aug 1945 and scrapped 1946
49	Kawasaki, Kobe	8 Nov 1926	28 Oct 1927	changed to I-22 in 1924; changed to I-122 in 1939; sunk by USS SKATE (SS 305) in Toyama Bay, Sea of Japan, 10 June 1945
50	Kawasaki, Kobe	19 Mar 1927	28 Apr 1928	changed to I-23 in 1924; changed to I-123 in 1939; sunk by USS GAMBLE (DM 15) 60 miles east of Savo Island, Solomons 29 Aug 1942
I-24	Kawasaki, Kobe	12 Dec 1927	10 Dec 1928	changed to I-124 in 1939; sunk by USS EDSALL (DD 219) and 3 Australian minesweepers in Clarence Strait, off Darwin 20 Jan 1942

Displacement:	1,142 tons standard
	1,383 tons surfaced
	1,768 tons submerged
Length:	279½ feet (85.2 m)oa
Beam:	24½ feet (7.5 m)
Draft:	14½ feet (4.39 m)
Propulsion:	2 diesels; 2,400 hp
	electric motors; 1,100 hp; 2 shafts
Speed:	14½ knots surfaced
	7 knots submerged
Range:	8,000 n.miles at 12 knots surfaced
	10,500 n.miles at 8 knots surfaced
	40 n.miles at 4.5 knots submerged
Depth:	200 feet (60 m)
Complement:	75 officers and men
Torpedo tubes:	4 21-inch (533-mm) bow
Torpedoes:	12 + 42 mines
Guns:	1 5.5-inch (140-mm)

These were the only specialized Japanese minelaying submarines (other submarines could lay mines from torpedo tubes). The design was based on the German U-125 of the UE II type provided to Japan after World War I. The lead ship was laid down in October 1924; all except the first ship were completed by the Kure Navy Yard. The submarines had two mine tubes aft, as did the USS ARGONAUT (SM 1/SS 166). At-sea endurance was 20 days.

During 1940 these submarines were modified to refuel seaplanes, being fitted with gasoline tanks. They retained their minelaying capability. Early in the war all were employed in minelaying operations in the Far East. From August 1943 the surviving I-121 and I-122 were employed at Kure to train submarine crews in the Inland Sea; they were shifted to Maizuru early in 1945.

The I-21 (later I-121) was one of four specialized minelaying submarines built by Japan. Their design was based on a German U-boat acquired after World War I. They were additionally modified to refuel seaplanes while retaining their mining capability. The I-121 was the only one of the class to survive the war. (Imperial War Museum)

The I-22 (later I-122) with her radio masts in place and a crane rigged for handling a small boat. (Holbrook)

1 LARGE SUBMARINE: KD2 TYPE

Number	Builder	Launched	Completed	Notes
51	Kure Navy Yard	12 June 1922	20 May 1925	changed to I-52 in 1924; changed to I-152 in 1942; stricken from the fleet 14 July 1942; scrapped 1948
I-52		cancelled 1922		
I-53		cancelled 1922		
I-54		cancelled 1922		
I-55		cancelled 1922		
I-56		cancelled 1922		

Displacement:	1,390 tons standard		Torpedo tubes:	8 21-inch (533-mm) 6 bow + 2 stern
	1,500 tons surfaced		Torpedoes:	16
	2,500 tons submerged		Guns:	1 4.7-inch (120-mm)
Length:	330¾ feet (100.8) oa			1 3-inch (76-mm)
Beam:	25 feet (7.6 m)			
Draft:	16¾ feet (5.1m)			
Propulsion:	2 diesels; 6,800 hp			
	electric motors; 2,000 hp; 2 shafts			
Speed:	22 knots surfaced			
	10 knots submerged			
Range:	10,000 n.miles at 10 knots surfaced			
	100 n.miles at 4 knots submerged			
Depth:	175 feet (53 m)			
Complement:	60 officers and men			

This was the second large, cruiser-type submarine built by Japan. Five additional KD2-type submarines were cancelled because of the Washington naval treaty. This design was based on the German U-139.

From 1940 onward the I-52 was employed as a training ship at Kure; she was deleted from active service on 14 July 1942.

4 SCOUTING SUBMARINES: J1 TYPE

Number	Builder	Launched	Completed	Notes
I-1	Kawasaki, Kobe	15 Oct 1924	10 Mar 1926	damaged by New Zealand KIWI and MOA and scuttled off Guadalcanal on 29 Jan 1943
I-2	Kawasaki, Kobe	23 Feb 1925	24 July 1926	sunk by USS SAUFLEY (DD 465) 50 miles west of New Hanover (off New Ireland) 7 Apr 1944
I-3	Kawasaki, Kobe	8 June 1925	30 Nov 1926	sunk by USN PT 59 off Guadalcanal 10 Dec 1942
I-4	Kawasaki, Kobe	22 May 1928	24 Dec 1929	probably sunk by USS SEADRAGON (SS 194) off Cape Esperance, Guadalcanal, 20 Dec 1942 (some sources credit USN PT 122)

Displacement:	1,970 tons standard
	2,135 tons surfaced
	2,791 tons submerged
Length:	320 feet (97.5 m) oa
Beam:	30¼ feet (9.2 m)
Draft:	16½ feet (5.0 m)
Propulsion:	2 diesels; 6,000 hp
	electric motors; 2,600 hp; 2 shafts
Speed:	18 knots surfaced
	8 knots submerged
Range:	24,000 n.miles at 10 knots surfaced
	60 n.miles at 3 knots submerged
Depth:	265 feet (80 m)
Complement:	68 officers and men
Torpedo tubes:	6 21-inch (533-mm) 4 bow + 2 stern
Torpedoes:	20
Guns:	2 5.5-inch (140-mm)

These submarines, a further development of the ex-U-139 and KD2 designs, were the first submarines designated as the *junsen* or cruiser type. The first three units were ordered as No. 74, 75, and 76, respectively; changed to I-series in 1924, prior to launching of the first unit. The lead ship was laid down in March 1923.

The I-1 conducted a test cruise of 25,000 miles without difficulty and successfully dived to a depth of 260 feet, the deepest a Japanese submarine had operated to that time. Endurance for the class was rated at 60 days. They had M.A.N. diesels purchased from Germany. The I-1 made 18.1 knots on trials, and the I-2 and I-3 made 19.1 knots.

Late in 1942 the I-1 and I-2 were modified for use as transports, with the after 5.5-inch gun removed, torpedo reloads reduced, and provisions made for carrying a 46-foot *daihatsu* landing craft, amphibious tanks, or cargo rafts.

The I-3 was one of the first cruiser-type submarines, developed from German submarine designs. Note the two 5.5-inch deck guns, the largest caliber mounted in Japanese submarines. (U.S. Naval Historical Center)

Although obsolescent when World War II began, the I-3 participated in the Pearl Harbor operation and was sunk while employed as a transport to carry supplies to troops on Guadalcanal. (Shizuo Fukui)

9 LARGE SUBMARINES: KD3A/KD3B TYPES

Number	Builder	Launched	Completed	Notes
64	Kure Navy Yard	5 Aug 1925	30 Mar 1927	changed to I-53 in 1924; changed to I-153 in 1942; surrendered 1945 and scrapped 1946
77	Sasebo Navy Yard	15 Mar 1926	15 Dec 1927	changed to I-54 in 1924; changed to I-154 in 1942; surrendered 1945 and scrapped
78	Kure Navy Yard	2 Sep 1925	5 Sep 1927	changed to I-55 in 1924; changed to I-155 in 1942; surrendered 1945 and scrapped
I-56	Kure Navy Yard	23 Mar 1928	31 Mar 1929	changed to I-156 in 1942; surrendered 1945; scuttled off Goto Island 1 Apr 1946
I-57	Kure Navy Yard	1 Oct 1928	24 Dec 1929	changed to I-157 in 1942; surrendered 1945; scuttled off Goto Island 1 Apr 1946
I-58	Yokosuka Navy Yard	3 Oct 1925	15 May 1928	changed to I-158 in 1942; surrendered 1945; scuttled off Goto Island 1 Apr 1946
I-59	Yokosuka Navy Yard	25 Mar 1929	31 Mar 1930	changed to I-159 in 1942; surrendered 1945; scuttled off Goto Island 1 Apr 1946
I-60	Sasebo Navy Yard	24 Apr 1929	25 Dec 1929	sunk by British JUPITER 25 miles west of Krakatoa Island, Sunda Strait, 17 Jan 1942
I-63	Sasebo Navy Yard	28 Sep 1927	20 Dec 1928	sunk in collision with I-60 in Bungo Strait 2 Feb 1939; refloated and scrapped 1940

Displacement:	1,635 tons standard
	1,800 tons surfaced
	2,300 tons submerged
Length:	330 feet (100.0 m) oa except
	I-56, I-57, I-59, I-60, I-63: 331⅓ feet (101.0 m) oa
Beam:	26 feet (8.0 m)
Draft:	15¾ feet (4.82 m) except
	I-56, I-57, I-59, I-60, I-63: 16 feet (4.9 m)
Propulsion:	2 diesels; 6,800 hp
	electric motors; 1,800 hp; 2 shafts
Speed:	20 knots surfaced
	8 knots submerged
Range:	10,000 n.miles at 10 knots surfaced
	90 n.miles at 3 knots submerged
Depth:	200 feet (60 m)

Complement:	60 officers and men
Torpedo tubes:	8 21-inch (533-mm) bow
Torpedoes:	16
Guns:	1 4.7-inch (120-mm)

These were long-range submarines. The four KD3A-type submarines had rounded bows; the five of the KD3B type had ship-like bows and were slightly longer; conning tower configurations also differed. The lead ship was laid down in April 1924. The I-63 sank with the loss of 81 men when she collided with the I-60.

From 1943 onward the survivors were employed as training submarines. The I-153 and I-154 were laid up (without crews) from 31 January 1944. Most units were refitted with snorkels during the latter part of the war.

The I-55 (later I-155) on her initial sea trials in Hiroshima Bay during September 1927. She has a net-cutting device fitted on her bow. (Imperial War Museum)

The "first" I-58 (later I-158) in Yokosuka Bay on 26 March 1928. (Imperial War Museum)

3 LARGE SUBMARINES: KD4 TYPE

Number	Builder	Launched	Completed	Notes
I-61	Mitsubishi, Kobe	12 Nov 1927	6 Apr 1929	sunk in collision with gunboat off Iki Island 2 Oct 1941; refloated in Feb 1942 and scrapped
I-62	Mitsubishi, Kobe	29 Nov 1928	24 Apr 1930	changed to I-162 in 1942; surrendered 1945; scuttled off Goto Island 1 Apr 1946
I-64	Kure Navy Yard	5 Oct 1929	30 Aug 1930	changed to I-164 in 1942; sunk by USS Triton (SS 201) 230 miles southeast of Kagoshima 17 May 1942

Displacement:	1,635 tons standard		Complement:	60 officers and men
	1,720 tons surfaced		Torpedo tubes:	6 21-inch (533-mm) 4 bow + 2 stern
	2,300 tons submerged		Torpedoes:	14
Length:	320½ feet (97.7 m) oa		Guns:	1 4.7-inch (120-mm)
Beam:	25½ feet (7.8 m)			
Draft:	15¾ feet (4.8 m)			
Propulsion:	2 diesels; 6,000 hp			
	electric motors; 1,800 hp; 2 shafts			
Speed:	20 knots surfaced			
	8.5 knots submerged			
Range:	10,800 n.miles at 10 knots surfaced			
	60 n.miles at 3 knots submerged			
Depth:	200 feet (60 m)			

This design was very similar to the previous KD3A/KD3B types, although slightly smaller with the number of torpedo tubes reduced by two. The I-61 was laid down in November 1926.

From March 1944 the I-62/162 was employed as a training submarine at Kure. In April of 1945 her deck gun was removed, and she was fitted to carry two *kaiten*.

The I-64/164 was numbered before her loss became known to the Japanese Navy.

3 LARGE SUBMARINES: KD5 TYPE

Number	Builder	Launched	Completed	Notes
I-65	Kure Navy Yard	2 June 1931	1 Dec 1932	changed to I-165 in 1942; sunk by U.S. naval aircraft 450 miles east of Saipan 27 June 1945
I-66	Sasebo Navy Yard	2 June 1931	10 Nov 1932	changed to I-166 in 1942; sunk by British submarine Telemachus off Singapore 17 July 1944
I-67	Mitsubishi, Kobe	7 Apr 1931	8 Aug 1932	lost during exercise off Bonin Islands 29 Aug 1940

Displacement:	1,575 tons standard		Torpedo tubes:	6 21-inch (533-mm) bow
	1,705 tons surfaced		Torpedoes:	14
	2,330 tons submerged		Guns:	1 3.9-inch (100-mm) antiaircraft
Length:	320½ feet (97.7 m) oa			1 13-mm MG
Beam:	26¾ feet (8.2 m)			
Draft:	15½ feet (4.7 m)			
Propulsion:	2 diesels; 6,000 hp			
	electric motors; 1,800 hp; 2 shafts			
Speed:	20.5 knots surfaced			
	8.25 knots submerged			
Range:	10,000 n.miles at 10 knots surfaced			
	60 n.miles at 3 knots submerged			
Depth:	230 feet (70 m)			
Complement:	75 officers and men			

These boats were slightly heavier than the similar KD4 type with a greater operating depth. The antiaircraft machine gun was fitted on the after end of the conning tower. The lead ship was laid down in December 1929. Eighty-seven men were lost with the I-67.

The I-65/165 was employed as a training submarine at Kure from December 1944. In April of 1945 she was refitted to carry two *kaiten* with the 3.9-inch gun removed.

The I-65 (later I-165) underway in Hiroshima Bay in 1932. She spent most of World War II in the training role. (Imperial War Museum)

1 SCOUTING SUBMARINE: J1M TYPE

Number	Builder	Launched	Completed	Notes
I-5	Kawasaki, Kobe	19 June 1932	31 July 1932	sunk by USS Wyman (DE 38) 360 miles east of Guam 19 July 1944

Displacement:	2,080 tons standard	Torpedo tubes:	6 21-inch (533-mm) bow
	2,243 tons surfaced	Torpedoes:	20
	2,921 tons submerged	Guns:	2 5.5-inch (140-mm)
Length:	320 feet (97.5 m) oa	Aircraft:	1 floatplane (until 1940)
Beam:	30¼ feet (9.2 m)		
Draft:	16½ feet (5.0 m)		
Propulsion:	2 diesels; 6,000 hp		
	electric motors; 2,600 hp; 2 shafts		
Speed:	18 knots surfaced		
	8 knots submerged		
Range:	24,000 n.miles at 10 knots surfaced		
	60 n.miles at 3 knots submerged		
Depth:	260 feet (80 m)		
Complement:	80 officers and men		

The I-5 was designed as a long-range scouting submarine and was the first Japanese submarine designed to carry an aircraft. Two hangars were fitted to port and starboard immediately abaft the conning tower. The fuselage and twin floats were stored in one hangar and the wings in the second. No catapult was provided. The arrangements for handling the aircraft were awkward, and the equipment was deleted in 1940.

The I-5 was laid down 30 October 1929.

8 LARGE SUBMARINES: KD6A/KD6B TYPES

Number	Builder	Launched	Completed	Notes
I-68	Kure Navy Yard	26 June 1933	31 July 1934	changed to I-168 in 1942; sunk by USS Scamp (SS 277) 60 miles off New Hanover (off New Ireland) 27 July 1943
I-69	Mitsubishi, Kobe	15 Feb 1934	28 Sep 1935	changed to I-169 in 1942; accidently flooded and sunk at Truk during U.S. air attack 4 Apr 1944
I-70	Sasebo Navy Yard	14 June 1934	9 Nov 1935	sunk by aircraft from USS Enterprise (CV 6) 200 miles northeast of Oahu 10 Dec 1941
I-71	Kawasaki, Kobe	25 Aug 1934	24 Dec 1935	changed to I-171 in 1942; sunk by USS Guest (DD 472) and Hudson (DD 475) 15 miles west of Buka Island, Solomons, 1 Feb 1944
I-72	Mitsubishi, Kobe	6 Apr 1935	7 Jan 1937	changed to I-172 in 1942; sunk by USS Southard (DMS 10) between San Cristóbal and Guadalcanal 11 Nov 1942
I-73	Kawasaki, Kobe	20 June 1935	7 Jan 1937	sunk by USS Gudgeon (SS 211) 240 miles west of Midway 27 Jan 1942
I-74	Sasebo Navy Yard	28 Mar 1937	15 Aug 1938	changed to I-174 in 1942; operational loss 3 Apr 1944
I-75	Mitsubishi, Kobe	16 Sep 1936	18 Dec 1938	changed to I-175 in 1942; sunk by USS Charrette (DD 581) and Fair (DE 35) 5 Feb 1944

Displacement:	I-68 to 73 1,400 tons standard
	<u>1,785 tons surfaced</u>
	2,440 tons submerged
	I-74, I-75 1,420 tons standard
	<u>1,810 tons surfaced</u>
	2,564 tons submerged
Length:	I-68 to 73: 343½ feet (104.7 m) oa
	I-74, I-75 344½ feet (105.0 m) oa
Beam:	27 feet (8.2 m)
Draft:	15 feet (4.57 m)
Propulsion:	<u>2 diesels; 9,000 hp</u>
	electric motors; 1,800 hp; 2 shafts
Speed:	<u>23 knots surfaced</u>
	8.25 knots submerged
Range:	I-68 to 73: 14,000 n.miles at 10 knots surfaced
	<u>I-74, I-75: 10,000 n.miles at 16 knots surfaced</u>
	65 n.miles at 3 knots submerged
Depth:	245 feet (75 m)
Complement:	70 officers and men
Torpedo tubes:	6 21-inch (533-mm) bow
Torpedoes:	14
Guns:	I-68 to 70 1 3.9-inch (100-mm) antiaircraft
	1 13-mm MG
	I-71 to 75 1 4.7-inch (120-mm)
	1 13-mm MG (except two in I-74, I-75)

These long-range fleet submarines had a greater surface speed and deeper operating depth than their predecessors. However, range and torpedo tubes were reduced. The lead ship of this type was laid down in June 1931.

Late in 1942 the I-171 and I-174 had the 4.7-inch gun removed (from forward of the conning tower) and, with some torpedoes deleted, they served as transports, carrying one 46-foot landing craft or other equipment on their decks.

Sailors clean the 3.9-inch antiaircraft gun on the I-169. Unlike the U.S., British, and French navies, the Japanese did not mount guns larger than 5.5-inch caliber on submarines. (*Ships of the World*)

The I-68 (later I-168) underway on trials in March 1934. This submarine sank the U.S. aircraft carrier YORKTOWN (CV 5) at Midway in June 1942. (Kazutishi Hando)

The I-73 was sunk by a U.S. submarine early in World War II through radio intercepts and decryption. This photo was taken in Ariake Bay on 24 April 1939. (Imperial War Museum)

1 SCOUTING SUBMARINE: J2 TYPE

Number	Builder	Launched	Completed	Notes
I-6	Kawasaki, Kobe	31 Mar 1934	15 May 1935	sunk by the USS WILLIAM C. MILLER (DE 259) off Saipan 14 July 1944)

Displacement:	1,900 tons standard	Complement:	80 officers and men
	<u>2,243 tons surfaced</u>	Torpedo tubes:	6 21-inch (533-mm) 4 bow + 2 stern
	3,061 tons submerged	Torpedoes:	17
Length:	323 feet (98.5 m) oa	Guns:	1 5-inch (127-mm) antiaircraft
Beam:	29¾ feet (9.0 m)		1 13-mm MG
Draft:	17½ feet (5.3 m)	Aircraft:	1 floatplane
Propulsion:	<u>2 diesels; 8,000 hp</u>		
	electric motors; 2,600 hp; 2 shafts		
Speed:	<u>20 knots surfaced</u>		
	7.5 knots submerged		
Range:	<u>20,000 n.miles at 10 knots surfaced</u>		
	60 n.miles at 3 knots submerged		
Depth:	265 feet (80 m)		

The I-6 was a further development of the I-5/J1M design, intended from the outset as a scouting submarine fitted to carry a single aircraft. A second deck gun originally to be positioned aft of the conning tower was not provided. A catapult was built into the after deck. Laid down October 1932.

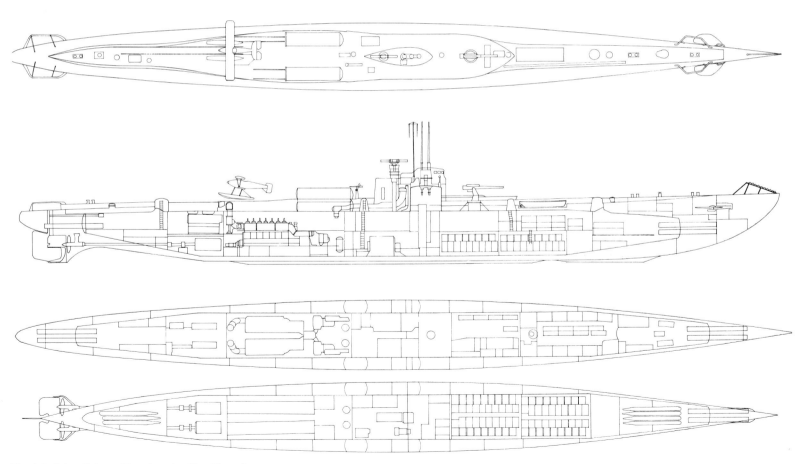

The I-6 of the J2 type. (Drawings by Alan Raven)

2 SCOUTING SUBMARINES: J3 TYPE

Number	Builder	Launched	Completed	Notes
I-7	Kure Navy Yard	3 July 1935	31 Mar 1937	damaged by USS Monaghan (DD 354) and grounded and scuttled off Kiska, Aleutians, 5 July 1943
I-8	Kawasaki, Kobe	20 July 1936	5 Dec 1938	sunk by USS Morrison (DD 560) and Stockton (DD 646) 65 miles southeast of Okinawa 31 Mar 1945

Displacement:	2,231 tons standard
	2,525 tons surfaced
	3,583 tons submerged
Length:	358½ feet (109.3 m) oa
Beam:	29¾ feet (9.0 m)
Draft:	17¼ feet (5.2 m)
Propulsion:	2 diesels; 11,200 hp
	electric motors; 2,800 hp; 2 shafts
Speed:	23 knots surfaced
	8 knots submerged
Range:	14,000 n.miles at 16 knots surfaced
	60 n.miles at 3 knots submerged
Depth:	330 feet (100 m)
Complement:	80 officers and men
Torpedo tubes:	6 21-inch (533-mm) bow
Torpedoes:	20
Guns:	1 5.5-inch (140-mm)
	5 13-mm MG (2 twin, 1 single)
Aircraft:	1 floatplane

These were the largest and in many respects the best-performing submarines built by Japan prior to the outbreak of World War II. They were long-range scouts. The I-7 was laid down on 12 September 1934 and the I-8 on 1 October 1934.

They were fitted as flagships for squadron commanders.

In early 1943 one of the 13-mm gun mounts was replaced by a twin 25-mm antiaircraft gun in both ships. In 1943 the I-8 was fitted with a *twin* 5.5-inch gun mount in place of the single mount, apparently for her voyage to Europe; this may have been the only submarine installation of its type. Late in 1944 the I-8 was converted to a *kaiten* carrier; the 5.5-inch gun, the hangar, and catapult were removed, and she was fitted to carry four human topedoes.

The I-8 was fitted with an unusual twin 5.5-inch gun mount, presumably for her voyage to Europe. (The British submarine X-1 of 1925 carried *two* twin 5.2-inch gun mounts, and the French Surcouf of 1930 had a twin 8-inch mount. The British M-class submarines of 1918 each had a single 12-inch gun.) In this view the I-8 is departing Lorient, France, en route to Singapore on 28 November 1943. (Courtesy of Royal Navy Submarine Museum)

The I-8 had a long and active career. The officers of the I-8 and I-10 were charged as war criminals for killing the survivors of merchant ships they sank. This view shows the I-8 entering Kagoshima Bay on 12 September 1939. (Imperial War Museum)

The I-7 and her sister ship I-8 were the largest Japanese submarines built prior to World War II. The I-7 launched the Glen reconnaissance plane that overflew Pearl Harbor on 16 December 1941 to determine the results of the earlier air-submarine attack. (*Ships of the World*)

The I-8 with a Watanabe E9W1 floatplane on her catapult. Note the twin aircraft storage hangars aft of the conning tower. This photo was taken about 1941; the E14Y1 monoplane replaced the Watanabe aircraft. (*Ships of the World*)

1 EXPERIMENTAL SUBMARINE: NO. 71

Number	Builder	Launched	Completed	Notes
71	Kure Navy Yard	Aug 1938	Aug 1938	scrapped 1940

Displacement:	195 tons standard
	213 tons surfaced
	240 tons submerged
Length:	140½ feet (42.8 m) oa
Beam:	10¾ feet (3.3 m)
Draft:	10⅓ feet (3.1 m)
Propulsion:	1 diesel; 1,200 hp
	electric motor; 1,800 hp; 1 shaft
Speed:	13.25 knots surfaced (see notes)
	21.25 knots submerged
Range:	3,830 n.miles at 12 knots surfaced
	33 n.miles at 7 knots submerged
Depth:	265 feet (80 m)
Complement:	11 officers and men
Torpedo tubes:	3 18-inch (457-mm) bow
Torpedoes:	3
Guns:	none

This was an experimental high-speed submarine. At the time of her construction, the No. 71 was the world's fastest undersea craft. On the surface her low displacement and low-powered diesel made her difficult to handle, and she fell short of the designed 18-knot surfaced speed and 25-knot submerged speed.

Laid down in December 1937. Her designation Vessel No. 71 was for deception purposes. She was "launched" by being lowered into the water by crane.

Following extensive evaluation, the No. 71 was scrapped. Data from the evaluation contributed to the design of the high-performance HA-201 and I-201 classes.

Submarine No. 71 was a revolutionary high-speed submarine, serving as the prototype for later Japanese attack submarines. She predated the more-publicized German Type XXI high-speed submarine. (*Ships of the World*)

3 HEADQUARTERS SUBMARINES: A1 TYPE

Number	Builder	Launched	Completed	Notes
I-9	Kure Navy Yard	20 May 1940	13 Feb 1941	sunk by USS Frazier (DD 607) off Kiska, Aleutians, 11 June 1943
I-10	Kawasaki, Kobe	20 Sep 1939	31 Oct 1941	sunk by USS David W. Taylor (DD 551) and Riddle (DE 185) 65 miles east of Saipan 4 July 1944
I-11	Kawasaki, Kobe	28 Feb 1941	16 May 1942	operational loss off Ellice Island 11 Jan 1944
# 700	Kawasaki, Kobe	cancelled 1942		
# 701	Kawasaki, Kobe	cancelled 1942		

Displacement:	2,434 tons standard		Torpedoes:	18
	2,919 tons surfaced		Guns:	1 5.5-inch (140-mm)
	4,149 tons submerged			4 25-mm (2 twin)
Length:	372¾ feet (113.7 m) oa		Aircraft:	1 floatplane
Beam:	31⅓ feet (9.5 m)			
Draft:	17½ feet (5.3 m)			
Propulsion:	2 diesels; 12,400 hp			
	electric motors; 2,400 hp; 2 shafts			
Speed:	23.5 knots surfaced			
	8 knots submerged			
Range:	16,000 n.miles at 16 knots surfaced			
	90 n.miles at 3 knots submerged			
Depth:	330 feet (100 m)			
Complement:	100 officers and men			
Torpedo tubes:	6 21-inch (533-mm) bow			

These were very large submarines intended to serve as flagships for groups of submarines. The design was developed from the J3 type with increased range, additional accommodations and working space provided for a squadron commander, and special radio equipment. The aircraft hangar and catapult were installed forward of the conning tower, with the hangar faired into the superstructure.

The I-9 was laid down in January 1939.

Two similar submarines ordered in 1942 were cancelled before construction began.

20 SCOUTING SUBMARINES: B1 TYPE

Number	Builder	Launched	Completed	Notes
I-15	Kure Navy Yard	7 Mar 1939	30 Sep 1940	sunk by USS McCalla (DD 488) north of San Cristóbal, Solomons, 2 Nov 1942
I-17	Yokosuka Navy Yard	19 July 1939	24 Jan 1941	sunk by New Zealand Tui and 2 USN aircraft 40 miles southeast of Noumea Bay, Noumea, 19 Aug 1943
I-19	Mitsubishi, Kobe	16 Sep 1939	28 Apr 1941	probably sunk by USN aircraft 18 Oct 1943
I-21	Kawasaki, Kobe	24 Feb 1940	15 July 1941	sunk by aircraft from USS Chenango (CVE 28) off Tarawa 29 Nov 1943
I-23	Yokosuka Navy Yard	24 Nov 1939	27 Sep 1941	operational loss February 1942
I-25	Mitsubishi, Kobe	8 June 1940	15 Oct 1941	sunk by USS Patterson (DD 392) off New Hebrides Islands, Solomons, 3 Sep 1943
I-26	Kure Navy Yard	10 Apr 1940	6 Nov 1941	operational loss east of Leyte, Philippines, Oct 1944
I-27	Sasebo Navy Yard	6 June 1941	24 Feb 1942	sunk by British Paladin and Petard 60 miles northwest of Addu Atoll 12 Feb 1944
I-28	Mitsubishi, Kobe	17 Dec 1940	6 Feb 1942	sunk by USS Tautog (SS 199) 45 miles south of Truk 17 May 1942
I-29	Yokosuka Navy Yard	29 Sep 1940	27 Feb 1942	sunk by USS Sawfish (SS 276) in Balintang Channel, Philippines, 26 July 1944
I-30	Kure Navy Yard	17 Sep 1940	28 Feb 1942	sunk by mine 3 miles east of Keppel Harbor, Singapore, 13 Oct 1942
I-31	Yokosuka Navy Yard	13 Mar 1941	30 May 1942	sunk by USS Edwards (DD 619) and Farragut (DD 348) off Kiska, Aleutians, 12 May 1943
I-32	Sasebo Navy Yard	17 Dec 1941	26 Apr 1942	sunk by USS Manlove (DE 36) and PC 1135 50 miles south of Wotje 24 Mar 1944
I-33	Mitsubishi, Kobe	1 May 1941	10 June 1942	lost during sea trials 20 miles southwest Iyo Nada, Inland Sea, 13 June 1944
I-34	Sasebo Navy Yard	24 Sep 1941	31 Aug 1942	sunk by British submarine Taurus 10 miles off Penang Island 13 Nov 1943
I-35	Mitsubishi, Kobe	24 Sep 1941	31 Aug 1942	sunk by USS Frazier (DD 607) and Meade (DD 602) off Tarawa 23 Nov 1943
I-36	Yokosuka Navy Yard	1 Nov 1941	30 Sep 1942	surrendered Aug 1945; scuttled off Goto Island 1 Apr 1946
I-37	Kure Navy Yard	22 Oct 1941	10 Mar 1943	sunk by USS Conklin (DE 439) and McCoy Reynolds (DE 440) northwest of Kossol Passage, Leyte, 19 Nov 1944
I-38	Sasebo Navy Yard	15 Apr 1942	31 Jan 1943	sunk by USS Nicholas (DD 449) 85 miles south of Yap Island 12 Nov 1944
I-39	Sasebo Navy Yard	15 Apr 1942	22 Apr 1943	sunk by USS Boyd (DD 544) in Gilbert Islands 26 Nov 1943

Displacement:	2,198 tons standard		Range:	14,000 n.miles at 16 knots surfaced
	2,584 tons surfaced			96 n.miles at 3 knots submerged
	3,654 tons submerged		Depth:	330 feet (100 m)
Length:	356½ feet (108.7 m) oa		Complement:	94 officers and men
Beam:	30½ feet (9.3 m)		Torpedo tubes:	6 21-inch (533-mm) bow
Draft:	16¾ feet (5.1 m)		Torpedoes:	17
Propulsion:	2 diesels; 12,400 hp		Guns:	1 5.5-inch (140-mm)
	electric motors; 2,000 hp; 2 shafts			2 25-mm (2 single)
Speed:	23.5 knots surfaced		Aircraft:	1 floatplane
	8 knots submerged			

These were long-range scouting submarines, intended to work with the A1 and C1 submarines. The B1 design was developed from the KD6 type; like the A1 type, the B1 had the hangar and catapult forward of the conning tower with the main gun aft (except that the positions were reversed in the I-17). These were streamlined submarines with the hangar faired into the conning tower. The original B1 design provided for four 25-mm antiaircraft guns, but only two single mounts were actually installed. Endurance was rated at 90 days.

This was numerically the largest class of I-boats to be completed. The I-15 was laid down in January 1938.

After the I-30 was mined, part of her cargo was recovered, and she was later salvaged. The I-33 was sunk at Truk by an aircraft bomb on 26 September 1942; later raised and refitted at Kure, she was returned to service on 1 June 1944 and lost on the 13th. (She was raised in 1953 and scrapped.)

After floatplane operations became too dangerous because of U.S. air capabilities and radar, some units had the hangar and catapult deleted in favor of a second 5.5-inch gun in front of the conning tower. Late in 1944 the I-36 and I-37 had their aircraft equipment and deck gun removed, and were modified to each carry four *kaiten.* The I-36 was again modified in early 1945 to carry six of the human torpedoes.

The conning tower of the I-36 after removal of her aircraft hangar. Note the camouflage paint scheme. She was one of the first submarines modified to carry *kaiten* human torpedoes. (Anthony J. Watts)

The conning tower of the I-30 upon her arrival at Lorient. The photo shows clearly the conning-tower windows, twin 25-mm antiaircraft gun mount, radio aerial, and 5.5-inch gun aft of the conning tower. (K.R. MacPherson)

The lead B1-type scouting submarine, the I-15, on her initial sea trials on 15 September 1940. This was the largest series of aircraft-carrying submarines built by Japan. (Imperial War Museum)

The I-26 was typical of the World War II-era scouting submarines, carrying a floatplane with moderate-size gun and torpedo batteries. The I-26 sank the U.S. light cruiser JUNEAU (CLAA 52). (*Ships of the World*)

The I-17 at launching on 19 July 1939. Her conning tower and hangar have not yet been fitted with a streamlined superstructure. (Imperial War Museum)

5 ATTACK SUBMARINES: C1 TYPE

Number	Builder	Launched	Completed	Notes
I-16	Mitsubishi, Kobe	28 July 1938	30 Mar 1940	sunk by USS ENGLAND (DE 635) 140 miles northeast of Choiseul, Solomons, 19 May 1944
I-18	Sasebo Navy Yard	12 Nov 1938	31 Jan 1941	sunk by USS FLETCHER (DD 445) and aircraft from USS HELENA (CL 50) 200 miles south of San Cristóbal, Solomons, 11 Feb 1943
I-20	Mitsubishi, Kobe	25 Jan 1939	29 Sep 1940	operational loss in New Hebrides 10 Oct 1943
I-22	Kawasaki, Kobe	23 Dec 1938	10 Mar 1941	operational loss in Solomons 1 Oct 1942
I-24	Sasebo Navy Yard	12 Nov 1939	31 Oct 1941	sunk by USS PC 487 50 miles northeast of Attu, Aleutians, 11 June 1943

Displacement: 2,184 tons standard
2,554 tons surfaced
3,561 tons submerged
Length: 358½ feet (109.3 m) oa
Beam: 30 feet (9.1 m)
Draft: 17½ feet (5.3 m)
Propulsion: 2 diesels; 12,400 hp
electric motors; 2,000 hp; 2 shafts
Speed: 23.5 knots surfaced
8 knots submerged
Range: 14,000 n.miles at 16 knots surfaced
60 n.miles at 3 knots submerged
Depth: 330 feet (100 m)
Complement: 95 officers and men
Torpedo tubes: 8 21-inch (533-mm) bow
Torpedoes: 20
Guns: 1 5.5-inch (140-mm)
2 25-mm (2 single)

These submarines were to be the third component of the A1/B1/C1 long-range submarine attack groups; the C1 was the smallest of the three designs, but still significantly larger than U.S. World War II fleet submarines. The C1 also evolved from the KD6 design. The eight torpedo tubes were served from two forward torpedo rooms, one above the other. The deck gun was fitted forward of the conning tower, and there were fittings on the after deck for carrying one Type A midget submarine.

The lead ship was laid down on 15 September 1937.

Late in 1942 the I-16 was refitted as a transport submarine with modifications permitting a 46-foot *daihatsu* landing craft to be carried abaft the conning tower.

The I-16 was one of the five modern attack submarines that carried midgets in the Pearl Harbor attack. In this photograph, she is underway at high speed in Hiroshima Bay, on trials during March 1940. Some of the five C1-type submarines had hardly completed trials before they sortied for the Pearl Harbor raid. (Imperial War Museum)

10 LARGE SUBMARINES: KD7 TYPE

Number	Builder	Launched	Completed	Notes
I-76	Kure Navy Yard	7 June 1941	4 Aug 1942	changed to I-176 in 1942; sunk by USS Franks (DD 554), Haggard (DD 555), and Johnston (DD 557) in Buka Passage, between Buka and New Guinea, 16 May 1944
I-77	Kawasaki, Kobe	20 Dec 1941	26 Dec 1942	changed to I-177 in 1942; sunk by USS Samuel S. Miles (DE 183) in Palau Islands 3 Oct 1944
I-78	Mitsubishi, Kobe	24 Feb 1942	26 Dec 1942	changed to I-178 in 1942; sunk by USS SC 669 off Espiritu Santo, Solomons, 29 May 1943
I-79	Kawasaki, Kobe	16 July 1942	18 June 1943	changed to I-179 in 1942; accidentally sunk Iyo Nada, Inland Sea, 14 July 1943; refloated 1957
I-80	Yokosuka Navy Yard	7 Feb 1942	15 Jan 1943	changed to I-180 in 1942; sunk by USS Gilmore (DE 18) 120 miles southwest of Kodiak Island, Aleutians, 26 Apr 1944
I-81	Kure Navy Yard	2 May 1942	24 May 1943	changed to I-181 in 1942; sunk by U.S destroyers in St. Georges Channel, Bismarck Archipelago, 16 Jan 1944
I-82	Yokosuka Navy Yard	30 May 1942	10 May 1943	changed to I-182 in 1942; sunk by USS Wadsworth (DD 516) south of Espiritu Santo, Solomons, 1 Sep 1943
I-83	Kawasaki, Kobe	21 Jan 1943	3 Oct 1943	changed to I-183 in 1942; sunk by USS Pogy (SS 266) 30 miles south of Cape Ashizuri, Bungo Strait, Japan, 28 Apr 1944
I-84	Yokosuka Navy Yard	12 Dec 1943	15 Oct 1943	changed to I-184 in 1942; sunk by aircraft from USS Suwannee (CVE 27) 20 miles southeast of Guam 19 June 1944
I-85	Yokosuka Navy Yard	16 Sep 1943	23 Sep 1943	changed to I-185 in 1942; sunk by USS Newcomb (DD 586) and Chandler (DMS 9) east of Saipan 22 June 1944

Displacement:	1,630 tons standard	Torpedoes:	12
	1,833 tons surfaced	Guns:	1 4.7-inch (120-mm)
	2,602 tons submerged		2 25-mm (1 twin)
Length:	346 feet (105.5 m) oa		
Beam:	27 feet (8.25 m)		
Draft:	15 feet (4.6 m)		
Propulsion:	2 diesels; 8,000 hp		
	electric motors; 1,800 hp; 2 shafts		
Speed:	23 knots surfaced		
	8 knots submerged		
Range:	8,000 n.miles at 16 knots surfaced		
	50 n.miles at 5 knots submerged		
Depth:	265 feet (80 m)		
Complement:	86 officers and men		
Torpedo tubes:	6 21-inch (533-mm) bow		

These were medium-range attack submarines also developed from the KD6 design. The original design provided for two 25-mm twin mounts; the 4.7-inch gun was substituted for one 25-mm mount. Endurance was 75 days. Note the small number of torpedo reloads. The lead ship was laid down on 15 September 1937.

Early in 1943 the I-176, I-177, and I-181 were modified for use as transports. The 4.7-inch deck gun was removed, fittings were provided for carrying a 46-foot landing craft, and, with some reload torpedoes removed, the ships were employed in the cargo-transport role.

The I-176 (formerly I-76) was the only Japanese submarine to sink a U.S. submarine, torpedoing the USS Corvina (SS 226) off Truk in 1943.

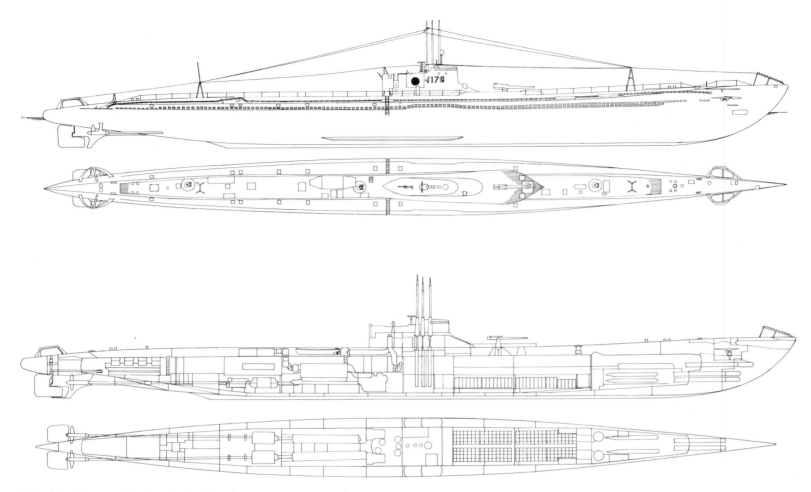

I-176 of the KD7 type. (Drawings by Alan Raven)

6 SCOUTING SUBMARINES: B2 TYPE

Number	Builder	Launched	Completed	Notes
I-40	Kure Navy Yard	1942	31 July 1943	sunk by USS RADFORD (DD 446) off Makin, Gilbert Islands, 25 Nov 1943
I-41	Kure Navy Yard	1943	18 Sep 1943	sunk by USS LAWRENCE C. TAYLOR (DE 415) and aircraft from USS ANZIO (CVE 57) east of Samar, Philippines, 18 Nov 1944
I-42	Kure Navy yard	1943	3 Nov 1943	sunk by USS TUNNY (SS 282) 6 miles southwest of Angaur, Palau Islands, 23 Mar 1944
I-43	Sasebo Navy Yard	1943	5 Nov 1943	sunk by USS ASPRO (SS 309) 280 miles east of Guam 15 Feb 1944
I-44	Yokosuka Navy Yard	1943	31 Jan 1944	sunk by aircraft from USS TULAGI (CVE 72) 29 Apr 1945
I-45	Sasebo Navy Yard	1943	28 Dec 1943	sunk by USS WHITEHURST (DE 634) 120 miles east of Surigao Strait, Philippines, 29 Oct 1944
#702 to 709		cancelled 1942		

Displacement:	2,320 tons standard
	2,624 tons surfaced
	3,700 tons submerged
Length:	356½ feet (108.7 m) oa
Beam:	30½ feet (9.3 m)
Draft:	17 feet (5.18 m)
Propulsion:	2 diesels; 11,000 hp
	electric motors; 2,000 hp; 2 shafts
Speed:	23.5 knots surfaced
	8 knots submerged
Range:	14,000 n.miles at 16 knots surfaced
	96 n.miles at 3 knots submerged
Depth:	330 feet (100 m)
Complement:	100 officers and men
Torpedo tubes:	6 21-inch (533-mm) bow

Torpedoes:	17
Guns:	1 5.5-inch (140-mm)
	2 25-mm (1 twin)
Aircraft:	1 floatplane

These submarines were a refinement of the B1 design, being slightly larger. Endurance was 90 days. The lead ship was laid down in March 1942.

During the war some units had the aircraft hangar and catapult, forward of the conning tower, replaced by a second 5.5-inch deck gun. Late in 1944 the I-44 had her aircraft facilities and 5.5-inch gun removed during conversion to a *kaiten* carrier, being modified to transport six of the human torpedoes.

3 ATTACK SUBMARINES: C2 TYPE

Number	Builder	Launched	Completed	Notes
I-46	Sasebo Navy Yard	1943	29 Feb 1944	sunk by USS HELM (DD 388) and GRIDLEY (DD 380) off Leyte, Philippines, 28 Oct 1944
I-47	Sasebo Navy Yard	1943	10 July 1944	surrendered Aug 1945; scuttled off Goto Island 1 Apr 1946
I-48	Sasebo Navy Yard	1944	5 Sep 1944	sunk by USS CONKLIN (DE 439), CORBESIER (DE 438), and RABY (DE 698) 25 miles northeast of Yap, western Caroline Islands, 23 Jan 1945
I-49		cancelled 1943		
I-50		cancelled 1943		
I-51		cancelled 1943		
#710 to 713		cancelled 1942		

Displacement:	2,184 tons standard
	2,557 tons surfaced
	3,564 tons submerged
Length:	358½ feet (109.3 m) oa
Beam:	29¾ feet (9.0 m)
Draft:	17½ feet (5.3 m)
Propulsion:	2 diesels; 12,400 hp
	electric motors; 2,000 hp; 2 shafts
Speed:	23.5 knots surfaced
	8 knots submerged
Range:	14,000 n.miles at 16 knots surfaced
	60 n.miles at 3 knots submerged
Depth:	330 feet (100 m)
Complement:	95 officers and men

Torpedo tubes:	8 21-inch (533-mm) bow
Torpedoes:	20
Guns:	1 5.5-inch (140-mm)
	2 25-mm (2 single)

The C2 design was almost identical to the prewar C1 attack submarines. Endurance was 90 days. The I-46 was laid down in November 1942.

These submarines were not fitted to carry a midget submarine as was the C1 type; however, in late 1944 the I-47 and I-48 had their 5.5-inch gun removed and were modified to carry four *kaiten,* with the I-47 refitted in early 1945 to embark six of the human torpedoes.

The large attack submarine I-47 at Kure after the war. Inboard of her are the submarines I-36 and I-402. (U.S. Navy)

1 HEADQUARTERS SUBMARINE: A2 TYPE

Number	Builder	Launched	Completed	Notes
I-12	Kawasaki, Kobe	1943	25 Apr 1944	operational loss in Central Pacific Jan 1945

Displacement:	2,390 tons standard	Complement:	100 officers and men
	2,934 tons surfaced	Torpedo tubes:	6 21-inch (533-mm) bow
	4,172 tons submerged	Torpedoes:	18
Length:	372¾ feet (113.7 m) oa	Guns:	1 5.5-inch (140-mm)
Beam:	31⅓ feet (9.5 m)		4 25-mm (2 twin)
Draft:	17½ feet (5.3 m)	Aircraft:	1 floatplane
Propulsion:	2 diesels; 4,700 hp		
	electric motors; 1,200 hp; 2 shafts		
Speed:	18 knots surfaced		
	6.25 knots submerged		
Range:	22,000 n.miles at 16 knots surfaced		
	70 n.miles at 3 knots submerged		
Depth:	330 feet (100 m)		

The I-12 was similar to the A1 design except that inferior propulsion machinery was provided, resulting in a significant reduction in speed. However, additional fuel was carried, providing a major increase in range. Additional submarines of this type were planned; see AM type (below). The I-12 was laid down in November 1942.

3 SCOUTING SUBMARINES: B3/B4 TYPE

Number	Builder	Launched	Completed	Notes
I-54	Yokosuka Navy Yard	1943	31 Mar 1944	sunk by USS Richard M. Rowell (DE 403) 70 miles east of Surigao Strait, Philippines, 26 Oct 1944
I-56	Yokosuka Navy Yard	1943	8 June 1944	sunk by USS Collett (DD 730), Heermann (DD 532), McCord (DD 534), Mertz (DD 691), Uhlmann (DD 687), and aircraft from USS Bataan (CVL 29) 160 miles east of Okinawa 18 Apr 1945
I-58	Yokosuka Navy Yard	1944	7 Sep 1944	surrendered Aug 1945; scuttled off Goto Island 1 Apr 1946
I-62		cancelled 1943		
I-64		cancelled 1943		
I-65		cancelled 1943		
I-66		cancelled 1943		
# 5101 to 5132		cancelled 1943		

Displacement:	2,140 tons standard
	2,607 tons surfaced
	3,688 tons submerged
Length:	356½ feet (108.7 m) oa
Beam:	30½ feet (9.3 m)
Draft:	17 feet (5.18 m)
Propulsion:	2 diesels; 4,700 hp
	electric motors; 1,200 hp; 2 shafts
Speed:	17.75 knots surfaced
	6.5 knots submerged
Range:	21,000 n.miles at 16 knots surfaced
	105 n.miles at 3 knots submerged
Depth:	330 feet (100 m)
Complement:	94 officers and men
Torpedo tubes:	6 21-inch (533-mm) bow
Torpedoes:	19
Guns:	1 5.5-inch (140-mm)
	2 25-mm (1 twin)
Aircraft:	1 floatplane

This design was similar to the aircraft-carrying B1/B2 types, but with less-powerful diesels, providing less speed; however, additional diesel oil bunkers resulted in a significantly greater range than the earlier scouting submarines. Endurance was 90 days. The I-54 was laid down in July 1942.

The eight boats numbered 5115 to 5132 were to have been of a larger configuration with a surface displacement of 2,800 tons, two additional bow tubes (eight total with 23 torpedoes plus eight mines), and an improved propulsion plant providing a surface speed of 22.5 knots. None of the cancelled boats was laid down.

These submarines were later fitted with snorkels. Early in 1945 the I-56 and I-58 had their 5.5-inch gun, hangar, and catapult removed during conversion to *kaiten* carriers. Four *kaiten* could be carried aft of the conning tower.

The I-54 in Tokyo Bay during 1944 shows the long, clean lines of the B3-type scouting submarines. The hangar is semi-recessed forward of the conning tower and the catapult track is visible on the bow. Except for engines these submarines were similar to the B2 type. (Imperial War Museum)

The scouting submarine I-58 at Kure at the end of the war. The I-53 is alongside. Note the similarity to the C2 design shown on an earlier page. (U.S. Navy)

3 ATTACK SUBMARINES: C3/C4 TYPE

Number	Builder	Launched	Completed	Notes
I-52	Kure Navy Yard	1943	18 Dec 1943	sunk by aircraft from USS Bogue (CVE 9) 800 miles southwest of Azores 24 June 1944
I-53	Kure Navy Yard	1943	20 Feb 1944	surrendered Aug 1945; scuttled off Goto Island 1 Apr 1946
I-55	Kure Navy Yard	1943	20 Apr 1944	sunk by USS Wyman (DE 38) and Reynolds (DE 42) 400 miles east of Tinian 28 July 1944
I-57		cancelled 1943		
I-59		cancelled 1943		
# 5141 to 5180		cancelled 1943		

Displacement:	2,095 tons standard	Guns:	2 5.5-inch (140-mm) (2 single)
	2,564 tons surfaced		2 25-mm (1 twin)
	3,644 tons submerged		
Length:	356½ feet (108.7 m) oa		
Beam:	30½ feet (9.3 m)		
Draft:	16¾ feet (5.1 m)		
Propulsion:	2 diesels; 4,700 hp		
	electric motors; 1,200 hp; 2 shafts		
Speed:	17.75 knots surfaced		
	6.5 knots submerged		
Range:	27,000 n.miles at 12 knots surfaced		
	21,000 n.miles at 16 knots surfaced		
	105 n.miles at 3 knots submerged		
Depth:	330 feet (100 m)		
Complement:	94 officers and men		
Torpedo tubes:	6 21-inch (533-mm) bow		
Torpedoes:	19		

These submarines were similar to the C1/C2 types but with inferior engines and a reduced torpedo battery. Additional fuel stowage provided a greater range. The I-52 was laid down in March 1942.

Submarines with program numbers 5156 through 5180 were to be of an improved C4 design; surfaced displacement was to have been increased to 2,756 tons with more powerful engines providing 20.5 knots on the surface; the torpedo battery was to be returned to eight tubes with only one 5.5-inch gun fitted.

These submarines were later fitted with snorkels. The I-53 was modified early in 1945 to serve as a *kaiten* carrier; her 5.5-inch guns were removed and provisions made for carrying four and subsequently six *kaiten.*

2 AIRCRAFT-CARRYING SUBMARINES: AM TYPE

Number	Builder	Launched	Completed	Notes
I-1	Kawasaki, Kobe	10 June 1944	—	construction ceased Mar 1945 when 70% complete; sunk in storm at Kobe 18 Sep 1945
I-13	Kawasaki, Kobe	1944	16 Dec 1944	sunk by aircraft from USS Anzio (CVE 57) and USS Lawrence C. Taylor (DE 415) 550 miles east of Yokosuka 16 July 1945
I-14	Kawasaki, Kobe	1944	14 Mar 1945	surrendered at sea 27 Aug 1945; scrapped
I-15	Kawasaki, Kobe	12 Apr 1944	—	construction ceased Mar 1945 when 90% complete; scrapped 1945
#5094		cancelled 1943		
#5095		cancelled 1943		
#5096		cancelled 1943		

Displacement:	2,620 tons standard
	3,603 tons surfaced
	4,762 tons submerged
Length:	372¾ feet (113.7 m) oa
Beam:	38½ feet (11.7 m)
Draft:	19⅓ feet (5.9 m)
Propulsion:	2 diesels; 4,400 hp
	electric motors; 600 hp; 2 shafts
Speed:	16.75 knots surfaced
	5.5 knots submerged
Range:	21,000 n.miles at 16 knots surfaced
	60 n.miles at 3 knots submerged
Depth:	330 feet (100 m)
Complement:	108 officers and men
Torpedo tubes:	6 21-inch (533-mm) bow
Torpedoes:	12
Guns:	1 5.5-inch (140-mm)
	7 25-mm (2 triple, 1 single)
Aircraft:	2 floatplanes

These submarines were the largest built by the Japanese Navy except for the aircraft-carrying I-400/STo class. The lead ship was the I-13, laid down in February 1943 as a unit of the A2 type. She was redesigned during construction to increase the number of aircraft-carrying submarines available to supplement the I-400/STo class. Subsequently, six additional AM-type submarines were ordered. Endurance was 90 days.

Operationally these ships were originally intended for the scouting role (as were the B1/B2/B3/B4 types), but as the war continued, bomber/*kamikaze* strikes became a more obvious role. The aircraft hangar was fitted to the starboard side of the deck with the main conning tower extending from the port side; a catapult was fitted in the forward deck (with the deck gun aft). Both completed ships were fitted with snorkels.

The hull of the I-1 was raised and was scrapped in 1947.

1 AIRCRAFT SUPPORT SUBMARINE: SH TYPE

Number	Builder	Launched	Completed	Notes
I-351	Kure Navy Yard	1944	28 Jan 1945	sunk by USS Bluefish (SS 222) 100 miles east of Natuna Bear Island, South China Sea, 14 July 1945
I-352	Kure Navy Yard	23 Apr 1944	—	90% complete when sunk by USAAF B-29s at Kure 22 June 1945
I-353	Kure Navy Yard	cancelled 1943		
#730		cancelled 1942		
#731		cancelled 1942		
#732		cancelled 1942		

Displacement:	2,650 tons standard
	3,512 tons surfaced
	4,290 tons submerged
Length:	363¾ feet (111.0 m) oa
Beam:	33½ feet (10.2 m)
Draft:	20 feet (6.1 m)
Propulsion:	2 diesels; 3,700 hp
	electric motors; 1,200 hp; 2 shafts
Speed:	15.75 knots surfaced
	6.3 knots submerged
Range:	13,000 n.miles at 14 knots surfaced
	100 n.miles at 3 knots submerged
Depth:	300 feet (90 m)
Complement:	77 officers and men + 13 aircrew
Torpedo tubes:	4 21-inch (533-mm) bow
Torpedoes:	4
Guns:	4 3-inch (76-mm) mortars
	7 25-mm (2 twin, 3 single)

This submarine class was intended specifically to support seaplanes in forward areas where shore facilities were unavailable and surface ships could not operate. Their design began prior to World War II. They could carry 365 tons of aviation gas, 11 tons of fresh water, plus 60 550-pound bombs or 30 bombs and 15 aircraft torpedoes. Endurance was 60 days.

The designed armament was one 5.5-inch deck gun and four 25-mm MG; as the submarines were being built, the former guns were in short supply, and trench mortars were provided instead. Note that no reload torpedoes were normally embarked, but four could be carried in lieu of aircraft torpedoes. The last three submarines were to have been of a slightly larger configuration. Fitted with snorkel.

The I-351 was laid down in May 1943. None of the cancelled boats was laid down.

3 AIRCRAFT CARRYING SUBMARINES: STo TYPE

Number	Builder	Launched	Completed	Notes
I-400	Kure Navy Yard	1944	30 Dec 1944	surrendered at sea 27 Aug 1945; scuttled off U.S. coast 1946
I-401	Sasebo Navy Yard	1944	8 Jan 1945	surrendered at sea 29 Aug 1945; scuttled off U.S. coast 1946
I-402	Sasebo Navy Yard	1944	24 July 1945	surrendered Aug 1945; scuttled off Goto Island 1 Apr 1946
I-403		cancelled Mar 1945		
I-404	Kure Navy Yard	7 July 1944	—	construction ceased Mar 1945 when 90% complete; sunk by U.S. carrier aircraft at Kure 28 July 1945
I-405	Kawasaki, Kobe		—	construction ceased Mar 1945; scrapped
I-406 to I-417		cancelled Mar 1945		
#714		cancelled 1942		

Displacement:	3,530 tons standard
	5,223 tons surfaced
	6,560 tons submerged
Length:	400¼ feet (122.0 m) oa
Beam:	39⅓ feet (12.0 m)
Draft:	23 feet (7.0 m)
Propulsion:	4 diesels; 7,700 hp
	electric motors; 2,400 hp; 2 shafts
Speed:	18.75 knots surfaced
	6.5 knots submerged
Range:	30,000 n.miles at 16 knots
	37,500 n.miles at 14 knots surfaced
	60 n.miles at 3 knots submerged
Depth:	330 feet (100 m)
Complement:	144 officers and men
Torpedo tubes:	8 21-inch (533-mm) bow
Torpedoes:	20

Guns:	1 5.5-inch (140-mm)
	10 25-mm (3 triple, 1 single)
Aircraft:	3 floatplane (see notes)

These were the largest submarines to be built by any nation prior to the advent of nuclear propulsion. They were designed specifically to launch floatplane bombers against U.S. cities. STo indicated *sen-toku* or "special submarine."

The original STo design was begun in early 1942 and provided for a displacement of 4,550 tons surfaced with two floatplanes being carried. The design was enlarged to accommodate three floatplanes plus parts for a fourth. The deck structure arrangement and catapult was similar to the AM design, with the catapult forward of the hangar, having an 85-foot 4-inch track slightly offset to starboard. Aircraft could be prewarmed in the hangar while the submarine was submerged through a system circulating heated lubricating oil. The STo hull design was unusual, with a figure eight (8) configuration forward evolving into a horizontal figure eight (∞) amidships. This permitted the submarine to have two forward torpedo rooms, one above the other, while accommodating four diesel engines mounted side-by-side amidships. They could carry sufficient fuel to cruise farther than any other non-nuclear submarine and could embark supplies for an endurance of 90 days.

These submarines could carry 4 aircraft torpedoes, 3 1,760-pound bombs, and 12 550-pound bombs.

They were fitted from the outset with radar and snorkel (see page 61); they were provided with accommodations and communications equipment for use as squadron flagships, thus combining the features of the earlier A-B-C types of submarines.

The I-400 was laid down on 18 January 1943; only three of the four other units that were laid down were completed. The I-402 was modified during construction to serve as a submarine tanker to transport oil from the East Indies through the U.S. submarine blockade to Japan.

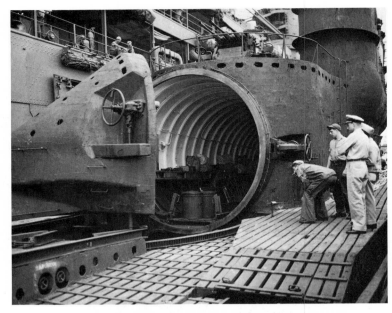

The hangar of the I-400 being examined by U.S. naval personnel. The conning tower is offset to port and the hangar to starboard. (U.S. Navy)

The conning tower of the I-402, showing searchlight, binoculars, surface-search radar (funnel-like device), air-search radar (top), and single 25-mm antiaircraft machine gun. (U.S. Navy)

The after superstructure of the I-400, showing two of the 25-mm triple gun mounts; note the curvature of the structure. (U.S. Navy)

The I-401 in Tokyo Bay with U.S. destroyers in the background. The aircraft crane on her foredeck could be lowered into the superdeck. Note the length of the conning tower-hangar structure. (U.S. Navy)

The Japanese I-400 submarines were the world's largest prior to the development of nuclear propulsion. Here the I-400 approaches the U.S. submarine tender PROTEUS (AS 19) in Japanese waters following her surrender at sea. Japanese submariners in the foreground look on. (U.S. Navy)

The catapult track and (left) retracted aircraft crane of an I-400 class submarine. (U.S. Navy)

The officers of the I-401 after the submarine's surrender. (*Ships of the World*)

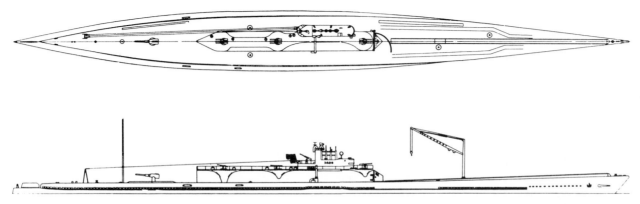

Sketch of the I-400 outboard profile and plan, from a report of the U.S. Navy Technical Mission to Japan. In the profile sketch, the
aircraft handling crane is in the raised position; the catapult is fitted forward of the elongated conning tower with the crane folding
down onto the deck, portside of the catapult. (U.S. Navy)

The diving control station of the I-400. (U.S. Navy)

Storage tube for aircraft floats on the starboard side of the I-400's aircraft hangar. (U.S. Navy)

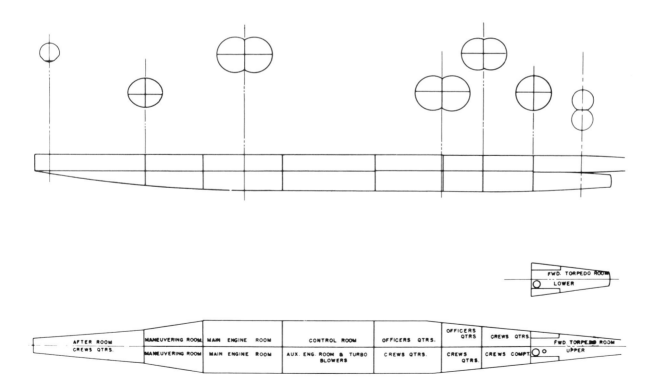

Sketch of the pressure hull and compartment plan of the I-400 class, from a report of the U.S. Navy Technical Mission to Japan. Note the unusual cross section of the pressure hull and the two-level arrangement of torpedo rooms. (U.S. Navy)

3 HIGH-SPEED ATTACK SUBMARINES: ST TYPE

Number	Builder	Launched		Completed	Notes
I-201	Kure Navy Yard		1944	2 Feb 1945	surrendered Aug 1945
I-202	Kure Navy Yard		1944	12 Feb 1945	surrendered Aug 1945; scuttled off Kongo Point 5 Apr 1946
I-203	Kure Navy Yard		1944	29 May 1945	surrendered Aug 1945
I-204	Kure Navy Yard	16 Dec	1944	—	90% complete when sunk by USAAF B-29s at Kure 22 June 1945
I-205	Kure Navy Yard	15 Feb	1945	—	80% complete when damaged by U.S. air attacks; scrapped
I-206	Kure Navy Yard	23 Mar	1945	—	construction ceased when 85% complete; sunk in storm at Kobe 25 Aug 1945; apparently raised and scrapped
I-207	Kure Navy Yard	—		—	construction ceased when 20% complete Mar 1945; scrapped 1945
I-208	Kure Navy Yard	—		—	construction ceased when 5% complete Mar 1945; scrapped 1945
I-209 to I-223		cancelled 1945			

Displacement:	1,070 tons standard
	1,291 tons surfaced
	1,450 tons submerged
Length:	259 (79.0 m) oa
Beam:	19 feet (5.8 m)
Draft:	18 feet (5.4 m)
Propulsion:	2 diesels; 2,750 hp
	electric motors; 5,000 hp; 2 shafts
Speed:	15.75 knots surfaced
	19 knots submerged
Range:	8,000 n.miles at 11 knots
	5,800 n.miles at 16 knots surfaced
	135 n.miles at 3 knots submerged
Depth:	360 feet (110 m)
Complement:	31 officers and men
Torpedo tubes:	4 21-inch (533-mm) bow
Torpedoes:	10
Guns:	2 25-mm MG (2 single)

These were high-speed attack submarines developed from the experimental submarine No. 71 (see page 100). The ST designation indicated *sen-taka* or "submarine, high [speed]."

The I-201 was twice as fast underwater as contemporary U.S. submarines; only the German Type XXI (operational from April 1945) was comparable in underwater speed. The ST design was characterized by (1) a streamlined hull, (2) large electric motors, and (3) a high-capacity battery, albeit with a rapid discharge rate. This was the only class of I-boats with an all-welded hull (only smaller HA-series and midget submarines were all welded; larger submarines were largely or all riveted). A snorkel was fitted, as were streamlined flaps to cover the camber hull openings when submerged. All deck fittings were recessed and the 25-mm guns retracted. The original design had no forward diving planes. Small planes were provided forward, however, during construction to improve control at low speeds and to help diving. At-sea endurance was 30 days.

Mass-production techniques were used in the ST program, with some one hundred units projected. The I-201 was laid down in March 1944; only seven other units of this design were laid down, all at the Kure dockyard. Extensive prefabrication and welding reduced building time to some ten months.

After sea trials the I-201 underwent a battery change, and there was extensive modification of her ballast and fuel tank arrangement. These features were included in the later units.

These submarines could travel underwater at 19 knots for 55 minutes, followed by 3 knots for 12 hours; these were also the deepest-diving submarines built by Japan. No operational patrols were made by these submarines.

The I-207 and I-208 were broken up on their building slips to facilitate the construction of *kaiten*. The I-209 through I-233 were cancelled for the same reason; none was laid down.

The I-202 at high surface speed. These ST-type submarines had the fastest underwater speed of any World War II undersea craft. The 25-mm machine guns retracted, and all deck fittings could be removed or were recessed to improve underwater performance. (U.S. Naval Historical Center)

The I-201 was the first of the high-speed ST-type submarines developed from the prewar submarine No. 71. No submarines of this class made war patrols before the conflict ended. (*Ships of the World*)

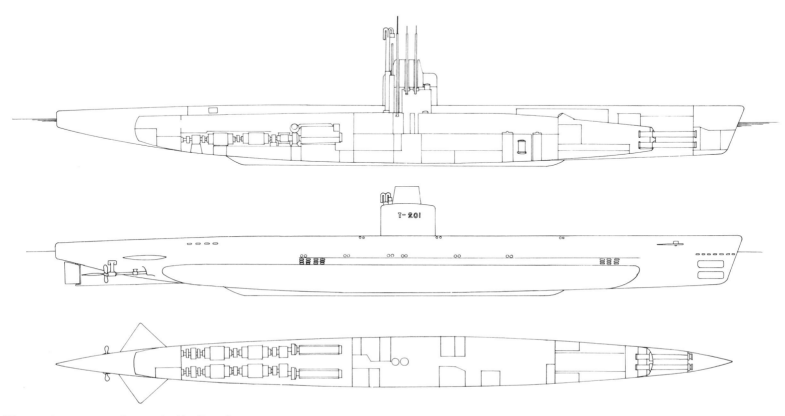

ST-type submarine I-201. (Drawing by Alan Raven)

2 EX-GERMAN CRUISER SUBMARINES: TYPE IXD₂

Number	(former)	Builder	Launched	Completed	to Japan	Notes
I-501	(U-181)	Deschimag, Bremen	30 Dec 1941	9 May 1942	May 1945	surrendered Aug 1945; scuttled off Singapore 12 Feb 1946
I-502	(U-862)	Deschimag, Bremen	5 June 1943	7 Oct 1943	May 1945	surrendered Aug 1945; scuttled off Singapore 12 Feb 1946

Displacement: 1,616 tons surfaced
               1,804 tons submerged
Length: 287½ feet (87.5 m) oa
Beam: 24½ feet (7.5 m)
Draft: 17¾ feet (5.3 m)
Propulsion: 4 diesels; 5,400 hp
               electric motors; 1,100 hp; 2 shafts
Speed: 19.25 knots surfaced
               7 knots submerged
Range: 23,700 n.miles at 12 knots surfaced
               57 n.miles at 4 knots submerged
Depth:
Complement: 57 officers and men
Torpedo tubes: 6 21-inch (533-mm) 4 bow + 2 stern
Torpedoes: 24
Guns: 1 37-mm antiaircraft
               4 20-mm MG (2 twin)

Four German U-boats and two ex-Italian submarines were taken over by the Japanese Navy in the Far East after the capitulation of Germany in May 1945. They were commissioned in the Japanese Navy on 15 July 1945.

The Type IXD₂ submarines were developed from the Type IX with increased fuel bunkers and higher surface speed. Eight vertical mine shafts for four mines each could be fitted as an alternative to torpedo reloads (i.e., six torpedoes plus thirty-two mines).

The I-501 and I-502 were at Singapore in August 1945 when surrendered to the Allies.

The U-862 was one of the long-range German IXD₂ submarines that operated in the Indian Ocean during World War II. Japanese-German submarine operations were the only area of military cooperation between the two major Axis nations. (Drüppel)

1 EX-ITALIAN TRANSPORT SUBMARINE: "MARCELLO" CLASS

Number	Builder	Launched	Completed	to Japan	Notes
I-503 (ex-COMMANDANTE ALFREDO CAPPELLINI)	OTO Muggiano, La Spezia*	14 May 1939	23 Sep 1939	10 Sep 1943/10 May 1945	surrendered Aug 1945; scrapped 1946

*OTO = Odero-Terni-Orlando.

Displacement:	910 tons surfaced
	1,220 tons submerged
Length:	239½ feet (73.1 m) oa
Beam:	23¾ feet (7.2 m)
Draft:	16¾ feet (5.1 m)
Propulsion:	2 diesels; 3,000 hp
	electric motors; 1,300 hp; 2 shafts
Speed:	17 knots surfaced
	8.5 knots submerged
Range:	9,500 n.miles at 9 knots surfaced
	80 n.miles at 4 knots submerged
Depth:	328 feet (100 m)
Complement:	58 officers and men
Torpedo tubes:	removed
Guns:	1 4-inch (102-mm)

The I-503 and I-504 were originally Italian submarines; they were converted to cargo ships at German-held yards in France during 1943 and sailed to the Far East in that role. When the fascist Italian government fell in 1943, both were taken over by the Japanese and handed to the Germans, being redesignated UIT-24 and UIT-25, respectively. The UIT-24 was fitted with a 4-inch deck gun at that time. With the capitulation of Nazi Germany in May 1945, they were in Far East ports and were again taken over by Japan and assigned I-series numbers. These were thus the only ships of the World War II era to fly the flags of all three Axis nations.

The CAPPELLINI was taken over by the Japanese at Sabang in September 1943 and was at Kobe in August 1945 when surrendered to U.S. forces.

(As combat submarines, the two Italian craft were fitted with eight torpedo tubes and carried 16 torpedoes; the CAPPELLINI had two 3.9-inch deck guns and the TORELLI had one.)

1 EX-ITALIAN TRANSPORT SUBMARINE: "MARCONI" CLASS

Number	Builder	Launched	Completed	to Japan	Notes
I-504 (ex-LUIGI TORELLI)	OTO Muggiano, La Spezia	6 Jan 1940	15 May 1940	10 Sep 1943/May 1945	surrendered Aug 1945; scrapped 1946

Displacement:	1,036 tons surfaced
	1,489 tons submerged
Length:	249¼ feet (76.0 m) oa
Beam:	22¼ feet (7.9 m)
Draft:	15½ feet (4.7 m)
Propulsion:	2 diesels; 3,600 hp
	electric motors; 1,240 hp; 2 shafts
Speed:	17.75 knots surfaced
	8.5 knots submerged
Range:	9,500 n.miles at 9 knots surfaced
	110 n.miles at 3 knots submerged
Depth:	300 feet (90 m)
Complement:	57 officers and men
Torpedo tubes:	removed
Guns:	removed

The TORELLI was at Singapore when taken over by the Japanese in September 1943, and was at Kobe when surrendered to U.S. forces in August 1945.

The Italian submarine LUIGI TORELLI was one of two submarines that served under the Italian, German, and Japanese flags. She was converted while in Italian service to a transport to operate between Europe and the Far East. Her Japanese designation was I-504. (Drüppel)

1 EX-GERMAN MINELAYING SUBMARINE: TYPE XB

Number	(former)	Builder	Launched	Completed	to Japan	Notes
I-505	(U-219)	Germania Werft, Kiel	6 Oct 1942	12 Dec 1942	May 1945	surrendered Aug 1945; scrapped 1947

Displacement: 17,630 tons surfaced
               2,177 tons submerged
Length: 294¾ feet (89.8 m) oa
Beam: 30¼ feet (9.2 m)
Draft: 13½ feet (4.7 m)
Propulsion: 2 diesels; 4,200 hp
               electric motors; 1,100 hp; 2 shafts
Speed: 16.5 knots surfaced
               7 knots submerged
Range: 14,550 n.miles at 12 knots surfaced
               93 n.miles at 4 knots submerged

Depth:
Complement: 52 officers and men
Torpedo tubes: 2 21-inch (533-mm) stern
Guns: 1 37-mm antiaircraft
               4 20-mm MG (2 twin)

The large fuel capacity of this submarine design permitted her use as a U-boat tanker. She was surrendered to Allied forces at Djakarta in August 1945.

The German U-219 was a long-range submarine of a type employed to refuel other submarines. She served briefly as the Japanese I-505 (Drüppel)

1 EX-GERMAN CRUISER SUBMARINE: TYPE IXD₁

Number	(former)	Builder	Launched	Completed	to Japan	Notes
I-506	(U-195)	A.G. Weser, Bremen	8 Apr 1942	5 Sep 1942	May 1945	surrendered Aug 1945; scrapped 1947

Displacement: 1,610 tons surfaced
               1,799 tons submerged
Length: 287½ feet (87.5 m) oa
Beam: 24½ feet (7.5 m)
Draft: 17¾ feet (5.3 m)
Propulsion: 2 diesels; 2,800 hp
               electric motors; 1,100 hp; 2 shafts
Speed: 15.75 knots surfaced
               7 knots submerged
Range: 9,900 n.miles at 12 knots surfaced
               115 n.miles at 4 knots submerged

Depth:
Complement: 57 officers and men
Torpedo tubes: removed
Guns: 1 37-mm antiaircraft
               4 20-mm MG (2 twin)

This submarine was converted in 1943 to the transport role. She could carry 252 tons of oil. Surrendered at Soerabaja in August 1945.

9 RO-Series Medium Submarines

This chapter describes the Japanese RO-series or medium submarines, beginning with the L4 type of 1923. These were the earliest RO-boats to see active service in the war in the Pacific. The previous submarines designated RO are described in chapter 6.

The two former German submarines transferred to Japan during the war were designated in the RO-series. The six other former German and Italian submarines had I-series designations (see chapter 8).

9 MEDIUM SUBMARINES: L4 TYPE

Number	Builder	Launched	Completed	Notes
59	Mitsubishi, Kobe	22 May 1922	17 Sep 1923	changed to RO-60 in 1924; stranded and wrecked at Kwajalein 29 Dec 1941
72	Mitsubishi, Kobe	19 May 1923	9 Feb 1924	changed to RO-61 in 1924; sunk by USS Reid (DD 369) and aircraft off Atka Island, Aleutians, 31 Aug 1942
73	Mitsubishi, Kobe	10 Sep 1923	24 July 1924	changed to RO-62 in 1924; surrendered Aug 1945; scrapped 1946
84	Mitsubishi, Kobe	24 Jan 1924	20 Dec 1924	changed to RO-63 in 1924; surrendered Aug 1945; scrapped 1946
RO-64	Mitsubishi, Kobe	19 Aug 1924	30 Apr 1925	sunk by mine in Hiroshima Bay 12 Apr 1945
RO-65	Mitsubishi, Kobe	25 Sep 1925	30 June 1926	sunk by U.S. aircraft in Kiska Harbor, Aleutians, 4 Nov 1942
RO-66	Mitsubishi, Kobe	25 Oct 1926	28 July 1927	sunk in collision with RO-62 off Wake Island 17 Dec 1941
RO-67	Mitsubishi, Kobe	18 Mar 1926	15 Dec 1926	surrendered Aug 1945; scrapped 1946
RO-68	Mitsubishi, Kobe	23 Feb 1925	29 Oct 1925	surrendered Aug 1945; scrapped 1946

Displacement:	988 tons standard
	996 tons surfaced
	1,322 tons submerged
Length:	250 feet (76.2 m) oa
Beam:	24½ feet (7.3 m)
Draft:	12⅓ feet (3.7 m)
Propulsion:	2 diesels; 2,400 hp
	electric motors; 1,600 hp; 2 shafts
Speed:	16 knots surfaced
	8 knots submerged
Range:	5,500 n.miles at 10 knots surfaced
	80 n.miles at 4 knots submerged
Depth:	200 feet (60 m)
Complement:	60 officers and men
Torpedo tubes:	6 21-inch (533-mm) bow
Torpedoes:	10
Guns:	1 3-inch (76-mm)
	1 MG

These submarines were similar to the RO-57/L3 class, but with major internal improvements. The number of torpedo tubes was increased by two, and the 3-inch gun was mounted forward of the conning tower. Endurance was 20 days. The No. 59 was laid down in December 1921.

From late 1942 the five surviving boats were assigned to training duties at Kure. No. 60 and 61 were cancelled in 1921.

The L4-type submarines, such as the RO-63 (formerly No. 84), were the oldest medium submarines to see significant combat in World War II. This photo was taken during sea trials in October 1924. (Imperial War Museum)

The RO-64 struck a mine and sank in the Inland Sea in 1945, going down with her crew of 50 men plus 30 trainees and instructors. (*Ships of the World*)

2 MEDIUM SUBMARINES: K5 TYPE

Number	Builder	Launched	Completed	Notes
RO-33	Kure Navy Yard	10 Oct 1934	7 Oct 1935	sunk by Australian Arunta 10 miles southeast of Port Moresby, New Guinea, 29 Aug 1942
RO-34	Mitsubishi, Kobe	12 Dec 1935	31 May 1937	sunk by USS O'Bannon (DD 450), Strong (DD 467) 40 miles off Russell Island, Solomons, 5 Apr 1943

Displacement:	700 tons standard 940 tons surfaced	Depth:	245 feet (75 m)	
		Complement:	75 officers and men	
Length:	239½ feet (73.0 m) oa	Torpedo tubes:	4 21-inch (533-mm) bow	
Beam:	22 feet (6.7 m)	Torpedoes:	10	
Draft:	10½ feet (3.25 m)	Guns:	1 3-inch (76-mm)	
Propulsion:	2 diesels; 3,000 hp electric motors; 1,200 hp; 2 shafts		1 13-mm MG	
Speed:	19 knots surfaced 8.25 knots submerged			
Range:	8,000 n.miles at 12 knots surfaced 90 n.miles at 3.5 knots submerged			

These were prototype submarines of an improved design intended for series production in wartime. They were generally similar to the K4 type with improved diesels and hence a greater surface speed.

The RO-33 was laid down in August 1933.

The RO-33 at rest, showing the saw-tooth rig forward for cutting through submarine nets.

18 MEDIUM SUBMARINES: KS TYPE

Number	Builder	Launched	Completed	Notes
RO-100	Kure Navy Yard	6 Dec 1941	23 Sep 1942	sunk by mine 2 miles west of Buin, Bougainville Island, 25 Nov 1943
RO-101	Kawasaki, Kobe	17 Apr 1942	31 Oct 1942	sunk by USS SAUFLEY (DD 465) and aircraft 100 miles east of San Cristóbal, Solomons, 15 Sep 1943
RO-102	Kawasaki, Kobe	17 Apr 1942	17 Nov 1942	probably sunk by USN PT 150 and PT 152 5 miles off Lae, New Guinea, 14 May 1943
RO-103	Kure Navy Yard	6 Dec 1942	21 Oct 1942	probably sunk by mine 28 July 1943
RO-104	Kawasaki, Kobe	11 July 1942	25 Feb 1943	sunk by USS ENGLAND (DE 635) 250 miles north of Kavieng, New Ireland, Bismarck Archipelago, 23 May 1944
RO-105	Kawasaki, Kobe	11 July 1942	5 Mar 1943	sunk by USS ENGLAND (DE 635) 200 miles north of Kavieng 31 May 1944
RO-106	Kure Navy Yard	30 May 1942	26 Dec 1942	sunk by USS ENGLAND (DE 635) 250 miles north of Kavieng 22 May 1944
RO-107	Kure Navy Yard	30 May 1942	26 Dec 1942	sunk by USS TAYLOR (DD 468) 15 miles east of Kolombangara Island, Solomons, 12 July 1943
RO-108	Kawasaki, Kobe	26 Oct 1942	20 Apr 1943	sunk by USS ENGLAND (DE 635) 110 miles northeast of Manus Island 26 May 1944
RO-109	Kawasaki, Kobe	1942	30 Apr 1943	sunk by USS HORACE A. BASS (DE 691) south of Okinawa 25 Apr 1945
RO-110	Kawasaki, Kobe	1943	6 July 1943	sunk by Australian IPSWICH and LAUNCESTON, and Indian JUMNA 17 miles south of Vizgapatam, eastern India, 11 Feb 1944
RO-111	Kawasaki, Kobe	1943	19 July 1943	sunk by USS TAYLOR (DD 468) 210 miles north of Kavieng 11 June 1944
RO-112	Kawasaki, Kobe	1943	15 Sep 1943	sunk by USS BATFISH (SS 310) off Camiguin Island, north of Luzon, Philippines, 11 Feb 1945
RO-113	Kawasaki, Kobe	1943	12 Oct 1943	sunk by USS BATFISH (SS 310) off Babuyan Island, north of Luzon 12 Feb 1945
RO-114	Kawasaki, Kobe	1943	20 Nov 1943	sunk by USS MELVIN (DD 680) and WADLEIGH (DD 689) 80 miles west of Tinian 17 June 1944
RO-115	Kawasaki, Kobe	1943	30 Nov 1943	sunk by USS BELL (DD 587), JENKINS (DD 447), O'BANNON (DD 450), and ULVERT M. MOORE (DE 442) 125 miles southwest of Manila, Philippines, 31 Jan 1945
RO-116	Kawasaki, Kobe	1943	21 Jan 1944	sunk by USS ENGLAND (DE 635) 225 miles north of Kavieng 24 May 1944
RO-117	Kawasaki, Kobe	1943	31 Jan 1944	sunk by USN B-24 (PB4Y-1) 350 miles southeast of Saipan 17 June 1944

Displacement:	525 tons standard		Complement:	38 officers and men
	601 tons surfaced		Torpedo tubes:	4 21-inch (533-mm) bow
	782 tons submerged		Torpedoes:	8
Length:	199¾ feet (60.9 m) oa		Guns:	1 3-inch (76-mm) antiaircraft
Beam:	19½ feet (6.0 m)			
Draft:	11½ feet (3.5 m)			
Propulsion:	2 diesels; 1,000 hp			
	electric motors; 760 hp; 2 shafts			
Speed:	14.25 knots surfaced			
	8 knots submerged			
Range:	3,500 n.miles at 12 knots surfaced			
	60 n.miles at 3 knots submerged			
Depth:	245 feet (75 m)			

This class was intended for coastal defense operations. Accordingly, they had a limited range and at-sea endurance (21 days). The original design called for two 25-mm guns, but the 3-inch weapon was installed instead.

The RO-100 was laid down in June 1941. At least nine more submarines of this type were projected.

The medium submarine RO-109. She was sunk by U.S. forces off of Okinawa in April 1945.

18 MEDIUM SUBMARINES: K6 TYPE

Number	Builder	Launched		Completed		Notes
RO-35	Mitsubishi, Kobe	4 June	1942	31 Mar	1943	sunk by USS Patterson (DD 392) between New Hebrides and Solomon Sea 25 Aug 1943
RO-36	Mitsubishi, Kobe	14 Oct	1942	27 May	1943	sunk by USS Melvin (DD 680) 75 miles east of Saipan 13 June 1944
RO-37	Mitsubishi, Kobe	30 June	1942	30 June	1943	sunk by USS Buchanan (DD 484) 130 miles east of San Cristóbal, Solomons, 22 Jan 1944
RO-38	Mitsubishi, Kobe	24 Dec	1942	24 July	1943	sunk by USS Cotten (DD 669) 24 Nov 1943
RO-39	Sasebo Navy Yard	6 Mar	1942	12 Sep	1943	sunk by USS Walker (DD 517) 10 miles east of Wotje Island 2 Feb 1944
RO-40	Mitsubishi, Kobe	6 Mar	1942	28 Sep	1943	sunk by USS Phelps (DD 360) and Sage (AM 111) 45 miles northwest of Kwajalein 16 Feb 1944
RO-41	Mitsubishi, Kobe	5 May	1943	26 Nov	1943	sunk by USS Haggard (DD 555) 320 miles southeast of Okinawa 23 Mar 1945
RO-42	Sasebo Navy Yard	25 Oct	1943	31 Aug	1943	sunk by USS Bangust (DE 739) east of Kwajalein 11 June 1944
RO-43	Mitsubishi, Kobe	5 June	1943	16 Dec	1943	sunk by aircraft from USS Anzio (CVE 57) 50 miles west of Iwo Jima 26 Feb 1945
RO-44	Zosensho, Tamano		1943	13 Sep	1943	sunk by USS Burden R. Hastings (DE 19) 110 miles east of Eniwetok 16 June 1944
RO-45	Mitsubishi, Kobe		1943	11 Jan	1944	sunk by USS Macdonough (DD 351) Stephen Potter (DD 538), and aircraft from USS Monterey (CVL 26) 65 miles south of Truk 30 Apr 1944
RO-46	Mitsubishi, Kobe		1943	11 Feb	1944	sunk by USS Sea Owl (SS 405) off Wake Island 18 Apr 1945
RO-47	Zosensho, Tamano		1943	31 Jan	1944	sunk by USS McCoy Reynolds (DE 440) southwest of Yap, western Caroline Islands 25 Sep 1944
RO-48	Mitsubishi, Kobe		1943	31 Mar	1944	probably sunk by USS William C. Miller (DE 259) 75 miles west of Saipan 14 July 1944
RO-49	Zosensho, Tamano		1943	19 May	1944	sunk by USS Hudson (DD 475) 60 miles west of Okinawa 5 Apr 1945
RO-50	Zosensho, Tamano		1943	31 July	1944	surrendered Aug 1945; scuttled off Goto Island 1 Apr 1946
RO-51		cancelled	1943			
RO-52		cancelled	1943			
RO-53		cancelled	1943			
RO-54		cancelled	1943			
RO-55	Zosensho, Tamano		1944	30 Sep	1944	sunk by USS Thomason (DE 203) off Luzon 7 Feb 1945
RO-56 (formerly RO-75)	Zosensho, Tamano		1944	15 Nov	1944	sunk by USS Monssen (DD 798) and Mertz (DD 691) 45 miles east of Okinawa 9 Apr 1945
RO-70 to RO-74		cancelled	1943			
RO-76 to RO-99		cancelled	1943			
RO-200 to RO-227		cancelled	1943			
#715 to 723		cancelled	1942			

Displacement:	960 tons standard
	1,115 tons surfaced
	1,447 tons submerged
Length:	264 feet (80.5 m) oa
Beam:	23 feet (7.0 m)
Draft:	13⅓ feet (4.05 m)
Propulsion:	2 diesels; 4,200 hp
	electric motors; 1,200 hp; 2 shafts
Speed:	19.75 knots surfaced
	8 knots submerged
Range:	11,000 n.miles at 12 knots surfaced
	45 n.miles at 5 knots submerged
Depth:	265 feet (80 m)
Complement:	61 officers and men
Torpedo tubes:	4 21-inch (533-mm) bow
Torpedoes:	10
Guns:	1 3-inch (76-mm) antiaircraft
	2 25-mm AA MG (1 twin)

This class was an improvement of the K5 design. The major changes were the increases in fuel carried and hence range, more powerful machinery, a greater operating depth, and modification for firing Type 95 torpedoes, the first RO-series submarines to have that weapon. The original design did not provide for a deck gun, but all units were completed with a high-angle 3-inch gun forward of the conning tower. Endurance was 40 days.

This class introduced the Tamano yard to submarine construction (formerly the Tama Shipyard of Mitsui Company).

Hull #645 was laid down as the RO-75, but was renumbered RO-56 in 1943. The RO-35 was laid down in October 1941.

U.S. submarine specialists at the end of World War II described this design as "well worked out and compact."

Further construction of RO-series submarines was cancelled in 1943 because of their high losses to U.S. antisubmarine forces.

The RO-56 was also lost in the futile effort to counter the U.S. assault against Okinawa. (*Ships of the World*)

The K6 represented the last type of medium submarines built by the Japanese. The RO-46 and other RO-series submarines fell easy victim to U.S. antisubmarine forces. (Imperial War Museum)

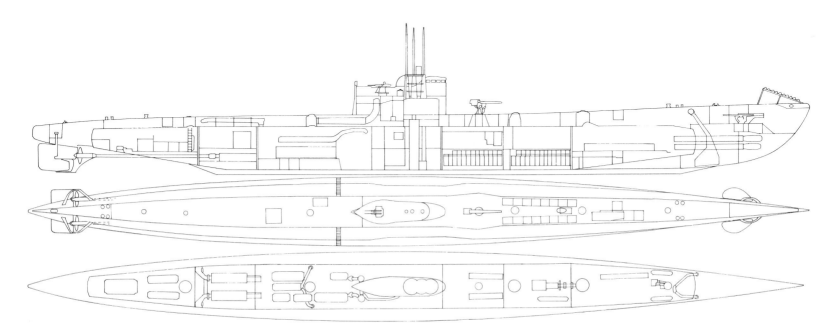

RO-35 of K6 type (Drawing by Alan Raven)

2 EX-GERMAN SUBMARINES: TYPE IXC

Number	(former)	Builder	Launched	Completed	to Japan	Notes
RO-500	(U-511)	Deutsche Werft, Hamburg	22 Sep 1941	8 Dec 1941	July 1943	surrendered Aug 1945; scuttled in Maizuru Gulf 30 Apr 1946
RO-501	(U-1224)	Deutsche Werft, Hamburg	7 July 1943	20 Oct 1943	15 Feb 1944	sunk by USS Francis M. Robinson (DE 220) 400 miles south of Azores 13 May 1944

Displacement:	RO-500 1,120 tons surfaced
	1,232 tons submerged
	RO-501 1,144 tons surfaced
	1,247 tons submerged
Length:	252 feet (76.7 m) oa
Beam:	22¼ feet (6.7 m)
Draft:	15½ feet (4.7 m)
Propulsion:	2 diesels; 4,400 hp
	electric motors; 1,000 hp; 2 shafts
Speed:	RO-500 18 knots surfaced
	7 knots submerged
	RO-501 18.33 knots surfaced
	7.33 knots submerged
Range:	11,400 n.miles at 12 knots surfaced
	63 n.miles at 4 knots submerged
Depth:	490 feet (150 m)
Complement:	48 officers and men
Torpedo tubes:	6 21-inch (533-mm) 4 bow + 2 stern
Torpedoes:	22
Guns:	RO-500 1 4.1-inch (105-mm)
	2 20-mm MG (2 single)
	RO-501 1 37-mm antiaircraft
	4 20-mm MG (2 twin)

The U-511 and U-1224 were specifically transferred as gifts to Japan at the direction of Adolph Hitler. The basic Type IX design evolved from the U-81 of World War I.

Upon arrival in Japan in August 1943, the RO-500 was examined by the Japanese Navy and, after trials, employed in training until the end of the war. She was surrendered at Maizuru. The RO-501 departed Kiel on 30 March 1944 and was sunk en route from Germany to Japan.

When transferred to Japanese service, she was temporarily renamed Satsuki No. 1.

The RO-500 upon transfer to the Japanese Navy in 1943. Formerly the U-511, she survived the transit to Japan and was employed as a training craft after being examined by Japanese engineers.

10 Small and Midget Submarines

Several classes of small submarines constructed in Japan during World War II were assigned the HA-series designation. The HA-101 and HA-201 classes were seagoing submarines, the former small transport craft (listed in chapter 12) and the latter high-speed attack craft.

The other HA-series craft were midget submarines, intended to be carried into the forward area by fleet submarines of the C1 type and by converted seaplane carriers and special transports. Subsequently, they were also based at shore stations, and the Type 1 high-speed landing ships were configured to carry two Type C or D midgets. These were not intended as suicide craft, but were to be recovered after their attacks.

The Japanese began the development of midget submarines in the 1930s in the strictest secrecy. Two unnamed experimental models were built at the Kure Navy Yard, and after trials they were followed by the Type A production series of the same basic design. The early midgets were generally referred to as *ko-hyoteki* or "A targets" to disguise their real purpose; several other code names were also used in the interests of secrecy.

The Type 1 landing ship No. 5 carrying two midget submarines. The configuration of these ships often led to their being mistakenly identified as destroyers. Several destroyers and one cruiser were fitted to carry *kaiten*, but not midget submarines.

10 HIGH-SPEED SUBMARINES: STS TYPE

Number	Builder	Completed	Notes
HA-201	Sasebo Navy Yard	31 May 1945	scuttled
HA-202	Sasebo Navy Yard	31 May 1945	scuttled
HA-203	Sasebo Navy Yard	26 June 1945	scrapped
HA-204	Sasebo Navy Yard	25 June 1945	wrecked 29 Oct 1945
HA-205	Sasebo Navy Yard	3 July 1945	scrapped
HA-206	Kawasaki, Tanagawa	—	scuttled
HA-207	Sasebo Navy Yard	14 Aug 1945	scuttled
HA-208	Sasebo Navy Yard	4 Aug 1945	scuttled
HA-209	Sasebo Navy Yard	4 Aug 1945	target
HA-210	Sasebo Navy Yard	11 Aug 1945	scuttled
HA-211	Kawasaki, Tanagawa	—	scrapped
HA-212	Kawasaki, Kobe	—	scrapped
HA-213	Mitsubishi, Kobe	—	scrapped
HA-214	Mitsubishi, Kobe	—	scrapped
HA-215	Sasebo Navy Yard	—	scuttled
HA-216	Sasebo Navy Yard	16 Aug 1945	scuttled
HA-217	Sasebo Navy Yard	—	scuttled
HA-218	Sasebo Navy Yard	—	scrapped
HA-219	Sasebo Navy Yard	—	scuttled
HA-220	Kawasaki, Tanagawa	—	scrapped
HA-221	Kawasaki, Kobe	—	scrapped
HA-222	Kawasaki, Tanagawa	—	scrapped
HA-223	Kawasaki, Kobe	—	scrapped
HA-224	Mitsubishi, Kobe	—	scrapped
HA-225	Mitsubishi, Kobe	—	scrapped
HA-226	Mitsubishi, Kobe	—	scrapped
HA-227	Mitsubishi, Kobe	—	scrapped
HA-228	Sasebo Navy Yard	—	scuttled
HA-229	Sasebo Navy Yard	—	scrapped
HA-230	Sasebo Navy Yard	—	scrapped
HA-231	Sasebo Navy Yard	—	scrapped
HA-232	Sasebo Navy Yard	—	scrapped
HA-233	Kawasaki, Tanagawa	—	scrapped
HA-234	Kawasaki, Kobe	—	scrapped
HA-235	Kawasaki, Kenshu	—	scrapped
HA-236	Kawasaki, Kobe	—	scrapped
HA-237	Mitsubishi, Kobe	—	scrapped
HA-238	Mitsubishi, Kobe	—	scrapped
HA-239 to HA-240	Mitsubishi, Kobe	not started	
HA-241 to HA-245	Sasebo Navy Yard	not started	
HA-246	Kawasaki, Tanagawa	—	scrapped
HA-247 to HA-249	Kawasaki, Kobe	not started	
HA-250 to HA-253	Mitsubishi, Kobe	not started	
HA-254 to HA-258	Sasebo Navy Yard	not started	
HA-259 to HA-262	Kawasaki, Kobe	not started	
HA-263 to HA-266	Mitsubishi, Kobe	not started	
HA-267 to HA-271	Sasebo Navy Yard	not started	
HA-272 to HA-275	Kawasaki, Kobe	not started	
HA-276 to HA-279	Mitsubishi, Kobe	not started	

Displacement:	320 tons standard
	429 tons surfaced
	493 tons submerged
Length:	173¾ feet (53.0 m) oa
Beam:	13 feet (4.0 m)
Draft:	11¼ feet (3.4 m)
Propulsion:	1 diesel; 400 hp
	electric motor; 1,250 hp; 1 shaft
Speed:	11.8 knots surfaced
	13.9 knots submerged
Range:	3,000 n.miles at 10 knots surfaced
	100 n.miles at 2 knots submerged
Depth:	330 feet (100 m) (see notes)
Complement:	22 to 26 officers and men
Torpedo tubes:	2 21-inch (533-mm) bow
Torpedoes:	4
Guns:	1 7.7-mm MG

These were small, high-speed attack submarines intended for coastal defense of the Japanese home islands. They had a relatively high underwater speed and deep operating depth, having, like the I-201/ST class, evolved from the experimental submarine No. 71. Diving planes were fitted amidships on the hull and not on the bow. Although their range and endurance (15 days) were limited, on trials the HA-201 travelled 5,000 miles at 10 knots. Japanese naval constructors stated that a safe working depth was 500 feet.

The HA-201/STS was the largest submarine class built by Japan, with a total of 90 units being planned for construction, i.e., the above-listed ships plus ten not assigned to specific shipyards. The design period in 1944 was extremely brief. The submarines were largely fabricated with electric welding, with other mass-production techniques planned to provide a building rate of 13 submarines per month with a construction period of only three months. Snorkels were fitted to some units. The HA-201 was laid down on 1 March 1945, and a total of 22 units were launched, ten being completed.

No submarines of this class made operational patrols. The HA-201 and HA-202 were scuttled by the U.S. Navy off Goto Island on 1 April 1946; the unfinished HA-206 sank in a storm at Kobe on 25 August 1945; the HA-207, HA-210, HA-216, HA-217, HA-219, and HA-228 were scuttled by the U.S. Navy off Kongo Point on 5 April 1946; and the HA-209 was taken to the United States and expended as a target on 19 November 1945.

The HA-204 with safety railing rigged. (*Ships of the World*)

The high-speed small submarine HA-202 on sea trials in May 1945. Note the clean lines and similarity to the larger I-201 class.

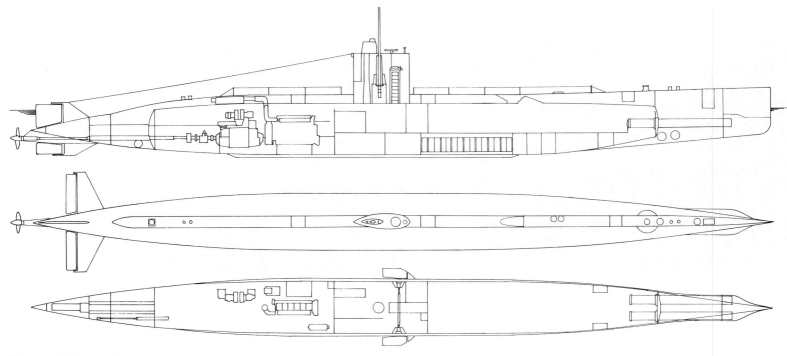

HA-201 of STS type (Drawing by Alan Raven)

62 MIDGET SUBMARINES: TYPE A

Number	Builder	Built	Notes
(2 units)	Kure Navy Yard	1934	experimental prototypes
HA-1	Kure Navy Yard	1936	experimental prototype
HA-2	Kure Navy Yard	1936	experimental prototype
HA-3 to HA-44	Ourazaki, Kure	1938−1942	
HA-46 to HA-61	Ourazaki, Kure		

Displacement:	
	46 tons submerged
Length:	78½ feet (23.9 m) oa
Diameter:	6 feet (1.8 m)
Propulsion:	electric motor; 600 hp; 1 shaft (contra-rotating propellers)
Speed:	23 knots surfaced
	19 knots submerged
Range:	80 n.miles at 6 knots surfaced
	18 n.miles at 19 knots submerged
Depth:	100 feet (30 m)
Complement:	2 men
Torpedo tubes:	2 18-inch (457-mm) bow
Torpedoes:	2

These were the world's first true midget submarines, being fitted with two torpedo tubes forward. They were intended to be carried into the forward area by specially configured submarines or surface ships, or to operate from shore bases; therefore, they had no means of recharging their electric storage batteries. Also, because generators were not fitted, the batteries could not be charged by the large submarine carrying the midget. All-welded construction. The first two units were built without conning towers; they were provided later. The original speed of those two units was 24 knots maximum *submerged*. The torpedoes were loaded through the muzzles of the tubes.

The HA-3 to HA-44 were intended to be carried by submarines and surface ships; the HA-46 to HA-61 were ordered in 1942 for coastal defense and were to operate from shore bases.

The factory at Ourazaki, Kure, was built specifically to produce midget submarines.

Losses: 5 boats lost at Pearl Harbor on 7 Dec 1941; 3 at Diego Suarez on 30 May 1942; 4 at Sydney Harbor on 31 May 1942; 8 off Guadalcanal in 1942; and 3 off the Aleutians in 1942-1943.

The Nishimura prototype midget submarine No. 2 in 1935. (Courtesy *Ships of the World*).

Stern view of the Nishimura prototype midget submarine No. 2 in August 1935. (Courtesy *Ships of the World*).

The Type A midget submarine that washed up on the eastern coast of Oahu after the attack on Pearl Harbor. Five midgets were carried to Pearl Harbor by C1-type attack submarines. The midgets scored no successes in the attack. (U.S. Navy)

A midget submarine on the deck of the landing ship No. 5. Guards are provided to protect the torpedoes from damage. This photo was taken on 17 August 1944. (K. R. MacPherson)

The Type A midget submarine HA-36 is lifted by a crane at Ourazaki, near Kure. Note the absence of bow or amidships diving planes. (K. R. MacPherson)

The conning tower of the Type A midget washed ashore on Oahu with various features identified on the photograph by U.S. Navy specialists. (U.S. Navy)

A midget submarine is launched from the landing ship No. 5. A second craft is at left. No surface ships launched midgets or *kaiten* in combat; rather, those small attack craft operated from submarines or shore bases. (Shizuo Fukui)

A Type A midget that was salvaged from Pearl Harbor. Note the contra-rotating propellers. (U.S. Navy)

A U.S. Navy diver examines the propellers of a Type A midget submarine on the bottom off Pearl Harbor. (U.S. Navy)

16 MIDGET SUBMARINES: TYPES B and C

Number	Builder	Built	Notes
HA-45	Ourazaki, Kure	1942-1943	prototype (Type B)
HA-62 to HA-76	Ourazaki, Kure	1943-1944	Type C

Displacement:	
	49¾ tons submerged
Length:	81¾ feet (24.9 m) oa
Diameter:	6 feet (1.8 m)
Propulsion:	1 diesel; 40 hp
	electric motor; 600 hp; 1 shaft (contra-rotating propellers)
Speed:	6.5 knots surfaced
	18.5 knots submerged
Range:	300 n.miles at 6 knots surfaced
	120 n.miles at 4 knots submerged
Depth:	100 feet (30 m)
Complement:	2 or 3 men
Torpedo tubes:	2 18-inch (457-mm) bow
Torpedoes:	2

These were improved midget submarines, their most significant change from the Type A being the provision of a 40-kilowatt diesel generator for charging the electric storage batteries. A full recharge of the battery, however, required 18 hours.

The HA-45 was the prototype and designated Type B, the subsequent production models being designated Type C. The HA-45 was begun in October 1942 and completed in February 1943.

Losses: 4 boats sunk off Cebu, 2 at Zamboanga, and 2 off Davo in the Philippines, all 1944-1945.

Approx. 115 MIDGET SUBMARINES: KORYU TYPE D

Number	Builder	Built	Notes
HA-77	Ourazaki, Kure	1944-1945	prototype
(39 units)	Harima, Aioi	1945	none completed
(30 units)	Hitachi, Mukajima	1945	2 completed
(47 units)	Kawasaki, Kobe	1945	none completed
(100 units)	Kure Navy Yard	1945	60 completed
(50 units)	Maizuru Navy Yard	1945	14 completed
(118 units)	Mitsubishi, Nagasaki	1945	3 completed
(12 units)	Niigata Iron Works	1945	none completed
(50 units)	Tamano Zosensho, Tamano	1945	30 completed
(50 units)	Yokosuka Navy Yard	1945	6 completed

Displacement:	
	59⅔ tons submerged
Length:	86 feet (26.2 m) oa
Beam:	6¾ feet (2.0 m)
Draft:	9½ feet (2.8 m)
Propulsion:	1 diesel; 150 hp
	electric motor; 500 hp; 1 shaft (contra-rotating propellers)
Speed:	8 knots surfaced
	16 knots submerged
Range:	1,000 n.miles at 8 knots surfaced
	125 n.miles at 25 knots submerged
Depth:	330 feet (100 m)
Complement:	5 men
Torpedo tubes:	2 18-inch (457-mm) bow
Torpedoes:	2

These were a further improvement of the midget submarine design, featuring a 100-kilowatt diesel generator resulting in a greater operating range, with a full battery self-charge possible in eight hours, or less than one-half the time required in the Type C midget. Submerged endurance was 40 minutes at 16 knots and 50 hours at 2.5 knots. Also, the crew was increased to five men.

The shortage of 18-inch torpedoes at the end of the war led to some of these craft being fitted with an explosive charge for use as a *kaiten* suicide submarine. Some Type D midgets were provided a taller conning tower and two periscopes for use in the training of *kaiten* pilots.

A total of 540 of this type were planned to be in service by September 1945, with a maximum production rate of 180 units per month through mass-production techniques. The HA-77 was laid down in June 1944 and completed in January 1945.

About eighty *Koryu* Type D midget submarines are shown in this dry dock at Kure after the end of the war. A total of 540 submarines of this type were planned, and 115 are reported to have been completed when the war ended. None saw action. (U.S. Navy)

244 MIDGET SUBMARINES: KAIRYU TYPE

Number	Builder	Built	Notes
(2 units)	Yokosuka Naval Repair School	1943-1944	experimental prototypes
(10 units)	Fujinagata, Osaka	1945	none completed
(41 units)	Hakodate Docks	1945	none completed
(10 units)	Hayashikane, Shimonoseki	1945	none completed
(5 units)	Hitachi, Innoshima	1945	none completed
(8 units)	Kasado Iron Works, Hitachi	1945	2 completed
(35 units)	Mitsubishi, Yokohama	1945	35 completed
(10 units)	Osaka Shipbuilding	1945	none completed
(4 units)	Sakurajima, Osaka	1945	none completed
(50 units)	Urago Dock, Tokyo	1945	none completed
(10 units)	Uranosaki	1945	none completed
(237 units)	Yokosuka Navy Yard	1945	207 completed

Displacement:	19¼ tons submerged
Length:	55½ feet (16.9 m) oa
Beam:	4½ feet (1.37 m) excluding amidships planes
Draft:	4½ feet (1.37 m)
Propulsion:	1 gasoline motor; 85 hp
	electric motor; 80 hp; 1 shaft (single propeller)
Speed:	7.5 knots surfaced
	10 knots submerged
Range:	450 n.miles at 5 knots surfaced
	36 n.miles at 3 knots submerged
Depth:	480 feet (146 m)
	330 feet (100 m) with torpedoes
Complement:	2 men
Torpedoes:	2 18-inch (457-mm) carried externally amidships
Warhead:	1,300 pounds without torpedoes

Two experimental prototypes based on the midget submarine Type A were built in 1943–1944, being constructed at the Yokosuka Naval Repair School. Subsequently, series production was ordered, with 20 of the early units being used for training. Small diving planes were fitted amidships instead of at the bow. An explosive warhead was to be fitted to most units because of a shortage of torpedoes.

Production began in February 1945 with the units being prefabricated in three sections and launched by crane; construction time was approximately 30 days. A total of 760 boats was planned for completion by September 1945. None undertook operational missions before the war ended; all completed units were scrapped. Listed above are the units actually assigned to shipyards for construction.

An enlarged, 40-ton version was planned but not built.

The *Kairyu* was the only midget submarine considered from the outset as a suicide weapon. Seven hundred and sixty of these submersibles were planned to help resist the Allied landings in Japan. (U.S. Navy)

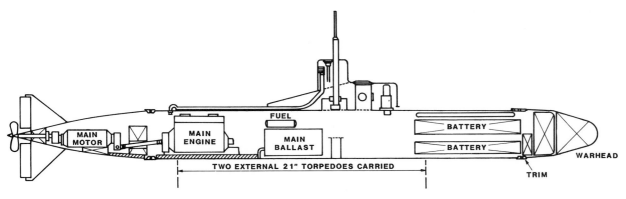

Kairyu-type submarine

A damaged *Kairyu* at a Japanese shipyard at the end of the war. The port-side amidships fin is just visible projecting from the water. (U.S. Navy)

11 Human Torpedoes

Although Britain, Germany, Italy, and Japan all made extensive use of midget submarines and manned torpedo-like craft in World War II, only Japan developed them from the outset as suicide vehicles. The *kaiten* concept was the product of the collaboration of two young naval officers, Ensign Sekio Nishina and Lieutenant (junior grade) Hiroski Kuroki. These men were pilots of midget submarines, and during the latter half of 1942 they developed plans for the one-man "human" torpedo based on the high-performance Type 93 oxygen-driven torpedo.[1]

Their plans were complete in January 1943. After extensive attempts to gain permission to do so, they were allowed to build a prototype with the understanding that a means be provided for the pilot to be ejected before the torpedo struck. In February 1944 the Naval General Staff gave permission for the *kaiten* to be developed and produced as a weapon. After the disastrous losses in the June 1944 battle of the Marianas, a high priority was given to the *kaiten* project.

To help maintain secrecy, the *kaiten* was referred to outside of a small group of officers and technicians as the "Circle Six Metal Fitting."

Kaiten could be fitted with either training/exercise warheads or explosive warheads. There were no oxygen bottles carried in Japanese submarines, hence the *kaiten* were charged at their base before being loaded on board ship. In forward areas *kaiten* on submarines sometimes had their oxygen containers charged through hoses from alongside cruisers or destroyers.

Late in the war several destroyers were modified to launch two or four *kaiten* over the stern, and the light cruiser KITAKAMI was modified in 1944 to carry eight *kaiten* on tracks that ran over the stern.

[1]Nishina was killed in a training accident, and Kuroki was lost on an operational mission.

330 KAITEN: TYPE 1

Builders:	Haikkari Navy Yard
	Kure Navy Yard
	Maizuru Navy Yard
	Sasebo Navy Yard
	Yokosuka Navy Yard
Displacement:	18⅓ tons submerged
Length:	48⅓ feet (14.7 m)
Diameter:	3¼ feet (1.0 m)
Propulsion:	oxygen + kerosene motor; 550 hp; 1 shaft
Speed/range:	12 knots for 85,300 yards
	20 knots for 47,000 yards
	30 knots for 25,100 yards
Warhead:	3,400 pounds

These were modified Type 93 torpedoes with a compartment inserted amidships for a single pilot, controls, and periscope. There was a telephone connection to the mother submarine, but no radio or sonar was provided. The *kaiten* was released from within the submarine after the pilot was given navigation information and target data.

The early submarines modified to carry *kaiten* required that some of the pilots board the craft while the submarine was on the surface; subsequently, all submarines had tubes provided through the pressure hull so that *kaiten* pilots could enter their craft through the lower hatch while the mother submarine was submerged.

Reportedly, 330 Type 1 *kaiten* were produced—100 in 1944 and 230 of the Mod 1 variant in 1945. The latter had an improved hatch closing mechanism and improved controls.

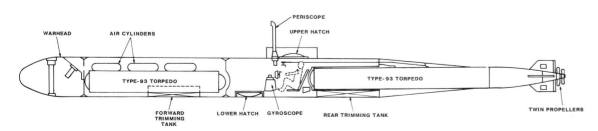

Kaiten Type 1

Few KAITEN: TYPE 2

Builders:	Hikari Navy Yard
	Kure Navy Yard
	Yokosuka Navy Yard
Displacement:	18⅓ tons submerged
Length:	54 feet (16.46 m)
Diameter:	4½ feet (1.37 m)
Propulsion:	hydrogen-peroxide + kerosene motor; 1,500 hp; 1 shaft
Speed/range:	20 knots for 90,700 yards
	30 knots for 54,600 yards
	40 knots for 27,300 yards
Warhead:	3,400 pounds

The *kaiten* Type 2 offered the promise of much higher performance than the Type 1. One or two pilots were planned for operational missions. The program was cancelled because the hydrogen-peroxide motors could not be produced in large numbers.

1 KAITEN: TYPE 3

Displacement:	18⅓ tons submerged
Length:	54 feet (16.46 m)
Diameter:	4½ feet (1.37 m)
Propulsion:	oxygen + kerosene motor; 1,800 hp; 1 shaft
Speed/range:	20 knots for 67,800 yards
	27 knots for 43,700 yards
	30 knots for 41,500 yards
Warhead:	3,400 pounds

One experimental unit of this type was built.

Approx. 50 KAITEN: TYPE 4

Displacement:	18 tons submerged
Length:	54 feet (16.46 m)
Diameter:	3½ feet (1.07 m)
Propulsion:	oxygen + kerosene motor; 1,500 hp; 1 shaft
Speed/range:	40 knots
Warhead:	3,960 pounds

This *kaiten* design provided a new all-oxygen engine and was developed because of the problems with the hydrogen-peroxide engine in the Type 2 craft. About 50 were built in 1945.

Approx. 6 KAITEN: TYPE 10

Displacement:	
Length:	approx. 30 feet (9.15 m)
Diameter:	3 feet (0.9 m)
Propulsion:	electric motor; 1 shaft
Speed/range:	7 knots for 35,000 yards
	30 knots maximum
Warhead:	660 pounds

This *kaiten* was based on surplus Type 92 torpedoes with a control section (of larger diameter) inserted amidships. Only an upper hatch was provided for the single pilot.

A *kaiten* Type 2 human torpedo on display at the Washington Navy Yard.

12 Transport Submarines

During 1942 the increasing need to supply isolated garrisons in the Pacific led the Japanese naval high command to order specialized cargo/transport submarines to replace the combat submarines being employed in that role. Although the Navy opposed diverting submarines to cargo/transport missions, operational submarines carried out numerous supply runs to bypassed troops with skill and determination. The submarines engaged in these operations were diverted from other important missions, and their losses during supply missions were considerable.

Subsequently, the Navy constructed three submarine classes specifically for the transport role—the D1 and D2 types, and the HA-101/SS type. The D type designation evolved from the large A/B/C series of the late 1930s (see chapter 8). Separate from the Navy's program to construct transport submarines, the Japanese Army built undersea craft intended for this role, as described in chapter 13.

12 TRANSPORT SUBMARINES: D1 TYPE

Number	Builder	Launched	Completed	Notes
I-361	Kure Navy Yard	1943	25 May 1944	sunk by aircraft from USS Anzio (CVE 57) 400 miles southeast of Okinawa 30 May 1945
I-362	Mitsubishi, Kobe	1943	23 May 1944	sunk by USS Fleming (DE 32) 320 miles north of Truk 18 Jan 1945
I-363	Kure Navy Yard	1944	8 July 1944	surrendered Aug 1945; sunk by mine east of Kyushu 29 Oct 1945
I-364	Mitsubishi, Kobe	1944	14 June 1944	sunk by USS Sea Devil (SS 400) 300 miles east of Yokosuka 16 Sep 1944
I-365	Yokosuka Navy Yard	1944	1 Aug 1944	sunk by USS Scabbardfish (SS 397) 75 miles southeast of Yokosuka 28 Nov 1944
I-366	Mitsubishi, Kobe	1944	3 Aug 1944	surrendered Aug 1945; scuttled off Goto Island 1 Apr 1946
I-367	Mitsubishi, Kobe	1944	15 Aug 1944	surrendered Aug 1945; scuttled off Goto Island 1 Apr 1946
I-368	Yokosuka Navy Yard	1944	25 Aug 1944	sunk by aircraft from USS Anzio (CVE 57) 35 miles west of Iwo Jima 27 Feb 1945
I-369	Yokosuka Navy Yard	1944	9 Oct 1944	surrendered Aug 1945; scrapped
I-370	Mitsubishi, Kobe	1944	4 Sep 1944	sunk by USS Finnegan (DE 307) 120 miles south of Iwo Jima 26 Feb 1945
I-371	Mitsubishi, Kobe	1944	2 Oct 1944	sunk by USS Lagarto (SS 371) in Bungo Strait 24 Feb 1945
I-372	Yokosuka Navy Yard	1944	8 Nov 1944	sunk by fast-carrier aircraft at Yokosuka 18 July 1945

Displacement:	1,440 tons standard
	1,779 tons surfaced
	2,215 tons submerged
Length:	248 feet (75.5 m) oa
Beam:	29¼ feet (8.9 m)
Draft:	15½ feet (4.7 m)
Propulsion:	2 diesels; 1,850 hp
	electric motors; 1,200 hp; 2 shafts
Speed:	13 knots surfaced
	6.5 knots submerged
Range:	15,000 n.miles at 10 knots surfaced
	120 n.miles at 3 knots submerged
Depth:	245 feet (75 m)
Complement:	75 officers and men + 110 troops
Torpedo tubes:	none (see notes)
Guns:	1 5.5-inch (140-mm)
	2 25-mm (2 single)

This class was designed from mid-1942 specifically as cargo/transport submarines. A total of 104 units were projected, but only the above-listed submarines were built. The D1/D2 types were the only Japanese Navy submarines to be built without torpedo tubes. The original design provided for two 21-inch tubes in the bow; however, after the I-361's sea trials they were removed and were not provided in later units. The 25-mm guns retracted to facilitate carrying landing craft. A snorkel was provided.

The D1 design provided for carrying 22 tons of cargo internally plus 110 troops, with two 42-foot landing craft and 60 tons of cargo carried externally on the hull casing abaft the conning tower. The cargo spaces were forward (in place of the torpedo room) and aft of the control room; the one aft of the control room had an endless chain conveyor sloping upward to the cargo hatch. The landing craft were of a special design, intended to withstand sea pressure to the submarine's operating depth. Endurance was 60 days.

The I-361 was laid down in February 1943.

Early in 1945 the I-361, I-363, I-366 to I-370, and I-372 were converted to carry five *kaiten*. The deck guns and landing craft fittings were deleted.

1 TRANSPORT SUBMARINE: D2 TYPE

Number	Builder	Launched	Completed	Notes
I-373	Yokosuka Navy Yard	1944	14 Apr 1945	sunk by USS Spikefish (SS 404) 190 miles southeast of Shanghai 14 Aug 1945
I-374	Yokosuka Navy Yard	1944	—	construction ceased when 40% complete Mar 1945; scrapped 1945
I-375	Yokosuka Navy Yard	cancelled 1945		
I-376	Yokosuka Navy Yard	cancelled 1945		
I-377	Yokosuka Navy Yard	cancelled 1945		
I-378	Yokosuka Navy Yard	cancelled 1945		

Displacement:	1,660 tons standard
	1,926 tons surfaced
	2,240 tons submerged
Length:	242¾ feet (74.0 m) oa
Beam:	29¼ feet (8.9 m)
Draft:	16½ feet (5.0 m)
Propulsion:	2 diesels; 1,750 hp
	electric motors; 1,200 hp; 2 shafts
Speed:	13 knots surfaced
	6.5 knots submerged
Range:	5,000 n.miles at 13 knots surfaced
	100 n.miles at 3 knots submerged
Depth:	330 feet (100 m)
Complement:	60 officers and men
Torpedo tubes:	none
Guns:	1 5.5-inch (140-mm)
	2 25-mm (2 single)

The D2 design was a refinement of the D1, with range reduced by the addition of internal fuel tanks that were to carry 150 tons of fuels as cargo. In addition, 110 tons of general cargo could be carried internally and on deck, with provisions for a single 42-foot landing craft on the after deck (vice two in the D1 design). The 25-mm guns could be retracted into the deck when the landing craft were on board. Endurance was 30 days. A snorkel was fitted.

The original design provided for two 3-inch mortars and seven 25-mm MG; the I-373 was completed with the armament shown above.

Only two units were laid down, the I-373 in August 1944 and the I-374 on 24 October 1944.

12 TRANSPORT SUBMARINES: SS TYPE

Number	Builder	Launched	Completed	Notes
HA-101	Kawasaki, Senshu	1944	22 Nov 1944	surrendered Aug 1945; scrapped
HA-102	Mitsubishi, Kobe	1944	6 Dec 1944	surrendered Aug 1945; scrapped
HA-103	Mitsubishi, Kobe	1944	3 Feb 1945	surrendered Aug 1945; scuttled off Goto Island 1 Apr 1946
HA-104	Kawasaki, Senshu	1944	1 Dec 1944	surrendered Aug 1945; scrapped
HA-105	Mitsubishi, Kobe	1944	19 Feb 1945	surrendered Aug 1945; scuttled off Goto Island 1 Apr 1946
HA-106	Kawasaki, Senshu	1944	15 Dec 1944	surrendered Aug 1945; scuttled off Goto Island 1 Apr 1946
HA-107	Kawasaki, Senshu	1944	7 Feb 1945	surrendered Aug 1945; scuttled off Goto Island 1 Apr 1946
HA-108	Kawasaki, Senshu	1945	6 May 1945	surrendered Aug 1945; scuttled off Goto Island 1 Apr 1946
HA-109	Mitsubishi, Kobe	1945	10 Mar 1945	surrendered Aug 1945; scuttled off Goto Island 1 Apr 1946
HA-110	Kawasaki, Senshu	12 Jan 1945	—	unfinished at end of war; hull scrapped
HA-111	Mitsubishi, Kobe	1945	13 July 1945	surrendered Aug 1945; scuttled off Goto Island 1 Apr 1946
HA-112	Mitsubishi, Kobe	15 Apr 1945	—	unfinished at end of war; hull scrapped

Displacement:	370 tons standard
	429 tons surfaced
	493 tons submerged
Length:	146 feet (44.5 m) oa
Beam:	20 feet (6.1 m)
Draft:	13 ¼ feet (4.0 m)
Propulsion:	2 diesels; 400 hp
	electric motor; 150 hp; 1 shaft
Speed:	10 knots surfaced
	5 knots submerged
Range:	4,000 n.miles at 8 knots
	3,000 n.miles at 10 knots surfaced
	120 n.miles at 3 knots submerged
Depth:	330 feet (100 m)
Complement:	21 officers and men
Torpedo tubes:	none
Guns:	1 25-mm MG

These small cargo/transport submarines were developed in reaction to the heavy losses of the larger D1 type. The SS type was designed specifically for mass production. The hull was entirely welded with modular construction permitting sections to be fabricated in shops and assembled on the slipways. The design was hastily developed and made use of existing propulsion machinery. As with the larger transport designs (D1/D2), no torpedo tubes were provided. Sixty tons of cargo could be carried. Some units were fitted with snorkel.

The HA-108 and some other units had stowage for 10 18-inch torpedoes in the superstructure and a tripod hoist fitted aft that could be used to rearm midget submarines.

The HA-101 was laid down in June 1944. Eighty-eight additional units were projected, but none was laid down as emphasis shifted to the I-201 and HA-201 attack submarine classes.

The small transport submarines HA-109 and HA-111 in Kure Harbor after the war. Submarines of this class made six supply runs during the war, four to Marcus Island, and one each to Borodino Island and Amami Oshima. All submarines returned safely to Japan. (U.S. Navy)

The HA-101, HA-102, and HA-104 awaiting their fate.

The conning tower of the HA-100 showing radar intercept antennas. (*Ships of the World*)

13　Army Submarines

During the war the Japanese Army initiated the construction of cargo/transport submarines to supply bypassed garrisons. The Army's submarine program was initiated without the knowledge of the Navy, and accordingly without Navy help.

After the war Vice Admiral Miwa, commander of the Sixth Fleet from July 1944 to May 1945, told U.S. officers that "when the Army planned building his own submarine, the Navy side opposed that plan; but the Army answered they were planning on building special submarine for supplying these islands and Army didn't want to use Navy submarine for supplying because Navy submarines had more important mission to fight with fleet, and the Navy agreed with that plan. The Navy explained to the Army that building of submarine was very difficult, and they wanted to show how to build them; but military did not want to be assisted by Navy, so military themselves built the submarines."

The Army constructed two classes of transport submarines, both designated in the YU-series, the YU indicating *yuso-tei* or transport craft. A third army submarine class was begun, but details are lacking, including whether any were actually completed.

12 TRANSPORT SUBMARINES: YU-1 CLASS

Number
YU-1 to YU-12

Builders:	Hitachi Shipbuilding
	Kasado Iron Works
	Kudamatsu
Displacement:	273 tons surfaced
	370 tons submerged
Length:	134 feet (40.85 m) oa
Beam:	13½ feet (4.1 m)
Draft:	9 feet (2.8 m)
Propulsion:	1 diesels; 360-400 hp
	electric motor; 75 hp; 1 shaft
Speed:	10 knots surfaced
	5 knots submerged
Range:	1,500 n.miles at 8 knots surfaced
Depth:	330 feet (100 m)
Complement:	13 officers and men
Torpedo tubes:	none
Guns:	1 37-mm antiaircraft

These submarines were laid down from 1943 onward at three shipyards. The YU-1 was launched 16 October 1943 (and sunk later that year). Cargo capacity was 40 tons.

Only the YU-10 and YU-12 are believed to have survived the war. They sank at Kuchinotsu after the war and were refloated and scrapped.

A YU-1 type supply submarine.

The Japanese Army submarine YU-1 at Lingayen Gulf in the Philippines being examined by U.S. officers in February 1945. (U.S. Navy)

A YU-1 type supply submarine. The design was kept simple to facilitate rapid construction.

Another view of the Army's YU-1, launched in October 1943 and sunk before the end of the year. There are no surviving records of the fate of this class except for the two surrendered units, the YU-10 and YU-12.

14 TRANSPORT SUBMARINES: YU-1001 CLASS

Number

YU-1001 to YU-1014

Builders:	Chosen Machine, Jinsen (Korea)
Displacement:	392 tons surfaced
Length:	160¾ feet (49.0 m) oa
Beam:	16½ feet (5.0 m)
Draft:	8½ feet (2.6 m)
Propulsion:	2 diesels; 700 hp
	electric motor; 2 shafts
Speed:	12 knots surfaced
	5 knots submerged
Range:	1,500 n.miles at 8 knots surfaced

Depth:	
Complement:	
Torpedo tubes:	none
Guns:	1 37-mm antiaircraft

These submarines were laid down from 1944 onward. The only major difference from the YU-1 class was the installation of a more powerful diesel engine. Cargo capacity and most other characteristics remained the same. The YU-1001 was launched in November 1944 and completed in March 1945.

The YU-1007, YU-1011, YU-1013, and YU-1014 were at Mikuriya in Nagasaki Prefect when the war ended. They were subsequently sunk in a storm but later refloated and scrapped. Most, if not all, others of this class were war losses, although details are not available.

The YU-1001 supply submarine. Note the 37-mm gun forward of the conning tower.

TRANSPORT SUBMARINES: YU-2001 CLASS

Number

YU-2001 . . .

Builders:	Ando Iron Works, Tokyo
Displacement:	392 tons surfaced
Length:	160¾ feet (49.0 m) oa
Beam:	
Draft:	
Propulsion:	2 diesels; 700 hp
	electric motors; 2 shafts

Speed:	12 knots surfaced
	5 knots submerged
Range:	
Depth:	
Complement:	
Torpedo tubes:	none
Guns:	none

These were improved transport submarines, with the YU-2001 laid down in 1945. Cargo capacity was 40 tons.

It is not known if any of these submarines were completed.

The YU-2001 was undergoing trials when the war ended.

14　Submarine Carriers and Tenders

The Japanese Navy, like several other navies, operated several submarine tenders or depot ships. These consisted of former merchant ships and built-for-the purpose ships. The purpose-built tenders were intended to operate in forward areas behind the battle fleet and thus had relatively heavy gun batteries and high speeds.

During the early stages of World War II, three seaplane carrier-tenders were converted to submarine carriers. The CHIYODA carried eight Type A midget submarines in the Battle of Midway, those craft intended to be based ashore for coastal defense after Japanese troops had secured the island. (The NISSHIN carried five motor torpedo boats in the Midway operation.)

The design and speed of Japanese submarine tenders and seaplane tenders permitted them to be rapidly converted to light aircraft carriers. The conversion of several submarine tenders to carriers, as well as the expansion of the size and operational area of the submarine fleet, required the acquisition of several merchant ships for use as submarine tenders.

2 SUBMARINE CARRIERS: "CHIYODA" CLASS

Name	Builder	Laid Down	Launched	Completed	Notes
CHITOSE	Kure Navy Yard	26 Nov 1934	29 Nov 1936	25 July 1938	converted to light aircraft carrier 1943–1944
CHIYODA	Kure Navy Yard	14 Dec 1936	19 Nov 1937	15 Dec 1938	converted to light aircraft carrier 1942–1943

Displacement:	11,023 tons
Length:	631½ feet (192.5 m) oa
Beam:	68¼ feet (20.8 m)
Draft:	24½ feet (7.47 m)
Propulsion:	2 geared turbines (44,000 shp) + diesels (12,800 hp) = 56,800 hp; 2 shafts
Speed:	29 knots
Complement:	
Guns:	4 5-inch (127-mm) dual-purpose (2 twin)
	12 25-mm MG
Aircraft:	24 floatplanes or 12 floatplanes + 12 midget submarines

These were the first ships designed by the Japanese Navy specifically for the role of seaplane carriers. In 1939 the CHITOSE was used in launching experiments with prototype midget submarines. Early in 1941 the CHIYODA was modified to carry midget submarines, her stern being cut open for the launching and recovery of the submarines (large steel doors were fitted). Submarine support equipment was added, and the submarines were handled internally on rails. The CHITOSE was similarly modified from July 1941.

With these changes, up to 12 midgets could be embarked. The midgets could be launched from the stern, two at a time, in 17 minutes while the ships were underway.

After the aircraft carrier losses of 1942, the decision was made to convert both ships to light carriers; the CHIYODA began conversion in December 1942 and the CHITOSE in January 1943. They retained their original names. Both carriers were sunk during the war.

The seaplane tender CHIYODA. She subsequently was modified to carry midget submarines. Like her sister ship CHITOSE, she was later converted to a light aircraft carrier and, subsequently, sunk by U.S. carrier planes in October 1944.

1 SUBMARINE CARRIER: "NISSHIN"

Name	Builder	Laid Down	Launched	Completed	Notes
NISSHIN	Kure Navy Yard	Nov 1938	30 Nov 1942	27 Feb 1942	sunk by U.S. land-based aircraft in Solomons 22 July 1943

Displacement: 11,317 tons standard
                 12,500 tons full load
Length: 631½ feet (192.5 m) oa
Beam: 64½ feet (19.7 m)
Draft: 23 feet (7.0 m)
Propulsion: 6 geared diesels; 47,000 hp; 2 shafts
Speed: 28 knots
Complement:
Guns: 6 5.5-inch (140-mm) (3 twin)
                 12 25-mm MG (4 triple)
Aircraft: 12 floatplanes + 12 midget submarines

The NISSHIN was built as a combination seaplane tender (carrying 12 to 20 floatplanes) and minelayer (700 mines). She was modified to handle midget submarines in 1942. In the latter configuration she retained an open deck with two catapults and cranes aft; the 5.5-inch twin mounts were all fitted forward of the bridge structure.

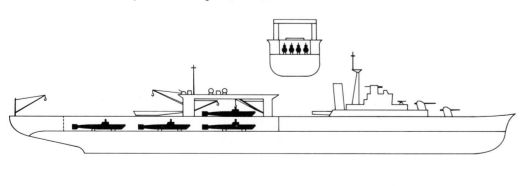

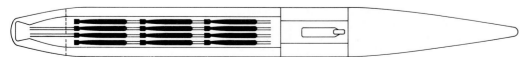

Midget submarine carrier NISSHIN.

1 SUBMARINE TENDER: "KARASAKI"

Number	Builder	Built	Notes
KARASAKI	Hawthorn, Leslie, Hebburn-on-Tyne (England)	1896	scrapped 1946

Tonnage:	9,570 tons
Length:	440 feet (134.1 m) oa
Beam:	49¾ feet (15.2 m)
Draft:	17¼ feet (5.26 m)
Propulsion:	reciprocating engines; 3,200 hp; 1 shaft
Speed:	12.5 knots

Complement:	
Guns:	1 3-inch (76-mm)
	1 3-inch (76-mm) antiaircraft
	1 3-pounder

The former Russian steamship EKATERINOSLAV, this ship was captured in 1904. She was renamed and served in several roles, including that of a submarine tender. In 1919 she escorted the former German U-boats being transferred to Japan from Europe. Her late 1930's armament is listed above.

1 SUBMARINE TENDER: "KOMAHASHI"

Name	Builder	Laid Down	Launched	Completed	Notes
KOMAHASHI	Sasebo Navy Yard	7 Oct 1912	21 May 1913	20 Jan 1914	sunk by U.S. carrier aircraft at Ise Bay, Honshu, 28 July 1945; refloated and scrapped

Displacement:	1,125 tons standard
Length:	227 feet (69.2 m) oa
Beam:	35 feet (7.6 m)
Draft:	17¾ feet (5.4 m)
Propulsion:	2 geared diesels; 1,200 hp; 2 shafts
Speed:	13.75 knots
Complement:	
Guns:	2 3-inch (76-mm) (2 single)
	1 3-inch (76-mm) antiaircraft

The small KOMAHASHI was built specifically as a submarine tender, the first ship built for that purpose in the Japanese Navy and probably the first of any navy. She served as a submarine tender until about 1920, when she became a base ship, being additionally employed as a survey ship. From 1926 the KOMAHASHI was used exclusively for surveying duty.

In 1933 her original steam reciprocating propulsion plant was replaced by two diesels.

She continued in the survey ship role, although officially classified as a submarine tender, until late 1944 when she again became a tender to midget submarines at Owari Bay (later Ise Bay) on the southern coast of Honshu.

Her 1930's armament is shown above.

The submarine tender KOMAHASHI shortly after her 1933 conversion to diesel propulsion. (Shizuo Fukui)

2 SUBMARINE TENDERS: "JINGEI" CLASS

Name	Builder	Laid Down	Launched	Completed	Notes
JINGEI	Mitsubishi, Nagasaki	16 Feb 1922	4 May 1923	30 Aug 1923	sunk by U.S. Navy carrier planes 30 miles north of Okinawa 10 Oct 1944
CHOGEI	Mitsubishi, Nagasaki	11 Mar 1922	24 Mar 1924	2 Aug 1924	surrendered Aug 1945; scrapped 1946

Displacement:	6,600 tons standard
Length:	426⅓ feet (130.0 m) oa
Beam:	56⅓ feet (17.2 m)
Draft:	21½ feet (6.5 m)
Propulsion:	2 geared turbines; 6,200 shp; 2 shafts
Speed:	18 knots
Complement:	
Guns:	4 5.5-inch (140-mm) (2 twin)
	2 3-inch (76-mm) antiaircraft (2 single)
Aircraft:	1 floatplane

These ships carried spare parts, torpedoes, and provisions for submarines, and had accommodations for submarine crewmen. They often served as flagships for submarine squadrons.

In 1944 the 3-inch guns were removed and 18 25-mm guns were installed.

The CHOGEI, which, like other large tenders, served as a submarine squadron flagship. (*Maru Magazine*)

The JINGEI.

The submarine tender JINGEI with five L4-type submarines in September 1929; from left are the RO-66, RO-67, RO-65, RO-62, and RO-61. (K. R. MacPherson)

1 SUBMARINE TENDER: "TAIGEI"

Name	Builder	Laid Down	Launched	Completed	Notes
TAIGEI	Yokosuka Navy Yard	12 Apr 1933	16 Nov 1933	31 Mar 1934	converted to light aircraft carrier RYUHO 1941–1942

Displacement:	10,000
Length:	707⅓ feet (215.5 m) oa
Beam:	59½ feet (18.1 m)
Draft:	17½ feet (5.33 m)
Propulsion:	4 geared diesels; 14,000 hp; 2 shafts
Speed:	20 knots
Complement:	400+ officers and men + 400 submarine crewmen
Guns:	4 5-inch (127-m) dual-purpose (2 twin)
	12 13-mm MG
Aircraft:	3 floatplanes

The TAIGEI was also built specifically to serve as a submarine tender. Upon completion she was top-heavy and rolled badly; in 1936–1937 she was modified to improve her stability.

In December 1941 she entered the yard for conversion to a light carrier and was renamed RYUHO; she was sunk during the war.

The submarine tender TAIGEI in 1938 after being extensively modified to improve her stability. She was subsequently converted to a light aircraft carrier. (*Maru Magazine*)

2 SUBMARINE TENDERS: "TSURUGIZAKI" CLASS

Name	Builder	Laid Down	Launched	Completed	Notes
TSURUGIZAKI	Yokosuka Navy Yard	3 Dec 1934	1 June 1935	15 Jan 1939	converted to light aircraft carrier SHOHO in 1941–1942
TAKASAKI	Yokosuka Navy Yard	20 June 1935	19 June 1936	—	completed as light aircraft carrier ZUIHO in 1941

Displacement:	9,500 tons
Length:	712 feet (227.0 m) oa
Beam:	59½ feet (18.1 m)
Draft:	22 feet (6.7 m)
Propulsion:	8 geared diesels; 56,000 hp; 2 shafts
Speed:	29 knots
Complement:	
Guns:	4 5-inch (127-mm) dual-purpose (2 twin)
	12 13-mm MG
Aircraft:	3 floatplanes

These were large submarine tenders, with one completed as an aircraft carrier and the other converted to a carrier beginning in January 1941. Both were sunk during the war.

Two additional ships of this class were cancelled in 1942, and three submarine tenders of a newer design were cancelled in 1943.

The submarine tender TSURUGIZAKI, also converted to a light aircraft carrier. (*Maru Magazine*)

2 SUBMARINE TENDERS: CONVERTED MERCHANT SHIPS

Number	Builder	Built	Notes
HEIAN MARU	Osaka Iron Works	1930	sunk by U.S. carrier aircraft at Truk 17 Feb 1944
HEI MARU	Yokohama Docks	1930	reclassified as transport Oct 1943 (subsequently sunk)

Tonnage:	HEIAN MARU 11,616 tons
	HEI MARU 12,000 tons
Length:	511½ feet (155.9 m) oa
Beam:	66 feet (20.1 m)
Draft:	
Propulsion:	
Speed:	17 knots
Guns:	2 4.7-inch (120-mm) (2 single)
	several MG

Seven merchant ships were converted to submarine tenders during World War II. Only limited data are available.

1 SUBMARINE TENDER: CONVERTED MERCHANT SHIP

Number	Builder	Built	Notes
NACHI MARU	Mitsubishi, Kobe	1926	surrendered Aug 1945

Tonnage:	1,605 tons
Length:	
Beam:	
Draft:	
Propulsion:	
Speed:	13.5 knots
Guns:	2 4.7-inch (120-mm) (2 single)
	several MG

Requisitioned by the Navy in 1943. Designated as submarine tender on 20 January 1945. Returned to commercial service after the war.

1 SUBMARINE TENDER: CONVERTED MERCHANT SHIP

Number	Builder	Built	Notes
NAGOYA MARU	Mitsubishi, Nagasaki	1932	reclassified as transport Apr 1942

Tonnage:	6,071 tons
Length:	406¾ feet (124.0 m) oa
Beam:	55½ feet (16.9 m)
Draft:	32½ feet (9.9 m)
Propulsion:	
Speed:	16 knots
Guns:	several MG

1 SUBMARINE TENDER: CONVERTED MERCHANT SHIP

Number	Builder	Built	Notes
RIO DE JANEIRO MARU	Mitsubishi, Nagasaki	1930	reclassified as transport Sep 1943

Tonnage:	9,627 tons
Length:	461¼ feet (140.6 m) oa
Beam:	62 feet (18.9 m)
Draft:	39½ feet (12.0 m)
Propulsion:	
Speed:	17 knots
Guns:	several MG

1 SUBMARINE TENDER: CONVERTED MERCHANT SHIP

Number	Builder	Built	Notes
MANJU MARU	Mitsubishi, Nagasaki	1925	reclassified as transport Mar 1943

Tonnage:	7,267 tons
Length:	430¾ feet (131.3 m) oa
Beam:	55¾ feet (17.0 m)
Draft:	36 feet (11.0 m)
Propulsion:	
Speed:	15.75 knots
Guns:	several MG

The ship was originally named SANTO MARU; renamed in 1941.

1 SUBMARINE TENDER: CONVERTED MERCHANT SHIP

Number	Builder	Built	Notes
TSUKUSHI MARU	Kawasaki, Kobe	1941	reclassified as transport Jan 1945

Tonnage:	8,135 tons
Length:	
Beam:	
Draft:	
Propulsion:	
Speed:	17 knots
Guns:	2 5-inch (127-mm) (2 single)
	several MG

1 SUBMARINE TENDER: CONVERTED MERCHANT SHIP

Number	Builder	Built	Notes
YASUKUNI MARU	Mitsubishi, Nagasaki	1930	sunk by USS TRIGGER (SS 237) northwest of Truk 31 Jan 1944

Tonnage:	11,930 tons
Length:	505 feet (153.96 m) oa
Beam:	64 feet (19.5 m)
Draft:	37 feet (11.28 m)
Propulsion:	
Speed:	17.5 knots
Guns:	2 4.7-inch (120-mm) (2 single)
	several MG

The seaplane tender/submarine carrier CHITOSE in July 1938 while still exclusively a seaplane tender. The light platform amidships supported derricks for lifting seaplanes. In this view there is a pair of floatplanes aft, and the 5-inch guns, behind open shields, are trained to starboard. (Imperial War Museum)

15 Submarine Construction and Losses

The following tables provide a month-by-month tabulation of the submarines placed in commission and lost by the Japanese Navy during World War II. Accounts of Japanese submarine losses vary even within official sources, and in several cases the exact date of loss is unknown.

In addition, several Japanese submarines of older types were fully or partially retired during the war. The I-33 was sunk in September 1942 by air attack, salvaged, and lost operationally in June 1944. She is counted *twice* in the loss totals.

| | SUBMARINES COMMISSIONED | SUBMARINES LOST | | | | | | | | TOTAL LOSSES |
		Land-based aircraft	Carrier-based aircraft	Land-based aircraft and surface ships	Carrier-based aircraft and surface ships	Surface ships	Submarines	Mines	Operational losses	
1941 Dec	(none)		I-70						RO-60, RO-66	3
1942 Jan	(none)					I-124, I-60, I-23	I-73			4
Feb	I-27, I-28, I-29, I-30									0
Mar	(none)									0
Apr	I-32									0
May	I-11, I-31						I-164, I-28			2
June	I-33									0
July	(none)									0
Aug	I-34, I-35, I-176			RO-61		I-123, RO-33				3
Sep	I-36, RO-100	I-33								1
Oct	RO-101, RO-103					I-22		I-30		2
Nov	RO-102	RO-65				I-172, I-15				3
Dec	I-177, I-178, RO-106, RO-107					I-3	I-4			2

SUBMARINES COMMISSIONED	SUBMARINES LOST								TOTAL LOSSES
	Land-based aircraft	Carrier-based aircraft	Land-based aircraft and surface ships	Carrier-based aircraft and surface ships	Surface ships	Submarines	Mines	Operational losses	
1943									
Jan I-38, I-180					I-1c				1
Feb RO-104				I-18d					1
Mar I-37, RO-35, RO-105, RO-109									0
Apr I-39, RO-108					RO-34				1
May I-181, I-182 RO-36					I-31, I-178, RO-102				3
June I-179, RO-37					I-9, I-24				2
July I-40, RO-38, RO-110, RO-111, RO-500a					I-7c, RO-107	I-168		RO-103 I-179	5
Aug RO-42			I-17		RO-35				2
Sep I-41, I-185, RO-39, RO-40, RO-44, RO-112			RO-101		I-25, I-182				3
Oct I-183, I-184, RO-113	I-19							I-20	2
Nov I-42, I-43, RO-41, RO-114, RO-115		I-21			I-35, I-39, I-40, RO-38	I-34	RO-100		7
Dec I-45, I-52, RO-43									0
1944									
Jan I-44, RO-45, RO-47, RO-116, RO-117					I-181, RO-37			I-11	3
Feb I-46, I-53, RO-46, RO-501a					I-171, I-175, I-27, RO-110, RO-39, RO-40	I-43			7
Mar I-54, RO-48					I-32	I-42			2
Apr I-12, I-55					I-2, I-180	I-183		I-169, I-174	5
May RO-49, I-361, I-362				RO-45	I-16, I-176, RO-104, RO-105, RO-106, RO-108, RO-116, RO-501				9
June I-56, I-364	RO-117	I-184, I-52			I-185, RO-111, RO-114, RO-36, RO-42, RO-44			I-33	10
July I-47, RO-50, I-363					I-5, I-6, I-10, I-55, RO-48	I-166, I-29			7
Aug I-365, I-366, I-367, I-368									0
Sep I-48, I-58, RO-55, I-370					RO-47	I-364			2
Oct I-369, I-371					I-177, I-45, I-46, I-54, I-26				5
Nov RO-56, I-372, HA-101				I-41	I-37, I-38	I-365			4
Dec I-13, I-400, HA-102, HA-104, HA-106									0

| | | SUBMARINES LOST | | | | | | | |
SUBMARINES COMMISSIONED	Land-based aircraft	Carrier-based aircraft	Land-based aircraft and surface ships	Carrier-based aircraft and surface ships	Surface ships	Submarines	Mines	Operational losses	TOTAL LOSSES
1945 Jan I-351, I-401					I-48, I-362, RO-115			I-12	4
Feb I-201, I-202, HA-103, HA-105, HA-107		I-368, RO-43			I-370, RO-55	I-371, RO-112, RO-113			7
Mar I-14, HA-109					I-8, RO-41				2
Apr I-373		I-44		I-56	RO-109, RO-49, RO-56	RO-46	RO-64		7
May I-203, (I-501)[a], (I-502)[a], (I-503)[b], (I-504)[b], (I-505)[a], (I-506)[a], HA-108		I-361							1
June (none)	I-165, (I-352)[e], (I-204)[e]			I-63		I-122			2 + 2
July I-402, HA-111		(I-404)[e], I-372		I-13		I-351			3 + 1
Aug (none)						I-373			1
111[f]	5 + 7[e]	9 + 1[e]	3	5	73	20	4	9	128 + 3

NOTES
[a]Ex-German submarine.
[b]Ex-Italian submarine.
[c]Scuttled after being damaged by surface ships.
[d]Aircraft from U.S. light cruiser.
[e]Incomplete when sunk.
[f]Plus six ex-German and ex-Italian submarines taken over in May 1945.

The end of the Imperial Japanese Navy's submarine force was marked by black surrender flags flown from surfaced, unarmed submarines heading for port in August 1945. This view, taken from the after gun deck of the giant I-400, shows the black flag flying above various antennas and frustrated officers. (U.S. Navy)

16 Submarine Torpedoes

Japanese torpedoes of the World War II era had the longest ranges, the highest speeds, and the largest warheads of any naval torpedoes. Further, Japanese submarine torpedoes did not have the exploder problems that plagued U.S., British, and German torpedoes during the war.

The best-known and most potent Japanese torpedo was the *surface-launched* Type 93 Long Lance. This was an oxygen-propelled weapon with a 24-inch diameter carrying a warhead of 1,078 pounds of high explosive. The Type 93 could travel 22,000 yards at a speed of 49 knots or 44,000 yards at 36 knots. In contrast, the most-capable U.S. destroyer torpedo of the war was the Mark 15, a 21-inch-diameter weapon with an 825-pound warhead. At 45 knots it could run 6,000 yards, and at 26.5 knots its range was out to 15,000 yards. (The large size and high performance of the Type 93 made it readily adaptable for the *kaiten* human torpedo.)

The standard U.S. submarine torpedo in World War II was the Mark 14, which was in development from 1931 and entered service in 1938. The Mark 14 was a 21-inch torpedo with a 643-pound warhead; maximum speed was 46.3 knots for 4,500 yards, and its low speed was 31.1 knots for 9,000 yards. These characteristics were inferior to the standard Japanese submarine torpedoes of the war, as described below.

All Japanese torpedoes had warheads comprised of 60 percent trinitrotoluene and 40 percent hexanitrodiphenylamine.

Most Japanese torpedoes were designated by the year of development. The year was based on the beginning of the Japanese Empire founded by Jimmu in 660 B.C.E. Thus, the Type 93 was based on the Japanese calendar year 2593, corresponding with the Western calendar year 1933.

TYPE 6

This torpedo was designed in 1917; it was used by submarines of the RO-60 class during World War II.

Diameter:	21-inch
In service:	1918–1933 except for the RO-60 class
Propulsion:	air-kerosene (radial engine)
Speed/range:	36 knots for 7,660 yards
	32 knots for 11,000 yards
	26 knots for 16,400 yards
Warhead:	484 pounds

TYPE 89

This torpedo was developed in 1929 and was in use by Japanese submarines until the end of 1942.

Diameter:	21-inch
In service:	1931–1942
Propulsion:	air-kerosene (reciprocating engine)
Speed/range:	45 knots for 6,000 yards
	43 knots for 6,500 yards
	35 knots for 11,000 yards
Warhead:	660 pounds

TYPE 92

This torpedo was a complement to the oxygen-propelled Type 95 series. Late in the war, surplus Type 92 torpedoes were converted to Type 10 *kaiten*. Research was carried out on an acoustic homing version of the Type 92, but it never entered service. This version was fitted with two hydrophones and a guidance package to home on warship propeller noises.

Diameter:	21-inch
In service:	1940–1945
Propulsion:	Electric
Speed/range:	28–30 knots for 7,500 yards
Warhead:	660 pounds

TYPE 92 MOD 1

This modification of the Type 92 was developed in 1934 and entered service in 1942. Although its performance was low compared to the Type 95, it was easily produced.

Diameter:	21-inch
In service:	1942–1945
Propulsion:	Electric
Speed/range:	28–30 knots for 7,660 yards
Warhead:	660 pounds

TYPE 92 MOD 2

This torpedo was designed in 1942 based on a German torpedo design. In 1942 the Germans transferred ten torpedoes and drawings to Japan.

The torpedo room of the C3-type submarine I-53. Japanese Type 93 surface-ship torpedoes and Type 95 submarine torpedoes were the most capable available to any navy at the start of World War II.

TYPE 95 MOD 1

The Japanese Navy looked into the possiblity of oxygen-propelled torpedoes in 1917, but that effort soon ceased. Research was started again in 1928, and the 24-inch Type 93 torpedo was designed in 1933. The submarine-launched Type 95, based on the same principles as the Type 93, was developed in 1935. The Type 95 torpedoes were manufactured at the Hikari and Kawatana Naval Arsenals, and by the commercial firm of Nagasaki Heiki Co.

Diameter:	21-inch
In service:	1939–1944
Propulsion:	oxygen + kerosene
Speed/range:	49 knots for 9,840 yards
	45 knots for 13,000 yards
Warhead:	891 pounds

TYPE 95 MOD 2

Problems with the pressurization of the oxygen container vessels in the Type 95 Mod 1 led to design of the Mod 2 in 1943.

Diameter:	21-inch
In service:	1944–1945
Propulsion:	oxygen + kerosene
Speed/range:	49 knots for 6,000 yards
	45 knots for 8,200 yards
Warhead:	1,210 pounds

TYPE 96

Because of the problems with the Type 95 Mod 1 torpedo, this weapon was developed in 1942 (before the Type 95 Mod 2). The fuel was only 38 percent oxygen vice 100 percent in the Type 95. About 300 Type 96 torpedoes were in service for one year from 1942 to 1943 before being succeeded in service by the Type 95 Mod 2.

Diameter:	21-inch
In service:	1942–1944
Propulsion:	oxygen + kerosene
Speed/range:	48 knots for 4,900 yards
Warhead:	891 pounds

TYPE 97

This torpedo was developed in 1937 for use by midget submarines. This torpedo and the similar Type 98 were manufactured by the Kure Naval Arsenal.

Diameter:	18-inch
In service:	1939–1942
Propulsion:	oxygen + kerosene
Speed/range:	45 knots for 6,000 yards
Warhead:	770 pounds

TYPE 98

Also referred to as the Type 97 (Special), this torpedo was developed in 1942 because of problems with the Type 97 and was in service from 1942 to 1944. It used 38 percent oxygen.

TYPE 02

This torpedo was developed for midget submarines, being a modified Type 91 Mod 3 aircraft torpedo. It was designed in 1942 and produced from 1944 onward. Manufactured by the Kure, Maizuru, and Yokosuka Naval Arsenals.

Diameter:	18-inch
In service:	1944–1945
Propulsion:	air + kerosene
Speed/range:	39 knots for 3,300 yards
Warhead:	770 pounds

TYPE 02 (SPECIAL)

This was similar to the Type 91, designed in 1944 to supplement the Type 02 torpedo.

Diameter:	18-inch
In service:	
Propulsion:	air
Speed/range:	39 knots for 2,190 yards
Warhead:	770 pounds

Bibliography

OFFICIAL HISTORIES AND REPORTS

Hinsley, F.H., E.E. Thomas, C.F.G. Ransom, and R.C. Knight. *British Intelligence in the Second World War.* Vol. 3, Part 1. London: Her Majesty's Stationery Office, 1984.

H.M. Government, Admiralty, Historical Section. *Submarines* (3 vols.). London: 1955.

Roskill, S.W. *The War at Sea 1939–1945* (3 vols.). London: Her Majesty's Stationery Office, 1954–1961.

U.S. Army, Forces Far East Command, Headquarters, Military History Section. *Japanese Monograph* series. The following are among the large number of reports that were written by former Japanese military officers:

No. 102 Submarine Operations in First Phase (Dec 1941–Apr 1942)
No. 110 Submarine Operations in Second Phase (Part 1)
No. 111 (Part 2)
No. 163 Submarine Operations in Third Phase (Parts 1–5)
No. 171 (Part 2)
No. 184 (Parts 3 to 5)
No. 145 Outline of Naval Armament and Preparations for War
No. 105 General Summary of Naval Operations, Southern Force
No. 145 Outline of Naval Armament and Preparations for War (Part I), No. 149 (Part II), No. 160 (Part III), No. 169 (Part IV), No. 172 (Part V), No. 174 (Part VI).

———. *The Imperial Japanese Navy in World War II.* February 1952. This report provides details of the organization and losses of the Japanese Navy in World War II.

U.S. Naval Technical Mission to Japan. The following are among the large number of reports prepared by U.S. and Royal Navy officers interrogating Japanese officers and examining Japanese equipment:

No. E-01 Electronic Targets, Japanese Submarine and Shipborne Radar, December 1945
No. E-17 Japanese Radio, Radar, and Sonar Equipment, February 1946
No. O-01-1 Ordnance Targets, Japanese Torpedoes and Tubes, Ship and Kaiten Torpedoes, April 1946
No. O-05 Ordnance Targets, Japanese Naval Mine Organization and Operational Techniques, January 1946
No. S-01-1 Ship and Related Targets, Characteristics of Japanese Naval Vessels, Submarines, January 1946
No. S-01-6 Ship and Related Targets, Characteristics of Japanese Naval Vessels, Submarines, Supplement I, January 1946
No. S-01-7 Ship and Related Targets, Characteristics of Japanese Naval Vessels, Submarines, Supplement II, January 1946
No. S-02 Ship and Related Targets, Japanese Suicide Craft, January 1946
No. S-17 Ship and Related Targets, Japanese Submarine Operations, February 1946

U.S. Navy, Battle Damage Reports of various ships.

U.S. Navy, Naval Historical Center, various official ships histories for U.S. vessels mentioned in the text.

U.S. Strategic Bombing Survey (Pacific Division). *Interrogations of Japanese Officials,* vol. II. [1946]; Interrogation of Vice Adm. Shigeyoshi Miwa on 10 October 1945, pp. 291–298. Adm. Miwa was commander of the 3rd Submarine Squadron when the war began and the commander of the Sixth Fleet from July 1944 to May 1945.

———. *Japanese Naval Shipbuilding.* 15 November 1946.

BOOKS

Aireview. *General View of Japanese Military Aircraft in the Pacific War.* Tokyo: Kanto-sha Co., 1956.

Busch, Harald. *U-Boats at War.* New York: Ballantine Books, 1955.

Cocchia, Aldo. *The Hunters and the Hunted.* Annapolis, Md.: U.S. Naval Institute, 1958. An account of Italian submarine operations in World War II.

Compton-Hall, Richard. *Submarine Warfare—Monsters & Midgets.* Poole, Dorset: Blandford Press, 1985. Technical and operational history of some of the more unusual Japanese submarines.

Francillon, R.J. *Japanese Aircraft of the Pacific War.* London: Putnam & Company, 1970.

Fukui, Shizuo. *Japanese Naval Vessels at the End of War.* Tokyo: Second Demobilization Bureau, 25 April 1947. An account of the Japanese naval ships surviving World War II by a distinguished naval constructor.

Hashimoto, Mochitsura. *Sunk!* New York: Henry Holt and Company, 1954. Commander Hashimoto commanded the submarine I-58, which sank the U.S. cruiser INDIANAPOLIS at the end of World War II.

Holmes, W.J. *Double-Edged Secrets.* Annapolis, Md.: Naval Institute Press, 1979. Captain Holmes was a principal member of the U.S.

Navy's code-breaking efforts in World War II, which are examined in this volume, including the impact on submarine warfare in the Pacific.

———. *Undersea Victory.* Garden City, N.Y.: Doubleday & Co., 1966. Subtitled "The Influence of Submarine Operations on the War in the Pacific," this is the best single-volume history of submarine activities in the Pacific, both U.S. and Japanese.

Ienaga, Saburo. *The Pacific War 1931–1945.* New York: Pantheon Books, 1978.

Ito, Masanori, with Roger Pineau. *The End of the Imperial Japanese Navy.* New York: W.W. Norton & Company, 1956. The late Mr. Ito was one of Japan's leading military journalists; Captain Pineau, a Japanese linguist, was principal assistant to historian Samuel Eliot Morison for his *History of U.S. Naval Operations in World War II.*

Jentschura, Hansgeorg, Dieter Jung, and Peter Mickel. *Warships of the Imperial Japanese Navy, 1869–1945.* Annapolis, Md.: Naval Institute Press, 1977. Translation from the original German.

Orita, Zenji, with Joseph D. Harrington. *I-Boat Captain.* Canoga Park, Calif.: Major Books, 1976. Commander Orita was executive officer of the I-15 at the time of Pearl Harbor and subsequently commanded the I-177 and I-47.

Rohwer, Jürgen. *Axis Submarine Successes 1939–1945.* Cambridge: Patrick Stephens Limited, 1983.

Roskill, Stephen. *Naval Policy Between the Wars.* Vol. I: *The Period of Anglo-American Antagonism 1919–1929.* London: Collins, 1968. Captain Roskill was the official cabinet historian for the Royal Navy in World War II.

———. *Naval Policy between the Wars.* Vol. II: *The Period of Reluctant Rearmament 1930–1939.* Annapolis, Md.: Naval Institute Press, 1976.

Society of Naval Architects of Japan. *Plans of Ships of the Imperial Japanese Navy—History of Shipbuilding in Showa Era.* Tokyo: Hara Shobo Co., 1975.

Watts, A.J. *Japanese Warships of World War II.* London: Ian Allan, 1966.

Willmott, H.P. *Empires in the Balance: Japanese and Allied Pacific Strategies to April 1942.* Annapolis, Md.: Naval Institute Press, 1982.

———. *The Barrier and the Javelin: Japanese and Allied Pacific Strategies February to June 1942.* Annapolis, Md.: Naval Institute Press, 1983.

Yokota, Yutaka. *The Kaiten Weapon.* New York: Ballantine Books, 1962. Petty officer Yokota was a *kaiten* pilot.

MAGAZINE ARTICLES*

Alden, John D. "Japanese Submarine Losses in World War II," *Warship International*, No. 1, 1985, pp. 12–31. Also, commentary on the article by Vernon J. Miller, *Warship International*, No. 3, 1985, pp. 222–23.

Fujita, Nobuo and Joseph D. Harrington. "I Bombed the U.S.A." *USNIP,* June 1961, 64–69.

Fukudome, Shigeru. "Hawaii Operation." *USNIP,* December 1955, 1314–1331.

Fukaya, Hajime, and Martin E. Holbrook. "Three Japanese Submarine Developments." *USNIP,* August 1952, 862–867.

"I-400 Class Submarines Just After War," *Ships of the World*, No. 5, 1980, pp. 58–63.

"Japanese Warships in Retrospect," *Ships of the World* [series]
    "Cruiser *Suzuya* and Some of the I-Class Submarines," No. 8, 1974, pp. 18–21.
    "Ex-German Submarines after World War I," No. 7, 1973, pp. 20–22.
    "*Jun-Sen* I Type Submarines," No. 12, 1978, pp. 24–27.
    "*Kai-Dai* III Type Submarines," No. 8, 1978, pp. 24–27.
    "*Kai-Dai* IV—VI Type Submarines," No. 11, 1978, pp. 22–25.
    "Ro-16 Class Submarines," No. 3, 1974, pp. 14–17.
    "Submarine I-30 at Lorient, August 1942," No. 4, 1985, pp. 30–31.
    "Submarines I-51 & I-52," No. 5, 1978, pp. 24–28.

Lemieux, C.P. "*L-16* Sinking—No Mistake, Just Dirty Work." *USNIP,* June 1963, 118–120.

"Nishimura Type Midget Sub No. 2, 1935," *Ships of the World*, No. 9, 1980, pp. 52–53.

Ohtake, Toshikazu, "Warship Builders in Japan—Kawasaki Heavy Industries' Kobe Works," *Ships of the World*, No. 4, 1985, pp. 140–147.

Saville, Allison W. "German Submarines in the Far East." *USNIP,* August 1961, 80–92.

Tanabe, Yahachi, and Joseph D. Harrington. "I Sank the *Yorktown* at Midway." *USNIP,* May 1963, 58–65.

Torisu, Kennosuke, and Masataka Chihaya. "Japanese Submarine Tactics." *USNIP,* February 1961, 78–83. Also see commentaries by Robert P. Harbold, Jr., and Yoya Kawamura, *USNIP,* July 1962, 118–119.

Yokota, Yutaka, and Joseph D. Harrington. "Japan's Human Torpedo." *USNIP,* January 1962, 55–68. Also see commentary by Bruce McCandless, *USNIP,* July 1962, 119–120.

*USNIP = U.S. Naval Institute *Proceedings.*

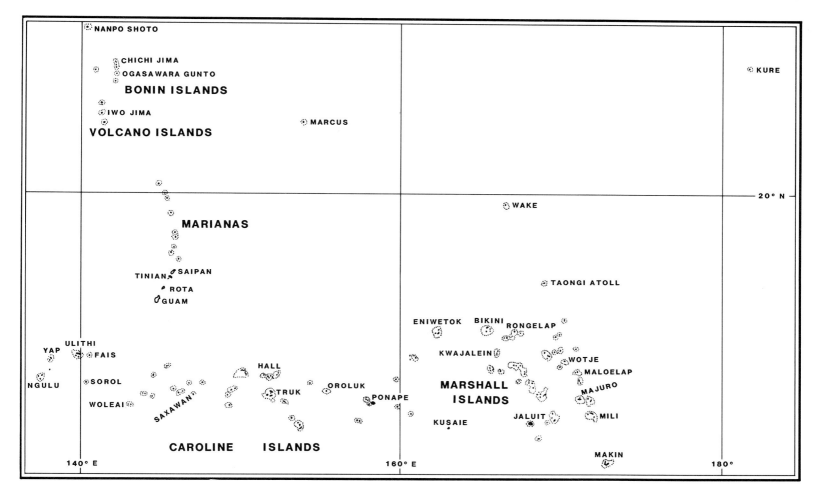

West Central Pacific

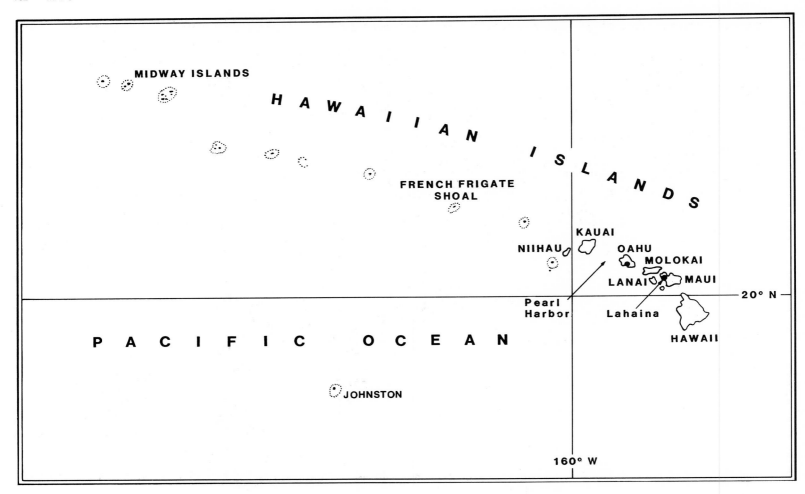

Hawaiian Islands

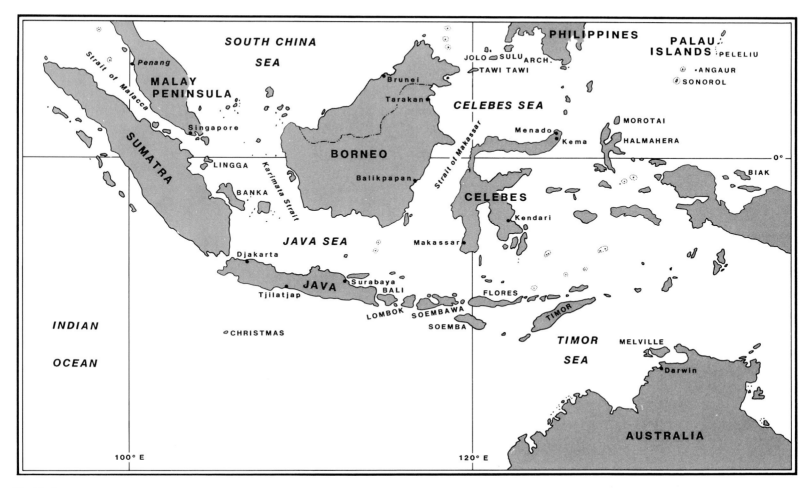

East Indies

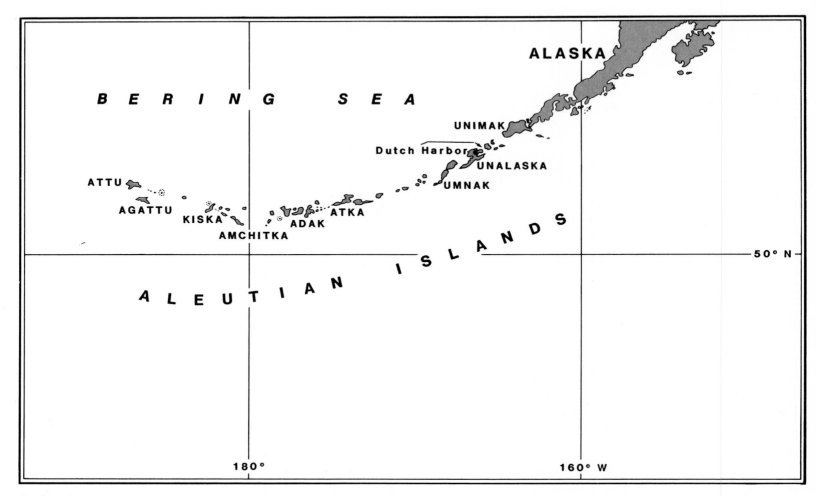

Aleutian Islands

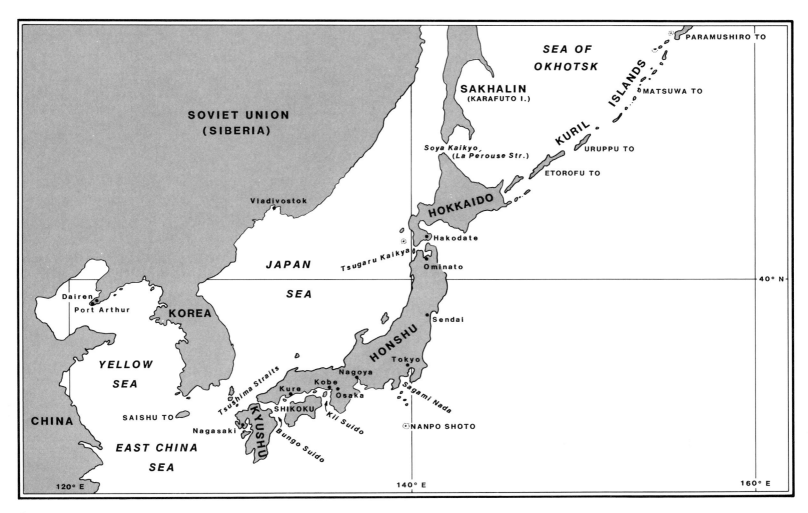

Japan

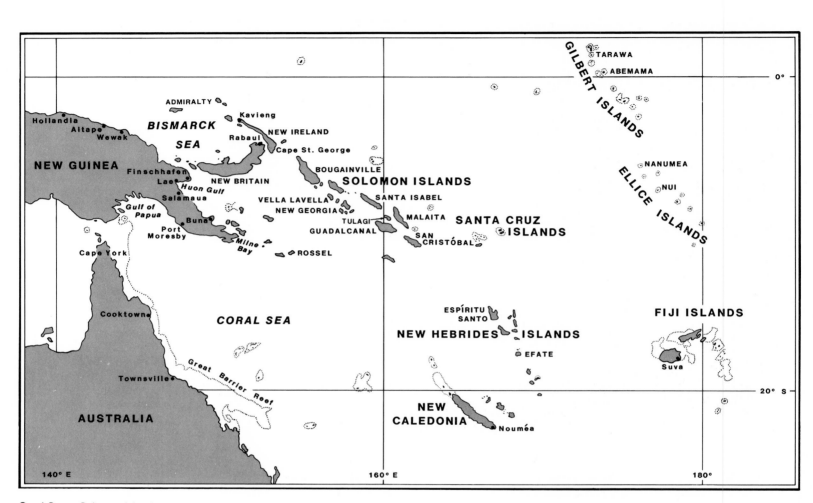

Coral Sea—Solomon Islands

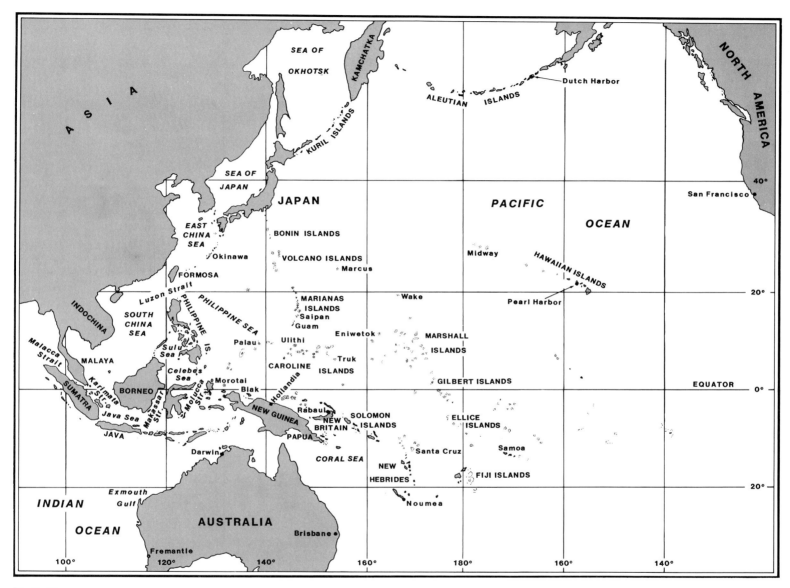

Pacific Ocean

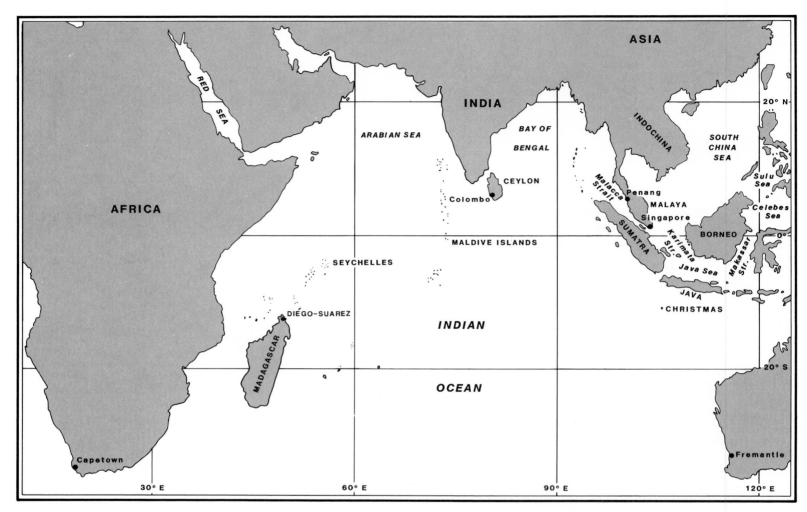

Indian Ocean

General Index

Ship Name Index

Ships in organizational tables are not indexed; see General Index for listings of midget submarines and human torpedoes (*kaiten*). Launch years are provided in parentheses for multiple submarines with the same number.
National abbreviations:

Aust. Australian
Brit. British
Fr. French
Ger. German
Ind. Indian
Neth. Netherlands
N.Z. New Zealand
Russ. Russian
Sov. Soviet
U.S. United States

Taken from the I-168, the I-169 is in the background, with the I-70 barely visible behind her. (*Ships of the World*)

The I-59 (later I-159) was one of the last submarines to depart on a war patrol in August 1945. She carried two *kaiten* human torpedoes on that mission, returning on 18 August after being at sea for two days. (Imperial War Museum)

The I-71 (later I-171) underway on the surface before World War II, showing the streamlined hull, radio aerials rigged aft, and small upper rudder. Sailors are on deck next to the conning tower, almost obscuring the deck gun. (Ted Stone from the James C. Fahey Collection)

The end of the Japanese submarine force: The I-14 (left) and I-400 moored alongside the U.S. submarine tender Proteus (AS 19). (U.S. Coast Guard)

An overhead perspective of the I-8, with her unusual twin 5.5-inch gun mounting, arriving at Lorient in August 1943. Japanese as well as German and Italian submarines were pressed into service carrying vital war supplies, equipment, and technical documents between Germany and Japan— albeit in small quantities. (Courtesy Royal Navy Submarine Museum)